George John Romanes

Christian Prayer and General Laws

George John Romanes
Christian Prayer and General Laws
ISBN/EAN: 9783743423473
Manufactured in Europe, USA, Canada, Australia, Japa
Cover: Foto ©Lupo / pixelio.de

Manufactured and distributed by brebook publishing software (www.brebook.com)

George John Romanes

Christian Prayer and General Laws

CHRISTIAN PRAYER

AND

GENERAL LAWS,

BEING THE

BURNEY PRIZE ESSAY FOR THE YEAR 1873,

With an Appendix,

THE

PHYSICAL EFFICACY OF PRAYER.

BY

GEORGE J. ROMANES, M.A.,

LATE SCHOLAR IN NATURAL SCIENCE OF GONVILLE AND CAIUS
COLLEGE, CAMBRIDGE.

London:
MACMILLAN AND CO.
1874.

[*All Rights reserved.*]

Cambridge:
PRINTED BY C. J. CLAY, M.A.
AT THE UNIVERSITY PRESS.

TO

P. W. LATHAM, M.A., M.D., F.R.C.P., ETC.,

AS A TOKEN OF THE AUTHOR'S GRATITUDE

FOR PROFESSIONAL AID OF THE HIGHEST VALUE

GENEROUSLY RENDERED

UNDER PECULIARLY ADVERSE CONDITIONS,

THIS ESSAY

IS AFFECTIONATELY INSCRIBED.

ADVERTISEMENT.

THE late RICHARD BURNEY, ESQ., M.A., of Christ's College, Cambridge, previously to his death on the 30th Nov. 1845, empowered his Cousin, Mr Archdeacon Burney, to offer, through the Vice-Chancellor, to the University of Cambridge, the sum of £3,500 Reduced Three per Cent. Stock, for the purpose of establishing an Annual Prize, to be awarded to the Graduate who should produce the best Essay on a subject to be set by the Vice-Chancellor.

On the day after this offer was communicated to the Vice-Chancellor, Mr Burney died; but his sister and executrix, Miss J. Caroline Burney, being desirous of carrying her brother's intentions into effect, generously renewed the offer.

The Prize is to be awarded to a Graduate of the University, who is not of more than three years' standing from admission to his first degree when the Essays are sent in, and who shall produce the best English Essay "on some moral or metaphysical subject, on the Existence, Nature, and Attributes of God, or on the Truth and Evidence of the Christian Religion." The successful Candidate is required to print his Essay; and after having delivered, or caused to be delivered, a copy of it to the University Library, the Library of Christ's College, the University Libraries of Oxford,

Dublin, and Edinburgh, and to each of the Adjudicators of the Prize, he is to receive from the Vice-Chancellor the year's interest of the Stock, from which sum the Candidate is to pay the expenses of printing the Essay.

The Vice-Chancellor, the Master of Christ's College, and the Norrisian Professor of Divinity, are the Examiners of the Compositions and the Adjudicators of the Prize.

In the event of the exercises of two of the Candidates being deemed by the Examiners to possess equal merit, if one of such Candidates be a member of Christ's College, the Prize is to be adjudged to him.

The thesis proposed by the Vice-Chancellor for the year 1873, was as follows:—

"*Christian Prayer considered in relation to the belief that the Almighty governs the World by general laws.*"

The prize was awarded to the author of the following Essay.

PREFACE.

As the subject of this Essay was expressly confined to Prayer in its relation to General Laws, I was precluded from discussing any of the purely *à posteriori* objections which have been urged against the doctrine of the physical efficacy of Prayer. Similarly, such of the *à priori* objections as are not founded on the conception of Natural Law, had to be neglected. The former category includes Mr Galton's article in the *Fortnightly Review* for August 1st, 1872,—an article which, in my opinion, is of greater argumentative worth than all the rest of the literature upon the same side put together;—and the latter, most of the views set forth by the Rev. Messrs. Robertson, Brooks, Knight, and others.

In making this apology, I should like it to be understood that I deem the limitation imposed by the Title of this Treatise a very wise one. The subject embraced by that Title is amply sufficient for a single Essay to discuss, if the discussion is to be in any wise exhaustive. And, I may add, in the present case it seems to me especially desirable that the discussion should be, as much as possible, of this character; seeing that this aspect of the Prayer-question is so closely allied to the yet more important question, regarding the antecedent improbability attaching to the occurrence of Miracles. As, therefore, in dealing with the former, I felt that I was also of necessity dealing with the latter; I trust that any arguments which, in view of the one question, may be thought to be over-elaborated, will, in view of the other, be acquitted of this charge.

It may be stated that all additions which have been made to this Essay since the decision of the Adjudicators was given, are shewn to be such by the date which is appended, thus [1874].

May, 1874.

CHAPTER I.

§ 1. HISTORY may be defined as the record of human thought. No doubt, as a science, history refers to the words and the deeds of previous generations, no less than to their intellectual processes: forasmuch, however, as the two former are but the sensible expressions of the latter, history may be considered as being, in its broadest and its truest sense, the record of our intelligence. If then this is the essential nature of history, it follows that the highest function devolving upon it to perform, is the registration of that which most characterizes human thought in its relation to time, viz., its progress. Hence it is that all other interest attaching to the study of history, dwarfs in the presence of this its highest function.

Taking a general survey of the world's intellectual progress as chronicled by history, the most striking feature presented is certainly the ever-increasing perception of the truth that Unity pervades Nature. The primitive religions (with the conspicuous exception of the Jewish and its derivatives) agreed, amid their discordance on all other subjects, in teaching Polytheism, or the doctrine of a multiplicity of powers in the Universe. Gradually, and in direct proportion to the progress of intelligence, the diffused and segregated influences previously believed in became more and more concentrated, and so few in number; until, in the days of the Classic Mythology, every deity, or class of deities, had its specified name. As the Classic Philosophy, however, gradually enfolded the Classical Religions, the multifarious gods and demi-gods of the former became less and less the objects of general credence, until they finally disappeared before the advance of Christianity. The latter, hand in hand with Philosophy, extirpated during the middle ages every vestige of the Polytheistic creeds, and the recognition among civilized men of the One God, as a Power if not a Person, became all but universal.

A great advance, however, yet remained to be achieved. Although a Unity of Power became thus generally acknowledged as a principle pervading the Universe, the variety of its manifestations appeared no less endless than were the gods and demons of the primitive religions. Indeed, as these gods and demons were but the personifying explanation of the more striking among these manifestations, the latter were more numerous than the former. So long, therefore, as man continued to regard the innumerable diversities occurring in nature as so many disconnected results, due to causes independent of one another, save through their dependence upon their common source; he had merely succeeded in divesting his mind of the superstitious belief in a multiplicity of personal agents. The disconnected results he perceived at this stage, presented themselves to his understanding as an infinitude of variations in the character of the Supreme Essence:—he saw a Unity of Being manifested in a Diversity of Operation.

Thus, although the intellect of man had doubtless made a great advance when it recognized Unity as an essential attribute of the Self-existing Substance, it was not until that intellect began to look without its own nature, and seriously to contemplate, in the objective Cosmos around it, the modes in which that Substance proximately manifested itself, that human intelligence began to see how the order of that Cosmos was maintained, not, as hitherto tacitly or avowedly supposed, by a multiplicity of ever-changing agencies continually emanating from the Indivisible Substance, but, as it were, by a Unity within a Unity:—by a Uniformity of Action within a Unity of Being.

The birth of the Physical Sciences thus marked an era in Philosophy of unparalleled importance. It then became "obvious to the deeper thinkers, that external nature lent itself readily to the subjective conditions under which alone observation is possible. Similarities without rendered possible conceptions within....There evidently was not a chaos without, a cosmos within, but the macrocosm responded to and harmonized with the microcosm[1]." And as thus at their birth, so throughout their development, the Physical Sciences have uninterruptedly tended to establish the doctrine, as the guiding principle of their methods, that all causes and effects with which they have to deal are mutually inter-related, and so inter-related, that, were the knowledge of them sufficiently extended, all natural phænomena would be reducible "to logical deduction from one permeating principle[2]:" and this cardinal doctrine of the Physical Sciences, thus primarily elaborated for their own guid-

[1] G. G. Scott, *Burney Prize*, 1868, p. 58.
[2] James Stuart.

ance, has throughout its progress continually reacted upon Philosophy; until the original and diffused conceptions as to cause and effect entertained by the latter, have gradually undergone a process of concentration, if not of agreement; each embodying more or less of the Physical conception, which has for its nucleus the doctrine of necessary, unconditional sequence, or, at least, of the perpetual uniformity of Natural Law.

§ 2. Thus, as in early times, Polytheism was gradually supplanted by Monotheism, so in later times, Anthropomorphism has been steadily superseded by modern Deism—belief in the immediate nature of the Supreme Government, by belief in the conduct of that Government through General Laws.

This one doctrine which all the sciences unite in teaching, and all the modern systems of philosophy unite in echoing, has now attained its highest phase of certainty. For, whatever may be the number and importance of the General Laws which yet remain to be discovered, their discovery, when made, cannot any further advance the doctrine we are considering; since men's minds are now, or ought to be, prepared for any amount of further development in this direction. Thus it is that the influence of Science upon Religion must now be considered as having ceased. For it has been in respect of this doctrine, and this doctrine alone, that Science has exerted upon Religion an influence of any kind—in this respect, and in this alone, is it true that the former has always been "the purifier" of the latter[1]. But in this respect it is most true; and the fact of its being so has ever been the cause, and the only cause, of that intense embitterment which has, from the first and un-

---

[1] Herbert Spencer, *First Principles*, p. 102.

interruptedly, characterized the relations between these two great departments of thought. "Of all antagonisms of belief, the oldest, the widest, the most profound, and the most important is that between Science and Religion[1]." Why is this? Not, surely, from any mere speculative interest attaching to the great question in dispute? Assuredly not. At each stage of advance men felt that the God, whom even their forefathers had called "a God that hideth Himself," was receding yet further and further into the dimness of mystery; and as concession after concession was wrung from Theology, men felt more and more that Prayer was in danger of being shewn, in cruel truth, but a "vain beating of the air." In proportion as the dominion of General Laws was advanced, men began to fear that Religion was losing all that made it religious; that belief in the "Living God" as the Upholder of the Universe, was becoming progressively absorbed by the antagonistic demonstration, that if such a God existed at all, His action must be removed to an indefinite degree. Men began to fear that the Deity their prayers addressed was in danger of being shewn a mere spiritual idol, fashioned by their own intellect and now in course of demolition, as the grosser idols "made with hands" had been before. For men began to feel that the attribute which in their minds was most characteristic of their spiritual Deity, was precisely that with which the former material deities had been most universally accredited—superintendence of physical phænomena; and this was just the attribute which the doctrine in question assailed. Men began to feel that the ardour of growing intelligence, which had previously melted down the grosser

[1] *Ibid.*, p. 11.

superstitions of their forefathers, had now begun to thaw out their own; that their more advanced conceptions as to the ultimate mystery of the Universe served but to merge the difficulty one stage higher; that these more advanced conceptions were now beginning to reveal yet a higher phase, and to shew that the theory of Personal Agency, which Superstition had embodied in one form and Religion in another, was a theory which, as it had ever been entertained without reason, so could now only be entertained against it; that the human intellect in its progress, had now at last caught sight of the great and fundamental truth that the Deity, whom all nations, races, and religions, from all time had delighted to invoke as "Father," was really only such to them in the sense that a cause is father to its effect; that the God of the Universe was the self-adjusting sufficiency of Nature; and that the Reign in Nature was the Reign of Law. Shall we say that men thought thus?—Shall we not rather say that never, "since the world began," have men thought thus so much as now? For we are not so much concerned with the masses of mankind, as with the leaders of their thought; and now, when men of Science, Literature and Philosophy, not in isolated instances, but as the intellectually orthodox position, bow to this Dominion of Law as being to them supreme, confessing as their belief that that Religion is only truly religious, which beyond this Dominion aspires to know naught else; now, when the demonstration of this Dominion has thus been steadily pushed to its highest phase of certainty, and the minds of men are confidently awaiting the discovery of other General Laws, and Laws which are yet more General;—now, surely, it becomes the duty of each individual to pause and consider for himself the bearing of this new doctrine upon the old faith. Is it true that "The Lord taketh pleasure in them that fear Him, in those that hope in His mercy"?—Or have we found the true reason why "the wicked live, become old, yea are mighty in power," why "the rod of God is not upon them," and why "they spend their days in wealth"? Even because we have proved that theirs is the only true philosophy, so tersely contained in the words that follow:—"What is the Almighty that we should serve Him? And what profit should we have if we pray unto Him?"

§ 3. In the present discussion it is desirable, for the sake of definition, that the following points should be noticed at the outset.

It is necessary to assume intelligence and regard for man as attributes of the First Cause: otherwise there is no room for argument. These attributes have indeed been wisely granted in the title of this Essay; but, even had they not been so granted, they would require to have been assumed.

From this assumption two ideas naturally arise. Firstly, as the intelligence of the First Cause is not an idea which Science or Philosophy is bound to accept, does not an assumption of this attribute tend to prejudicate the question at issue, *i. e.*, unfairly to invalidate the Scientific[1] and Philosophical objections to Christian Prayer[2]? The discussion of this point is of so great importance, that it had better, for the present, be deferred.

---

[1] For the sake of brevity, the word Science will throughout be used in the sense of Physical Science only.

[2] For the sake of brevity, the word Prayer will throughout be used (except when other qualifications are stated) in the sense of prayer for physical results.

Secondly, supposing an Intelligent First Cause to answer Prayer, does the wording of the belief set forth in the Title necessitate the further belief, that such answer must in all cases be granted through General Laws; or is that belief free from this necessity?—Can it consistently with itself suppose that the Almighty, while ruling the Universe by means of General Laws, makes an exception in the case of Prayer, and sometimes or always answers it by immediate action? Although this at first sight appears an important question with regard to our subject, examination will shew that it is not such in reality.

To begin with an illustration. When Christ, at a piteous human cry, by a word stilled the raging of the waters, His disciples[1] "marvelled, saying, What manner of man is this, that even the winds and the sea obey Him!" They stated their account of the surprising occurrence simply as it happened, and subsequent generations upon that account have formed two opinions as to the manner in which the wonder was performed. One of these opinions agrees with the impression which we must suppose to have been produced upon the witnesses, and has been best formulated by Hume[2], who defines a miracle as "a transgression of a Law of Nature by a particular volition of the Deity." The other opinion has been concisely formulated thus:—"A miracle is the superseding of a lower rule of working by a higher[3]." Now the point which concerns us at present is this,— whichever of these views we may suppose to be correct, one thing is certain (supposing, of course, the facts to

---

[1] It matters not who these ἄνθρωποι were.
[2] Essay on Miracles, note 2.
[3] Liddon.

have been as recorded), viz., that so far as the disciples had any means of knowing, one view might be as correct as the other. Even if we suppose (for the sake of the illustration) that the more refined idea of miraculous agency ever occurred to them, it is certain that the actual estimation they entertained of the work would not have been in the least modified; for if such ever did occur to them, they would immediately have reflected that, whatever the mode of causation employed might be, it was certainly beyond the scope of human understanding. The effect was all that they, from the very nature of their faculties, were able to appreciate; and whatever speculations they might entertain as to the cause, these would not have modified by a single letter that outburst of human astonishment, "What manner of man is this! for He commandeth even the winds and the water, and they obey Him."

Now let us apply this illustration to the case before us. We will suppose the same power to be still at work, and all things still the same, with this difference only—the ultimate effects must no longer *appear* to be miraculous in character. But let us remove this element of difference from the illustration, and it is an illustration no longer—it becomes identical with the case which it illustrates. We, no less than they, can only think of this inscrutable causality in terms of its effects—to us no less than to them is it true, that the question whether a *particular* result (supposing it to be produced in answer to Prayer) is brought about through the agency of General Laws, or independently of these Laws, is a question altogether beyond the scope of our faculties to decide.

Now the presence of the miraculous element causes,

as we have just seen, an important difference between the two cases; and for this reason. When this element is observably present, the mind at once feels that it is in proximity with a power sufficient either to suspend or to modify the ordinary course of Natural Law. Why? Because the production of this feeling is the end for which the miracle is wrought. Hence, when the proximity of this power is not intended to be sensibly recognized, then, manifestly, the ultimate effect will appear to result (whether or not it really does so) in the ordinary course of Natural Law. So that the two cases may be stated antithetically thus :—A miracle (supposing it to be real) is an ultimate result, in which a power is sensibly exhibited over the normal action of Natural Law; but whether exhibited by a suspension or by a modification of such Law is unknown. An answer to Prayer (supposing it to be real) is an ultimate result, in which there is no sensible exhibition of power over the normal action of Natural Law; and whether it is effected by a suspension or by a modification of such Law is unknown.

Hence, so far as the belief in government by General Laws is concerned, the question as to whether or not the case of an answer to Prayer differs from other modes of Divine action may be dropped; although it must subsequently be resumed in another connection. Further, it is hoped that the point has now been made clear, that whether or not Prayer is answered through the normal action of General Laws, it must equally in all cases, excepting in those of miracles, *appear* to be so answered.

§ 4. We may now briefly indicate the nature of the objections which it is the purpose of this Essay to discuss. It has already been pointed out that the greatest conquest of human thought which history records, is the recognition of the truth that General Laws pervade the observable Domain of Physical Nature; and it has been likewise shewn that this conquest has been effected solely through the agency of Science. Now, as this conquest was originally due to the scientific methods, so at the present day, a mind versed in these methods feels, with a force almost impossible to others, the magnitude of the present difficulty. There is, indeed, nothing easier to understand than the general nature of this difficulty, but it requires a scientific training to appreciate its weight. "It is hazardous ground for any general moral reasoner to take to discuss subjects of evidence which essentially involve that higher appreciation of *physical truth* which can be attained only by an accurate and comprehensive acquaintance with the connected series of the physical and mathematical sciences." It is only when a man has spent years of toil, in thoroughly acquainting himself with the investigations of others in the field of Natural Science, or in pursuing such investigations of his own, that the conviction is forced upon his mind as an axiom, that the operation of Law does not admit of differential rigidity. An ordinary man may assent to this proposition, but it is almost impossible for him to realize it—to feel that it is inconceivable that it should be otherwise—with the same intensity as a man, who has long been disciplined in taking minute quantitative cognizance of natural phænomena. Science asserts as loudly as she asserts any one of her most indisputable demonstrations, that "without the disturbance of a natural law quite as serious as the stoppage of an eclipse, or the rolling of the river St Lawrence up the Falls of Niagara, no act of humiliation, individual or national, can call one shower from heaven, or deflect towards us a single beam of the sun[1]." A man of Science will continue:—'I do not say what the Almighty can or cannot do, and it is for each of us, no doubt, to frame our own conceptions as to what He does; but I do say, and say most confidently, that supernatural power does not admit of degrees,—that every time the Litany is rehearsed in our churches, we ask for prodigies of power quite as great as any of those we have just heard read from the Old Testament. Such being, I will not say my faith, but my knowledge, I balance the probabilities in my own mind, and I discover the difference between them to be so ludicrously disproportionate, that I feel it is only a question of the time which must elapse, before an adequate knowledge of the Physical Sciences filters into the minds of the people at large, when the present wide-spread belief will be assigned to its place beside those in sorcery and witchcraft. Such being my persuasion, I long for a better inculcation of this knowledge among the masses; for men would then abandon this the last of their pernicious superstitions; they would then, instead of wasting their time and energy over senseless oblations, apply themselves to help themselves by the modes and means appointed in Nature; they would then perceive that the study of Nature's Laws conduces more to their well-being than ignorant addresses to the Law-Maker; for they would then begin to notice that *savants* have lived where saints have perished, and to acknowledge that the Anti-Christ of

---

[1] Prof. Tyndall, *Fragments of Science*, p. 36 ("Prayer and Natural Law").

Daniel is right where it is written of him, "In his estate he shall worship the god of forces."'

§ 5. Such is a type of the objections raised from the Physical Sciences. Before commenting on them, it is desirable in this place to state some further objections which have been raised from Metaphysics.

Without pausing to give the stereotyped proof of the existence of the First Cause, the Infinite, and the Absolute; we may proceed at once to the difficulties which are raised upon it.

'How can the Caused react upon the First Cause? for, if it does so, the latter has ceased to be the First Cause. It profits nothing to say that the First Cause acts from condescension, for then the desire of man becomes the true First Cause of the particular effect desired and executed. But if the First Cause ceases to be the First Cause of one effect, it ceases to be the First Cause of any effect; for the only meaning of the term First Cause is, that it is the First Cause of all effects.

'How can the Finite act upon the Infinite? for the Infinite must include all existence, and so all action; if, therefore, it is acted upon, it ceases to be the Infinite.

'How can the Relative influence the Absolute? for the only meaning of the term Absolute, is that which is beyond relation; whereas influence of necessity implies relation.'

'These remarks would apply to Prayer under any creed, that recognized the necessity of believing in the existence of the First Cause, the Infinite, and the Absolute. But how does the superadded belief in the government by General Laws affect the question? Manifestly it increases the difficulty of believing in the physical efficacy of Prayer; for it is a positive argument added to the negative ones above stated. It is just such a practical out-come as we should have expected from our metaphysical conclusions. The First Cause is now supposed to be removed indefinitely far off from this the sphere of its ultimate effects. Penetrate as we may into ever-increasing generalities, there is always a dim horizon of generalities lying beyond. To suppose, then, that Prayer is physically efficacious, becomes more mentally inconceivable than ever. We do but multiply impossibilities of thought by this addition to our creed; for we are now required to believe, not only that the Caused, the Finite, and the Relative, react upon the Uncaused, the Infinite, and the Absolute; but also that they thus react through the intervention of a practically infinite series of changes. If it is difficult to conceive of A acting immediately upon B; much more is it difficult to conceive of such action, when A is separated from B by a chain of practically infinite length. If it is hard to imagine a floating leaf at the origin of a great river, directing the course of the rushing stream; much more is it hard to imagine that same leaf, when it has eventually arrived through ever widening and deepening channels at the broad delta below, reacting against all that mighty length of current it has traversed, and, with the power of a deity, changing the course of that current at its fountain-head.'

§ 6. Such are the objections raised by the Physical and Metaphysical Sciences. If the former have been understated, it is merely from the want of space to render them more fully; for, myself a student of these Sciences, I am thoroughly alive to the potency of their influence upon the mind in this connection; and I know from experience the magnitude of the difficulty which a mind so influenced is obliged to encounter, when it endeavours to emancipate itself from the thraldom of its petty conceptions, and to take a broader and a deeper view of the mystery that surrounds us. Such being the case, I can offer no apology for confining the subject of this Essay to the almost exclusive consideration of these objections. On the one hand "in an age of physical research like the present, all highly cultivated minds and duly advanced intellects have imbibed, more or less, the lessons of the inductive philosophy[1];" and, on the other hand, this philosophy "is a system far enough from the surface to make it appear deep, but does not go sufficiently far down to reach the foundation[2]." There are, hence, numberless minds at the present time, too much prepared to deem the scientific aspect of the present question a foregone conclusion. And this tendency is increased by the fact, that the other aspect requires for its justification an honest effort of thought, in a direction in which, of all others, the scientific mind is least disposed to travel. For the latter reason my endeavour throughout will be, above all things to avoid abstruseness. Metaphysics, indeed, cannot be avoided (even were it desirable in a Burney Essay that they should)—the subject being purely metaphysical: but that abstruseness which so often occurs in this department of thought, and of which the scientific mind is so particularly intolerant, will, as far as possible, be avoided; not only for the last-named reason, but also because I conceive that an argument which admits of a thorough institution upon a lower

---

[1] *Essays and Reviews*, p. 133.
[2] Dr M'Cosh, *Method of Divine Government*, 7th edition, p. 183.

stage of speculative abstruseness, should not, on principle, be raised to a higher; since every advance in abstruseness is a further indication of the intrinsic difficulty of the subject, and so of the liability to error. Thus it is that, were I not persuaded that the objections to Prayer which we are about to examine admit of easy refutation by "common sense metaphysics," I should not have undertaken to write upon the subject at all; conscious as I am that this subject belongs to such a province, that it would then have required for its adequate treatment a writer who had given his principal attention to Philosophy.

§ 7. We must now recur to a question already propounded, viz., does not the assumption of the existence of the Almighty unfairly invalidate the scientific position? No doubt, in strict argument, a writer upon the present subject is not necessarily required to entertain this question: forasmuch, however, as I am convinced that it is mainly from a want of giving it due attention, that the objections we have to consider appear to some minds so plausible, I deem it highly desirable to expose its shallowness, for the sake of intensifying conviction by the removal of an unfair prejudication.

What is the character of Science considered as a department of thought? Clearly, in the first place, it is purely intellectual. The moral feeling of individuals may be moulded or affected by contact with Science, but this does not affect the character of Science itself; and so does not modify the weight of objections raised by Science to any belief external to itself. The present objections, then, in so far as they are scientific, must be purely intellectual. But not only is Science purely intellectual; it is likewise purely objective: it deals with the concrete and the actual, not with the abstract and the hypothetical. No doubt a mind engaged in scientific enquiry must frequently make draughts upon the Unknown; and the "imagination," guided by previous knowledge, is of indispensable "scientific use" when roaming in the regions of the Probable. Nay, it is not too much to assert that Science would have made no progress whatever, had not this its pioneer always preceded it into this region. But we must be careful to distinguish between the process of scientific thought, and the product of scientific thought, *i.e.*, scientific discovery. While it is necessary for a scientific investigator to quit the region of the Known for the Unknown —a journey implied by the very term "scientific research,"—yet in doing so he leaves, for the time being, the territory of Science proper; and he only extends that territory in the direction of his advance, when he has succeeded in reclaiming a portion of the Unknown or the Probable to the Known and the Proveable[1]. But, although there is thus a great difference between scientific thought and scientific discovery, they are alike in this,—they both refer to the Proximate: for the object of the former is the attainment of the latter, and the Discoverable must always be the Proximate. Hence, in whatever degree scientific thought wanders from the contemplation of the Proximate, in that degree it has ceased to be scientific—has become speculative.

Thus, Science is the child of Physical Law, and is but true to its genetic nature when it seeks to resolve all things into terms of matter, force, and motion.

---

[1] This statement is not strictly accurate, because a probability may be so high as to amount for practical purposes to a certainty.

Materialism is the philosophy of Science, not by convention, but of necessity; for Science deals exclusively with the Proximate, and the Proximate is Material. But after Science has attained its highest successes,—after it has reduced all things to terms of its ultimate ideas, and reconstructed these ultimate ideas again into the comprehensible "How" of all things,—even after it has shewn us the physical basis of life and the mechanical equivalent of thought,—Science has done nothing more than systematize our experience—it has left us still within the Proximate. "The utmost possibility for us, is an interpretation of the process of things as it presents itself to our limited consciousness; but how this process is related to the actual process we are unable to conceive, much less to know." If Physical Law is, as we have said, the mother of Science, it is no less certain that it is destined to be its tomb: it is to Science the alpha and the omega, the beginning and the end.

§ 8. Religion refers to the Ultimate or it refers to nothing. Further, that Ultimate is to Religion a Person[1]. This is true of the religious sentiment in general, but that special phase of it with which we are concerned is not a sentiment only. It is not the presence of the soul's aspirations, nor a recognition of our dependence upon a higher power, and the desire to express the consequent feelings of praise and thankfulness,—it is not even the beautiful adaptation of the Christian

---

[1] Spencer's definition of Religion, viz., "an *à priori* theory of the Universe" is true so far as it goes; but belief in personal agency in some form or other is of the essence of religion. In other words, to apply the term "Religion" to any other form of belief is merely to abuse it.

religion to these the highest wants of man—that has gained for that religion the adherence, through many centuries, of the choice of human intellect. Let us take what view we may regarding the truth of Christianity, but—in common argumentative justice, if not in ordinary respect for our own intellectual faculties—let us acknowledge that Christianity has done in the world's history what it has done, and is now what it is, in virtue of the evidence—be it true or be it false—in favour of a Revelation. This is not the place to vindicate that evidence, but it is necessary to dwell briefly upon its character. From what we have just stated, it must be seen that Christianity differs from Science in being partly moral and partly intellectual—there being a great difference between a Religion and evidence in favour of a Revelation. Considered as a whole, it may be defined as a department of thought having reference to the Ultimate. In so far as it is moral, it is independent of all other departments of intellectual enquiry; but in so far as it is intellectual, the condition of its existence is that of dependence upon other departments. Our present object is to see how this dependence is reduced to a *minimum*.

While the intellectual credentials of Christianity penetrate many departments of intellectual operation, such as history, philosophy, and morality; the evidence itself, considered in its totality, is rendered by this very diffusion, unique. The very multitude of the intellectual pillars on which it is supported makes it independent of each constituent individual; so that it cannot be destroyed without the destruction of all the chief departments of human thought. But not only is the evidence in favour of a revelation rendered independent of each department of thought by its diffusion through all: it is further insulated by its intrinsic character. For it is self-evident that the character of a department of thought is determined by the character of its object; consequently the Evidences, considered merely as such, *i.e.*, in reference to their one Object, are essentially distinct from all other departments of thought. Thus we find that the Christian Evidences are not only rendered independent (so far at least as the maintenance of their intellectual character admits), of all other departments of thought considered severally; but that they are further insulated from all such departments considered collectively.

§ 9. These considerations then, viz., that the Evidences are partly moral and partly intellectual,—that in so far as they are moral they have nothing whatever to do with Science, Science being purely intellectual,—that even in so far as they are intellectual they are rendered by their diffusion almost independent of Science,—and lastly that, considered as a department of thought, they are, in their intrinsic nature, distinct from all other departments considered collectively;— these considerations render obvious what we are now engaged in shewing, viz., that it is no disparagement to the objections raised by Science to assume that the First Cause possesses an intelligent regard for man. For these considerations clearly establish two positions: firstly, that any reasons we may have for believing this to be the case, are reasons *independent* of Science; and, secondly, that the department of the Evidences is so fundamentally *distinct* from that of Science, that the latter can have no voice in the general question as to whether the First Cause is, or is not, "the Almighty."

Now, no matter how small our "independent" reasons may be in favour of an affirmative to the general question, it can be no disparagement to this special objection to assume the conclusions to which these reasons tend. For we are not endeavouring to ascertain any probability relating to the general question, but merely to consider the two sides of this particular question; and to do this most fairly we should consider it as separate from the general one. Only if Science were able to demonstrate the falsehood of the Evidences of Christianity, and so to settle the general question in the negative, would the assumption of its affirmative be a disparagement to this special question. It may be asked,—But why are we not entitled to add whatever strength of improbability there is as to the general question, to the improbability we can shew to obtain regarding the special? We answer,—Because to do this would be to confuse the functions of the departments of thought with those of thought itself. After an individual mind has satisfied itself regarding the weight of the objections advanced by Science, it is then, no doubt, the duty of that mind to add this result to any improbability which it believes to exist on the side of an affirmative to the general question; but the only fair way of estimating the value of the special improbability, is to consider it apart.

§ 10. At the risk of being tedious I shall adduce an illustration, in order to render this point perfectly clear. Probabilities may be fairly likened to forces, existing only in relation to other forces: they are the resultants, both in direction and magnitude, of previous probabilities. Like forces, too, probabilities are usually complex; the resultant being caused by the incidence of numerous other probabilities, most of which are themselves the resultants of previous systems.

Now the probability that Prayer is ineffectual is compounded of two other probabilities; first, the probability that the πρῶτον κινοῦν is not even a Θεὸς ἄγνωστος, much less a Πατὴρ ἐλεήμων; and, second, the probability that if the First Cause has an intelligent regard for man, this regard should not manifest itself in answering Prayer; or, which is the same thing, the improbability that it should. Now concerning the first probability, Science has no voice—the evidence by which it is increased or decreased being, as we have seen, altogether without the range of scientific enquiry. Those who have most honestly examined that evidence, best know the number and complexity of the contending resultants of the many systems of probabilities which contribute to form the final resultant, the assumed direction and magnitude of which the title of the present Essay sets forth. Now, in making this assumption, we are in nowise invalidating the scientific objections; for the only business on which we are now engaged is to discover, as nearly as possible, the value of the scientific element in the system,—the other element belonging, as we have repeatedly seen, to a distinct and widely different *department*. As the total resultant regarding the specific question is not granted, it can only be ascertained by a composition of its constituents; and the fairest way of arriving at the true value of each constituent is to consider it separately—to assume the other constituent neutralized. When, by another line of investigation, an individual mind has, to the best of its ability, ascertained in the other department the resultant probability as to the general question, both in magnitude and direction; then, no doubt, it becomes the duty of that mind to compound that resultant with this probability established by Science as to the specific question, in order to obtain the ultimate and total result with regard to the latter; but it is no less clearly the duty of each *department* to abstain from encroaching upon the other. Before, however, such a mind can make this composition, it is necessary that it should know the measurement of this scientific constituent. For the sake, therefore, of measuring, in the fairest possible manner, the degree of strength residing in the scientific constituent, let us assume the other neutralized.

§ 11. We are now in a position to appreciate the nature of the purifying influence, which, as we saw at the commencement, Science has continuously exerted upon Religion. The human mind will not rest satisfied with the single contemplation either of the Proximate or of the Ultimate; and this necessity in the human mind of dual thought, because natural, must be deemed legitimate. But this duality of human thought is not confined to its process, it is projected more or less into its product—is not restricted to the intellect, but colours reciprocally the two corresponding departments of intellectual enquiry. This mutual diffusion of influence between the two departments is no doubt theoretically illegitimate, but is practically unavoidable. The consequence is that each department, in so far as it penetrates the other, becomes liable to be influenced by whatever changes that other department may have to undergo: but this liability is incurred only to the extent in which the penetration has obtained. Were the line of demarcation between the departments as clearly defined in thought as it is in reality, no such liability could exist: as it is, this liability increases in direct proportion to the want of this definition. Hence, as we should have expected, in all the accounts which history affords of the controversies between Science and Theology, the battle-ground has ever been this border-land of illegitimate diffusion; and it is within the precincts of this territory alone that the purifying agency of Science on Religion has been exerted. Briefly then, Religion transcends Science,—the former reposing upon the Ultimate, and the latter upon the Proximate. Any modification, therefore, which Science may impose upon religious ideas of the Proximate—ideas which are, in reality, extra-religious,—cannot influence religious ideas of the Ultimate—ideas which are, in reality, the only truly religious.

§ 12. We have arrived, then, at the following general conclusions. We have seen that it is no disparagement to the scientific objections, to discuss them upon the supposition that the First Cause has an intelligent regard for man:—on the contrary, to discuss them upon any other ground, or ground on which this supposition is not clearly defined, would be to endow these objections with an initial bias that would be argumentatively unjust.

We have also observed that the legitimate sphere of Science is rigidly confined within the Proximate, while that of Religion is similarly restricted to the Ultimate; and we have noticed, as a striking illustration of this point, a fact, which is, indeed, its necessary consequence, viz., that great difficulties are encountered when the two provinces are made artificially to overlap.

Lastly, we have observed that the purifying influence of Science on Religion, has ever been confined to the filtering of the scientific element from the religious when these had commingled,—to the correction of religious ideas as to the proximate government of God when these were erroneous, and which, in so far as they had obtained, were extra-religious.

The point, then, which we have specially to bear in mind throughout the following chapters is, that Science deals exclusively with the proximate government of the First Cause; while Religion refers to that Cause as a Person, to its character, its relations and intentions towards man[1],—but is in no wise concerned with causation.

[1] It will be seen that this definition of religion differs from that of Spencer, who maintains, in effect, that Religion becomes irreligious in the proportion in which it endeavours to explain the mystery it acknowledges—*i. e.*, in the proportion in which it aspires to deal with the character and intentions of the First Cause. It may be well to point out that this difference between the two definitions does not arise from any defect in the logical sequences by which they are respectively attained, but merely from a difference of premises. For while Mr Spencer tacitly ignores the possibility of a revelation, such possibility is in the present treatise recognized. The logical consequence of the former premise is, that religion is not merely irreligious but irrational, in proportion as it aspires to know the Unknowable; while the logical consequence of the latter premise is, that religion is not merely irreligious but irrational, in proportion as it fails to respond to whatever degree of evidence there may exist in favour of a revelation.

I cannot lose this opportunity of noticing the singularly unfortunate character of the term "Unknowable," as applied by Hamilton to designate the Ultimate, and afterwards appropriated by Spencer as a verbal epitome of the doctrine of Comte. It is unfortunate, because the assertion that the Ultimate is unknowable involves, not only the unphilosophical assumption that a revelation is in the nature of things impossible, but likewise a necessary contradiction—to wit, that we possess at least this much knowledge concerning the Ultimate, that if it is intelligent, it cannot reveal

The establishment, therefore, of the scientific doctrine of the government of the world by General Laws, which we at the beginning saw was the only sense in which Science has been the purifier of Religion, but which in the process has been throughout its development the only cause of antagonism between Religion and Science, is thus seen to be altogether foreign to Religion as a department of thought; and while, at each successive stage of Science's development, Religion seemed to be losing all that made it religious, by the withdrawal of the object of its worship within ever-increasing shades of distance,—this has only been the case because Religion has never fully recognized the magnitude of its office. Far beyond our faculties of sense, of thought, and of imagination, — indefinitely

itself or its wishes to man. [The Author finds that thus far he has been anticipated in his criticism by Mr J. Martineau. 1874.] The first-mentioned fallacy appears to reside in not recognizing the ambiguity which attaches to the verb *to know*, and its derivatives. As applied to causation—that is, in a scientific sense—it simply means *to have explained*,—that is, to have perceived a cause more ultimate than that to which the verb is applied. Now, as self-existence is clearly not susceptible of explanation, the Ultimate must of necessity be, in a scientific sense, unknowable. In other words, if the Ultimate is intelligent, its existence must, in this sense, be a mystery to itself; or, to descend to our own level, even if an intelligent First Cause were to impart a revelation of demonstrative value, this revelation could tell us nothing more of self-existence than that it is what it is. This fact, however, is widely different from that which the unqualified use of the term Unknowable conveys; viz., that not only the existence, but likewise the modes and the attributes of the Ultimate are beyond the limits of possible knowledge. It may be true that on philosophical grounds alone these modes and attributes are beyond these limits: it certainly does not follow, that in the nature of things a partial revelation of these modes and attributes is therefore impossible.

far without the region of this the proximate manifestation of His power, is the tabernacle of the dwelling-place of the Most High; and if Religion has felt that the extension of the dominion of General Laws has, in the smallest degree, affected its relation to its Object, it is only because Religion has failed to see that that Object is rendered none the less personal, because the further removed,—nor the less moral, because the more incomprehensible.

With these preliminaries thus well understood, let us now proceed to investigate the objections raised by Science to a practice sanctioned by Religion. It is a question which Science, as a department of thought referring to the Proximate, has a full and perfect right to raise; and it thus becomes a question, the discussion of which Religion, inasmuch as it is intellectual, is bound to entertain.

CHAPTER II.

§ 1. As the metaphysical objections are of a merely technical nature, it is better to dispose of them before discussing the physical.

It is a sufficient answer to the first of these objections, that the frame of mind conducing to any petition is as much an effect of the First Cause, as would the answer be if vouchsafed. For the petition being thus equally with its answer contained within the First Cause, we have no better reason to say that the former, any more than the latter, reacts upon that Cause. This difficulty is one which can only be raised by novices in speculative philosophy. They have an undefined notion of human will differing from all other created things in its freedom of action; and they carry this notion into the highest term of the speculative series: now, this term has been arrived at by a wholly different route from that by which the freedom of the will is inferred: placing, then, the one doctrine in opposition to the other, they point to the antithesis as an insuperable obstacle to the belief in the validity of Prayer. This difficulty, however, is no greater in the case of Prayer, supposing it efficacious, than in the case of any other effectual action of which the human will is capable. The only difference is that in the case of Prayer the difficulty is rendered more apparent, in consequence of the influence of the First Cause being directly involved, instead of being tacitly assumed[1].

§ 2. Taking the other two objections together, we have first to observe that there are two very different significations attaching to the words infinite and absolute. If they are used as subjects, they become mere abstractions; if they are used as predicates, they become intelligible concretes. We may, for instance, speak of infinite space, or absolute goodness, with a definite meaning; but when we speak of the Infinite, or the Absolute, as substantives, we employ indefinite abstractions. It would be a mistake, however, to brand the latter as "senseless abstractions[2]," since, as abstractions and when not unphilosophically treated, they are at least as valuable as any other

[1] The objection thus refuted has been advanced in a great variety of verbal forms. As the above statement of it, however, is the essence of all such, the refutation there given must be considered general. As an example of the various forms we may take the following. "Were they (the series of physical pre-arrangements) ever altered at the suggestion of a creature, either they were imperfect before the suggestion was made, or they were made less perfect by means of it. If previously perfect, the change would be undivine; if not perfect until the change, we could with difficulty believe in the perfection of Him who made it." "Belief in an all-comprehending Intelligence which saw the end from the beginning, and determined beforehand the history of every inorganic atom, and the evolution of each sentient structure, is a postulate of rational theology: and that in the guidance of the Universe its great Superintendent acts according to laws set up from everlasting is no less axiomatic." All such objections, involving as they do the more ultimate difficulty of fore-ordination and free-will, should be rigidly excluded from the present specific question; since they have no more bearing upon it than upon any other in which the human will is concerned.

[2] Mill, *Examination of Hamilton*, p. 45.

mere abstraction. Now, it seems to me that it is of the essence of an abstraction, to contain all the possible concretes of which it is the abstraction; and that it is of the essence of concretes that they should not be mutually annihilative: if so, it follows that no abstraction can contain two mutually annihilative concretes. An abstraction may thus be looked upon as a genus which contains all its possible concretes as species, and which is by this very fact precluded from containing the opposites of these species; since it is of the essence of these species that their opposites should be non-existent. If this view is correct, we can perceive and avoid errors occurring upon both sides of the issue between Hamilton, Mansel, Spencer, etc., on the one hand, and Mill on the other. The latter, it must seem, is perfectly right in shewing that it is as unphilosophical to attach any concrete meaning to these abstractions, as it would be to do so in the case of any other abstraction whatever,—to suppose that these abstractions themselves and as such have a concrete existence[1]. But Mr Mill is wrong in asserting that "the Infinite" must be at once "infinitely great," and "infinitely little;" and "the Absolute" "absolutely wise and absolutely stupid[2]." The Infinite may be *either* infinitely great or infinitely little, and the Absolute may be *either* absolutely wise or absolutely stupid; but neither can be *both* the one and the other, since the species are opposites, and so mutually exclusive.

Applying then these considerations to the case before us, it is evident that the objections can have no rational meaning, unless the terms in question are employed in their concrete sense. Now there is nothing inconceivable in the idea of an infinitely powerful and absolutely bene-

---

[1] *Ibid.* chap. IV. [2] p. 43.

ficent Being answering the petitions of His sentient creatures : on the contrary, this idea is the very ground from which these petitions take their rise.

To those, however, who are not satisfied with these views concerning the species of the Unconditioned, but adhere to their strictly logical significations, it must be sufficient to answer, as we answered when treating of the First Cause, that the difficulty which arises from our collision with the Infinite and the Absolute in this sense is not confined to Prayer, but extends to every subject concerning which it is possible to think. And this argument is here intensified by the fact, that the very same logical processes which prove the logical existence of the abstractions we are considering, likewise and as incontestably prove that they are mutually annihilative when predicated of the same Being.

All adjuncts to these metaphysical objections, such as the rhetorical metaphors of the type before given, rest upon the physical objections. To these, then, as constituting the subject of the present Essay, let us now, at length, proceed.

§ 3. Mr Herbert Spencer[1] has somewhere observed, that it is necessary to the discussion of any subject that it should be reduced to a single proposition. Hence it is fortunate that, in the present case, no one can experience any difficulty in throwing the scientific objections into this form. True it is that writers upon this subject almost invariably obscure the real question at issue, by introducing other and altogether distinct questions, such as the pernicious influence on man of belief in the efficacy of Prayer, the impossibility of answering contradictory petitions, the impiety of addressing suggestions

---

[1] *Principles of Psychology*, Vol. II.

to the Deity, and so forth. All such questions, however, being entirely extraneous to the one in hand, will be carefully excluded, as they should be from all writings professing to deal with the *scientific* objections to Prayer[1]. Now, into whatever verbal form we may choose to throw the proposition we have to consider, that proposition itself must possess two characters: it must be conditional, and it must be universal. No one can assert that the Almighty *does not* answer Prayer, but merely that *if* He does, He must interfere with the normal course of nature: also the proposition must be universal, in *no case whatever* can Prayer be answered without such interference.

The examination, then, of this proposition forms the main subject of this Essay. Let us first enquire whether it is adduced as establishing a necessity or merely a probability. The answer lies on the surface: if the proposition is adduced as establishing a necessity, it manifestly should not be thrown into a conditional form. That it must be thrown into a conditional form is self-evident; but, lest the reason why it must, should not be at once perceived, it may not be superfluous to give it. A necessity can only rest upon a demonstration; but from the nature of the case science is unable to demonstrate that Prayer is never answered, because the sphere of science is, as we have seen, restricted to the Proximate. All, therefore, that science can do is to argue from the known to the unknown, and thus, by analogy, to infer that Prayer is ineffectual. By the mere fact, however, of this appeal to analogy, science has ceased to be scientific—

[1] I have entertained the foregoing metaphysical objections, because the term "Almighty" includes the conceptions on which they are founded.

has become speculative; has ceased to prove, and endeavours only to presume.

But although analogical arguments cannot from their nature establish a necessity, they may, as we shall subsequently see, establish any degree of probability. Hence the business before us is critically and impartially to analyse the scientific proposition, with the view of ascertaining as nearly as possible the degree of probability which it contains.

§ 4. As the term "Physical Law," or its equivalents, must occur in the proposition we have thus to analyse, it becomes necessary to point out what has already been pointed out by other writers times without number, viz., the ambiguity which attaches to it. The only rational interpretation of the term admits, indeed, of an easy and precise definition, which may be thus stated:—A Physical Law is the formula of a physical sequence, which, so far as human observation extends, is invariable[1]. But from this definition there immediately arises the question,—Is this sequence necessary?—is that, which observation has determined to be invariable relatively, also invariable absolutely? These are, manifestly, questions which cannot be answered, and hence the ambiguity of the term. Now this ambiguity is not, as a rule, sufficiently recognized by disputants, and even when it is so, the balance of probability appears to some minds to preponderate towards an affirmative answer to those questions, as decidedly as to other minds it seems to tend towards a negative. Hence to those of the former school, the term Physical Law habitually bears the signification of

[1] The Duke of Argyle in his *Reign of Law* gives five distinct definitions of this term; but in so far as they do not embody the metaphysical conception of cause, the above definition includes them all.

a mere instrument of the Divine Will, perfectly obedient in its ministry, and indefinitely plastic in its operation; while to those of the latter, it no less constantly represents a practically independent directive influence of unalterable rigidity, upon which eternal order universally depends.

Without pausing to examine the respective merits of these rival creeds, we shall, for the sake of definition in argument, assume that the latter represents the truth. It is the belief entertained by those who raise the class of objections to Prayer which we are considering, and the belief upon which those objections are founded. The supposition, therefore, of its truth, while it endows these objections with their full weight, likewise, in so doing, affords the most unprejudiced ground for their discussion.

§ 5. We have recently seen that Science, in order to establish its universal proposition, is under the necessity of appealing to Analogy. The reason of this necessity is our inability to follow the sequence of cause and effect in any one line beyond some determinate point. The fact of this barrier to our progress existing on all sides, is but the practical expression of our ignorance of second causes. It now devolves upon us to estimate the probable amount of this ignorance. The endeavour is not, of course, to estimate the extent of the Unknown, which would be absurd; but merely, from the data afforded us by the known conditions of knowledge, to indicate by *à priori* considerations the *probabilities* there are as to that extent.

In dealing with this subject it would be as impossible to attain, as it would be undesirable to attempt, complete originality. So far, however, as the general doctrine of "the relativity of knowledge" admits of special development in its bearing upon the subject before us, so far is originality desirable. Further, as it is also desirable, for reasons before indicated, to avoid abstruseness as much as possible, the conclusions which by other writers have been attained by metaphysical considerations of a more or less technical kind, will now be reached by considerations more in accordance with the disposition of a mind accustomed to scientific thought. As the vastness of this subject, however, is only equalled by its vagueness, if these considerations are sometimes found to be deficient in precision, it must be remembered that they are only advanced in order to test the direction in which the general current of probability in this matter is flowing. Every oscillation of the needle need not be observed, if only it eventually points with certainty in one direction.

§ 6. One great section of writers upon miracles employ an argument against the *à priori* objection to them, which, although its manner of presentation usually admits of improvement, is nevertheless undoubtedly valid. In the form of an exhaustive statement the argument may be rendered thus:—The whole *à priori* objection to miracles, so far as it rests on the doctrine of General Laws, goes upon the implied supposition that a miracle, to be such, must be supernatural—*i.e.*, a violation of the established Laws of Nature. But this character is not necessary either for the nature, or for the object of a miracle. For the nature is maintained, and the object answered in the same degree, if the miracle is merely superhuman—*i.e.*, produced by secondary causes to the knowledge of which human experience can never attain. That such a class of secondary causes should exist, may appear more or less improbable, but can never be considered impossible, without assuming that our knowledge of physical causation is absolute.

Now this applies with equal force to the subject of the present Essay, and to develope it will be the object of the first step in the following examination. It must be observed that this first step in our argument is not intended to *prove* that such a class of second causes exists; but merely to shew that it is more or less probable that they may; and, further, that if they do, they must of necessity escape the scrutiny of Science.

§ 7. He who is most conversant with the natural sciences, either singly or collectively, and with the methods of scientific research, will be the man who will most readily admit how limited is the range of our scientific knowledge. The fact of the practical results of science having been so numerous and important, added to the fact that the field of scientific research affords the best opportunity for intellectual competition, and so the best background for throwing out into strong relief those individuals who possess the greatest powers of mind—these are the lenses which magnify science in the eyes of the people at large. But the natural philosopher, while he may justly plume the science which he follows on the enormous progress it has recently made, and as justly complain that the uninitiated are unable intelligently to appreciate its amount, is nevertheless conscious that the very training which enables him to value the attainments of science, compels him at the same time to feel, with an intensity impossible to the untrained, how utterly insignificant they really are. Considered relatively to former centuries, the dimensions to which science has developed in this are certainly astonishing; but, considered absolutely, these dimensions dwindle almost to nothing—serve but to indicate the magnitude of that which lies beyond. For every fresh discovery, and every new district that is opened by it for further investigation, while it enlarges the sphere of the Known, still more increases our perception of the magnitude of the Unknown. So that not only is it true that Discovery can never satisfy Inquiry, but, since the sphere of the Inquirable always encloses that of the Discoverable, the increase of the latter entails that of the former, not in a similar degree, but, as it were, in accordance with the law of areas varying as the radius squared. How long this process is to last, it would be foreign to our subject to inquire: we must observe, however, that there is much misapprehension in some quarters with regard to this matter. Mr Mill's arguments are irrefutable, and they lead to the conclusion that when all generalizations shall have been merged into the fewest possible number, the latter must still be numerous. To this we should add that, even when all the sciences shall have become purely deductive (if this be possible), although the sphere of the Researchable will then, comparatively speaking, have been filled up, the sphere of the Inquirable will never have been so large.

Thus the prime result of scientific investigation is to reveal to ourselves the denseness of our ignorance. So far no one will be more willing to go with us than a man of science. We will now ask him to go with us in the opposite direction. As he acknowledges that the greatest organizations of scientific thought land us in ignorance comparatively total, we will now ask him to reduce those organizations to terms of their ultimate ideas. In each of these, viz., space, time, matter, force, and motion, every reader of modern philosophy will recognize that which is wholly inconceivable. It is not a matter of knowing or not knowing, of understanding or not understanding; but, in dealing with these ultimate scientific ideas, all alike must acknowledge that they are mere symbols of thought, which must for ever remain utterly unthinkable. From this it follows that the only office of Science is the tracing back of phænomena to the point at which they emerge from the ocean of the Unknowable, and the following of their course forward until they are again engulfed by its waters. And if such is the indisputable nature of that which underlies all science, it follows that even what we think we know we do not understand—that all our knowledge, absolutely considered, is merely another phase of our ignorance. "We know phænomenally and yet, marvellous as it is, we know that we know phænomenally." We know that our ignorance is great, and yet we know that we know not how ignorant we are. Thus, whether we follow Science upwards to its highest generalizations, or downwards to its fundamental data, we find it alike embraced by ignorance—a sphere "hung upon nothing," floating in a boundless space of Nescience.

§ 8. In the last section we have briefly considered what may be termed our objective ignorance of second causes, or ignorance entailed by the nature of the things examined. We shall now briefly consider our subjective ignorance of second causes, or ignorance entailed by the nature of our faculties. The one class of considerations is, of course, but the obverse aspect of the other; but it is necessary that we should enter upon it, in order to bring out into a yet stronger relief the profound nature of our ignorance.

"Quicquid recipitur, recipitur ad modum recipientis." Nothing can be more evident than that we are entirely dependent for our knowledge of the Universe upon our five senses: what are the diameters and the directions of these our intellectual apertures?

§ 9. We shall first consider the negative aspect of the case. Descartes and Berkeley may be deemed the founders of the doctrine that man, being dependent upon his senses for his information regarding the external world, can know nothing of things as they are in themselves. The doctrine may be summarized thus:—We can only maintain consciousness in one of two states, viz., either in a state of sensation (including perception), or of reflection. Now the only change that can be produced in consciousness by external objects must be so produced through the medium of the senses; and, as consciousness can only exist in virtue of a change of states, it follows that external objects can only be represented to the reflective state, by first being presented to the sensational state. Hence, the mind receives nothing from external objects, save the changes in sensational states which the latter occasion. But it is evident that these sensational states cannot exist, as such, in the objects themselves—that they are merely subjective affections of the percipient mind. Hence, it is utterly impossible for man to know or to conceive of any objective reality as such; since, before he can be aware even of its existence, the reality must be translated into the appearance, which alone he can appreciate.

Now the reasoning so far is incontrovertible, and it may well appear strange how any dispute could have arisen out of it. The fact, however, is, that the confusion of thought upon this subject is not in anywise occasioned by the above considerations, but arises from endowing them with a force they do not possess. Although it is perfectly true that we cannot know anything in its reality, it is evidently a case of *non sequitur* to suppose that on this account no such reality exists. Whatever basis "material idealism" may have to stand upon, it best consults its own interests by refraining from the endeavour to press this truth into its service. The point then which we have to bear in mind as admitting of no dispute is, that we are precluded by the nature of our faculties from knowing any objective existence, as it is in its substantial reality. This truth has great importance for us at the stage we have now reached.

§ 10. Let us suppose that any object X is present to our senses, and that its attributes as apparent through their medium to the mind are A, B, C; and that the realities corresponding to A, B, C are respectively a, b, c. Now it is evident that although A, B, and C are each present to consciousness as simple and indecomposable attributes of X, it by no means follows that their corresponding realities are in truth elemental. On the contrary, the group a, b, c may be compounded to any extent in each of its divisions, *e.g.*, thus: a, a', a'', a'''; b, b'; c, c', c'': or a, a'; b, c, c'; a'', b', c'', a'''. Further, although X presents only the qualities A, B, C, it does not follow that its substantial actualities are confined to even complex groups in which the elements a, b, c are variously compounded; for other and wholly different elements, d, e, f, &c., may well be present in X, although not appreciated by the senses: and these latter elements may likewise occur in groups variously compounded. Thus, an entity which is phænomenally simple may be noumenally complex. Conversely, an entity which is phænomenally complex may be noumenally simple; for A, B, C, although apparently widely different attributes, may in reality be but slight modifications of a single element, a. Thus in no case does the testimony of the senses afford any guarantee that apparent differences or similarities are, either in kind or degree, even approximately identical or commensurate with the actual ones. "The only relation between the two (*i.e.* 'the mental modifications of Brown,' and 'the objects which excite them') is that of cause and effect[1]."

Now the bearing of these reflections on our present subject is very direct. For it must be the underlying realities, and not the superficial appearances, that are the true causes of the effects occurring in nature. No doubt it will appear at first sight that this distinction is immaterial, since, the causes and effects being alike to us phænomenal, the issue, so far as our knowledge of sequence is practically concerned, is the same as it would be were we acquainted with the corresponding realities—the sense, as it were, not being impaired by its translation into a language we can understand. That this view of the case is erroneous, we can readily perceive by the use of symbols.

Suppose X, Y, and Z to be three objects, possessing respectively the phænomenal attributes a, b, c; d, e, f; g, h, i; and the noumenal attributes 1 and $1'$, 2 and $2'$, 3 and $3'$, 4 and $4'$, 5 and $5'$, 6 and $6'$, 7 and $7'$, 8 and $8'$, 9 and $9'$; and let us suppose these three objects interacting upon one another as cause and effect, in such a manner that the resulting combination is X, Y, Z: the phænomenal attributes would then be present to the mind thus:—a, b, c; d, e, f; g, h, i; and the noumenal attributes might be arranged thus:—1 and $1'$, 2 and $2'$, 3 and $3'$, ... 9 and $9'$. But, although the latter might be

[1] Mill.

arranged thus, it does not follow that they must; for it is evident that one half of the figures, viz., those to which the dash is appended, may be transposed amongst themselves, and amongst the other half, with every variety of permutation, without the order 1, 2, 3; 4, 5, 6; 7, 8, 9 (that is, the order of which alone the senses can take cognizance) being in any way affected.

This is a simple case, but any amount of complexity can be conceived as existing, by adding to the groups 1 and $1'$, 2 and $2'$, 3 and $3'$, ... 9 and $9'$, other entities which the senses cannot perceive; and this may be done in the form of other groups, thus:—10 and $10'$, 11 and $11'$, 12 and $12'$, &c.; or by increasing previous groups, thus:—1 and $1'$, 2 and $2'$, 3 and $3'$, V, X, L; &c. Lastly, the noumenal groups may undergo the reverse process of simplification, thus:—

$$a, b, c, = 1 + \cdot 0001 + \cdot 000001.$$

Hence we are not justified in assuming that our appreciation of causes and effects is in all cases a fair measure of the inscrutable realities. For, although it is no doubt true that, in many cases, experience of superficial appearances informs us correctly of the underlying realities, it is, to say the least, perfectly conceivable,— especially in a complex series of causative interactions among objects, such as $A, B, C, ... Z$,—that the unobservable qualities, by a cumulative influence, should at last affect those realities which in turn affect consciousness. And, if this be admitted, it necessarily follows that there may be two series of causes and effects, $A, B, C, ... Y$; and $A, B, C, ... Y$; to all appearances identical, but which are in reality very dissimilar, (either in consequence of one series having inappreciable attributes which the other series has not, or from having the same inappreciable attributes differently arranged, or both these reasons,) and this dissimilarity, hitherto obscured, may, at the last stage in the sequence $A, B, C, \ldots\ldots Y, Z$, affect one of the observable attributes, and so become apparent; the final result being (to appearance) indifferently $A, B, C, \ldots\ldots Y, Z$; or $A, B, C, \ldots\ldots Y, Z'$; or $A, B, C, \ldots\ldots Y\alpha\beta\gamma$, &c.

§ 11. This reasoning will perhaps appear to a man of science, at first sight, almost ludicrous. If, however, he will take the trouble to analyse his emotions, he will find that the only excuse he can frame for them is, that experience never displays such irregularity in natural sequences. This fact, however, has no bearing upon the present argument, as we shall immediately perceive.

Without entering into the most vexed of all philosophical questions, the true nature of a cause, we find, upon the very threshold of the metaphysics of causation, a fact, which all modern philosophers of any ability agree in recognizing, and which affords a complete and sufficient answer to the argument grounded on the uniformity of experience. This fact is that the invariable sequences patent to experience, and which are ordinarily "dignified with the name of cause" and effects, can really only be supposed such in a metaphorical sense; or, at least, that we have no means of ascertaining in any one case, whether in an invariable sequence we have really perceived the true cause of a true effect. That a true cause in every case of such sequence does exist, is readily admitted; but that we cannot take cognizance of this true cause, or, at least, cannot know in any one case whether or not we have taken cognizance of it, is a doctrine upon which metaphysicians are ever tending more and more to agree. "The notion of causation is deemed, by the schools of metaphysics most in vogue at the present moment, to imply a mysterious and most powerful tie, such as cannot, or at least does not, exist between any physical fact and that other physical fact on which it is invariably consequent, and which is popularly termed its cause[1]."

There is nothing mystical about this conception—nothing that need repel a mind disciplined in regarding physical sequences as the most real and invariable objects which it can contemplate. The considerations already briefly advanced as to our entire dependence upon our senses for information regarding the external world—considerations which are surely the reverse of abstruse—are alone sufficient to indicate that there must be a broad distinction between the ontological and the phænomenal order of things, and so between an ontological and a phænomenal cause. "Quis enim me doceat quid sit substantia, nisi miseris illis verbis, *res subsistens?* Scientiam ergo nostram constat esse umbram in sole."

Thus much then being premised, it is evident that the objection founded upon the uniformity of experience, or, which is the same thing, upon the assertion that the sense of the real order is not impaired by being translated into the apparent, has no bearing upon our present argument. For if (to use the terms of Reid) an efficient cause must in every case include the physical, it is evident that the field in which the former operates is not that of the superficial appearances; or, returning to the symbols of Section 10, it is among the figures, and not among the letters, that the actual causes are at work. Now it is, no doubt, perfectly true that in all simple cases the real order (so

[1] Mill.

far at least as is practically necessary) is faithfully reflected into the experiential order. This fact is indeed indisputable, both on *à priori* and *à posteriori* grounds. It is indisputable on *à priori* grounds, because, unless this fact were a fact, human existence would have been impossible; since it would have become impossible to adjust internal relations to external with any degree of certainty. It is indisputable on *à posteriori* grounds, because experience is but the empirically corrected register of such efficient causes and of such of their mutual interactions, as present to consciousness the outward and visible aspect of physical causes. But although this fact is indisputably true when applied to comparatively simple cases of sequence, it by no means follows that it is likewise true when applied to complex cases—and it is only with complex cases that we are concerned, for the reasons mentioned in Chap. 1, Section 3. This is evident from the consideration that the utilitarian necessity for the trustworthiness of experience demands only that the register shall be correct for simple cases; and even were this not so, we may be sure that, if there are thus two currents of causation, a real and an apparent, a point of complexity *must* somewhere be reached at which it would become impossible for the former to keep pace with the latter; and if this point happened (so to speak) to have been below that at which the utilitarian *necessity* for the accurate representation of experience comes in, human existence would have been impossible.

Hence, it is evident that whatever degree of strength our present argument may be supposed to possess, it is wholly unaffected by the objection raised from the uniformity of experience. Experience must, in any case, be uniform; but this fact has nothing to do with the question at issue. The only bearing which experience has upon this question is that which has already been discussed, viz., the extent or degree of its ability to symbolize through the senses the interaction of efficient causes upon one another. This degree it is, as before observed, manifestly impossible even approximately to determine, since one term in the comparison is a negative of the most universal and inconceivable kind. It is hoped, however, that the foregoing brief discussion of this negative part of the subject is sufficient to indicate, that from the known conditions of obtaining such knowledge as we possess on the one hand, and the known imperfection both in kind and extent of those conditions on the other, we are amply justified in inferring, or rather the inference is forced upon us, that not only is all our knowledge of second causes merely symbolical, but that even of this symbolical knowledge our attainment is indefinitely small; and that even could we attain to the topmost pinnacle of such knowledge as with the medium of our present senses is potential, we should still be enveloped by a vast and seething cloud-land of mysterious though interoperating causes, the confines of which we could neither see, nor be able to conceive.

§ 12. Let us now turn to the positive aspect of the subject before us. We know what each of our senses perceives, and so can estimate precisely the amount of knowledge which would have been subtracted from the race, had any one of our senses been absent. If sight, for instance, had been wanting, we should have known of the existence of light only by the occurence of a few chemical reactions, such as the union of chlorine and hydrogen, the decomposition of carbonic anhydride in the presence of chlorophylle, of some of the silver and gold salts, and, as recently observed, the decreasing of the electric conductivity of metallic selenium[1]. How vast would have been the knowledge of the Universe thus excluded! Yet, on Darwinian principles, the occurrence of the eye depends, as it were, upon the merest accident, or rather on a concurrence of many accidents; and whether or not we subscribe to these principles, they may be taken as a fair index of the probable chances there are as to the presence or absence of a possible sense. Had then nerve-organization (not to go further back) never been sensitive to light, the peripheral portion of a sensory nerve could never have become modified into an ocellus. Further, had the perception of light not been for the benefit of species, or had the requisite variations never arisen, or had they arisen in an improper order or relation to other variations; or again, had the varying organisms not been subjected to adequate competition with other and kindred varying organisms; an ocellus could never have advanced in structure. Yet the degree of this advance is so great, that Mr Darwin himself admits the difficulty of believing it due to natural selection to be "insuperable by our imagination."

It detracts nothing from the force of this example to assert the obvious truth, that human intelligence would have been impossible had the race been destitute of vision. Indeed this assertion is merely a repetition of our argument. For the fact that, in the absence of the visual faculty, intelligence could never have become human, merely affords a high presumptive proof of the probability we are endeavouring to establish, viz., that

[1] There are many other chemical changes which light is able to effect; but as these are very minute and insignificant, they do not affect the illustration.

were we endowed with senses additional to those we possess, our intelligence would have been superhuman.

The sense of vision has been chosen as an example, because it stands mid-way in importance between that of touch and the other senses. The ancient doctrine of Democritus, that all the senses are but modifications of touch, although long rejected, is now universally recognized. Hence, as we before likened the sum of our sensual abilities to five intellectual apertures, so we now see that they may be diagrammatically represented as four small tubes, surrounding a fifth and larger one, and all alike pointing in the same direction.

§ 13. To these views it may be objected, that the fact of all animals possessing the same senses, is a sufficient pledge that no sense of any importance could be superadded. We reply, It is quite the contrary. The fact of all animals possessing the same senses, only proves that this possession represents the approximate *maximum* of adaptation between an individual and its environment, attainable by the plasticity of nerve-organization. The fact, therefore, that man possesses these senses in common with animals proves nothing, except that equally with them he is, in his animal capacity, adapted to his environment. Indeed, this fact only tends to intensify the present argument; for when we reflect upon the elaborate care (so to speak) with which nature has provided for the animal wants of creation, it becomes a highly significant consideration that man should have no additional senses. For I do not think it is too much to assert, that all the four sense-organs occur upon a fundamentally different type, in each of the sub-kingdoms in which they appear[1]. Yet, notwithstanding all this wealth of adap-

[1] By this is not, of course, meant that the same type never

tive power, man—the only animal endowed with reflective faculties—is unprovided with any special senses to minister to them. Why is this? Surely not because nerve-organization, being as we have just seen so marvellously plastic, is unable to respond to the demand; or that nothing remains to be taken sensible cognizance of beyond what we perceive. The counter hypothesis is certainly on *à priori* grounds the more rational, viz.,—that the four sense-organs having reference to the escape from enemies, and the procuring and examination of food, are of vital importance to the animal existence of their possessor, and so have undergone innumerable modifications; while any additional sense, having exclusive reference to the intellect, being useless to the animal, has never appeared in man.

Whether or not, therefore, we accept the theory of evolution, thus much seems plainly indicated, viz., that the quality of the senses on which we depend for our knowledge of second causes, is determined with reference to our animal welfare, and not to our intellectual curiosity. Could we perceive the vibrations which give rise to the phænomena of magnetism, in the same sensible manner as we can those which occasion light, how profoundly might our conceptions of the physical universe be modified. Under existing conditions, we only know the presence of these vibrations by the

---

occurs in different sub-kingdoms; but merely that each sub-kingdom has a characteristic type. The Vertebrate's eye is wonderfully imitated in the Cephalopoda, while the molluscous type of eye occurs in the Annulosa; yet no one would hesitate to say which is the characteristic type in each of these sub-kingdoms. Simi'arly, the otolithic type of ear occurs in at least three sub-kingdoms, but is characteristic of the Mollusca alone.

occurrence of a few phænomena analogous to those chemical decompositions, &c., upon which, as we previously saw, we should have depended for our knowledge of light, had we been destitute of vision. Had it not been for the apparent accident that a particular ore of a single metal, or that this metal when placed under very exclusive conditions, becomes affected by these vibrations in a sensible manner; we should have been ignorant of the very existence of a force in its nature as cosmical as heat.

From these considerations it becomes evident that, unless we make the highly improbable supposition that the portion of our environment which is potent to evolve[1] senses necessary for the maintenance of our animal existence, is the entire Universe of second causes, we must believe an unknowable of such causes to exist. Πάντων χρημάτων μέτρον ἄνθρωπος.

To this must be added the consideration, that with whatever degree of plasticity we may suppose nerve-organization to be endowed, it must have a limit somewhere; so that even if our senses were determined with reference to our intellectual instead of to our animal nature, we might still feel that an unknowable of second causes probably existed beyond our cognizance. Τὸ γιγνῶσκον κατὰ τὴν ἑαυτοῦ γιγνώσκει φύσιν.

§ 14. We have not yet exhausted the limitations which our nature imposes upon our knowledge. Whether or not we accept the theory of evolution, it is evident that *in things physical* our mental faculties are moulded by our sensual abilities; for our reflective states

---

[1] Whether a real force or a metaphorical is here given to this word is immaterial, the fact of our adaptation to our environment being all that we are concerned with. See § 15.

are all ultimately dependent upon our sensational states, —thought, humanly speaking, being impossible in the total and *perpetual* absence of sensation. To this it may be retorted,—' It does not follow that because thought is impossible in the absence of sensation, therefore in the presence of sensation thought has no other source from which to draw its ultimate materials.' And this rejoinder would be sufficiently cogent, were we speaking of thought in general, for then our proposition would be incapable of proof. Far from this, however, we are only dealing with our ability to apprehend physical phænomena, and that such ability is wholly dependent upon our sensational states, our hospital reports abundantly prove[1]. And if this is the case, the considerations just advanced seem to justify the belief that our mental faculties themselves are, in their appreciation of things physical, determined with exclusive reference to our animal requirements. No doubt by cultivation in certain directions, by habits of reflection acquired by individuals and ever intensified during transmission, and by the division of intellectual labour; the human mind has developed its innate faculties to a degree so far excelling that which is required for a mere animal existence, that it might well be supposed to refer to an altogether different order of things,—the animal existence being the adjunct to the mental, rather than the reverse. Nevertheless, a difference of degree, however great, does not constitute a difference of kind; and however far the

[1] For the psychological condition of a man born blind and suddenly restored to sight, see Adam Smith's *Metaphysics and External Senses:* for that of a person deaf and blind, "Laura Bridgman." Compare also Carpenter's *Human Physiology*, 7th Ed. p. 611.

human intellect may have succeeded in extending the lines of its initial endowments, it can never alter the nature of these endowments themselves. However unlike the growing organism may be to the germ from which it originated, the former is dependent upon the latter for its substance, its dimensions, and its form.

§ 15. The conclusions thus arrived at admit of easy confirmation from psychological deductions. Long before the evolution theory was thought of as applying to psychology, it was pretty generally recognized by students of the science that objective existence can only be perceived by the mind in certain modes relative to our faculties, sensational and intellectual, since objective existence can only be known by the mind "under modifications determined by these faculties themselves[1]." This general inference, however, it seems to me, admitted of the retort:—How are we to know that the mind is not originally endowed with powers of intuitively apprehending objective existences in their reality? Some one mode of internal perception must, as it were, have been chosen by the Deity as the endowment of human intelligence, and is it not, at least, just as probable that that mode is the one which most harmonizes with external realities, as that it should be any other single mode[2]?

[1] Hamilton.
[2] It is to be observed that in the absence of the evolution theory this question is unanswerable: it is not, however, on this account formidable. On the contrary, it is feeble to an indefinite degree, because embodying a conjecture which can never be raised even to the lowest stage of probability. All that upon this subject can be legitimately supplied by any system of psychology is, that the mind "instinctively infers unknown causes from known [because subjective] effects;" but whether or not the inference concerning

As the science of psychology is still, in respect of progress, in its infancy, and the theory of evolution, as distinguished from a mere speculation, not yet a generation old, we need not wonder that opinions may now legitimately vary as to the extent in which that theory affects that science. As, however, many among students of physical science recognize in the evolution theory a proximate, or scientific, explanation of the phænomena of mind; and as not a few among students of philosophy subscribe to the belief that "it is this theory alone which furnishes a solution of the controversies between the disciples of Locke and Kant;" it would be a serious omission not to point out in this place how that theory, if accepted, cuts to the root of natural realism, in so far as this is distinguished from cosmothetic idealism of the third order. It does so because it supplies the reason why intelligence has, in all its relations to the external world—sensational and otherwise—been moulded to the particular form in which it exists. Hence, if we accept this theory, we cannot, without violating the law of parsimony, look for other causes.

The law of intelligence is formulated by the author and master of the philosophy in question as being, "that the strengths of the inner cohesions between psychical states must be proportionate to the persistences of the outer relations symbolized[1]." Such being the case, the development of intelligence is "secured by the one simple principle that experience of the outer relations *produces* inner cohesions, and makes the inner

the character, as distinguished from the existence, of these causes is correct, and if so to what degree—these are matters, not of probability, but of opinion.

[1] *Psychology*, Vol. I. p. 439.

cohesions strong in proportion as the outer relations are persistent[1]." Again, "what do we say of cases in which the inner order does not completely answer to the outer order? We say that they imply a low degree of intellect, or a limited experience, or but a partial enlightenment. And the disappearance of these discrepances between thoughts and facts, we speak of as an advance in intelligence[2]."

If then these are the conditions under which human intelligence has become existent, it follows deductively from the nature of these conditions, that intelligence can never contemplate physical events from other than a single stand-point; and that this stand-point is determined with exclusive reference to our animal necessities. Whatever degree of advance intelligence is destined to make in the future, we may be sure that it can never rise above its source—can never take cognizance of other relations in its environment than those which pertain, however remotely, to that class under which and by which alone it has been evolved. If there exist any such other relations (and we cannot but suppose that there must), their perception has, as it were, been carefully sifted away from our intelligence,—that class alone being eliminated, as the objects of possible thought, which there was a dire necessity for retaining.

§ 16. It is almost unnecessary to point out that the foregoing considerations have no reference to man's spiritual nature, since whatever view we take of this—whether we consider it as separate from, or as including his animal intelligence,—his moral obligations would be equally unaffected by the proximate source of his intel-

---

[1] *Psychology*, Vol. I. p. 440.
[2] *Ibid*. p. 410.

lectual faculties. Man would be none the less human were his origin proved to be derivative, nor would conscience be the less supreme even though evolved. All we are now engaged in shewing is, that in the interpretation of natural phænomena we are restricted to the use of intellectual faculties, whose character is determined with reference to our animal wants and not to our mental desires. And just as we appear to have a connecting link between the sensible and the insensible in magnetism, so we appear to have a similar link between the intelligible and the unintelligible in the interstellar ether. We are bound to think of it as possessing some of the essential properties of matter, and not others: it thus becomes semi-intelligible, because partially opposed to faculties which refer exclusively to the material order. We might add that in the case of consciousness and the intellectual operations, we happen, as it were by accident, to be acquainted with the existence of a wholly unintelligible order, because, so far as we know or are able to conceive, wholly removed from the material.

It thus becomes evident that, even apart from the evolution theory, not only is there probably a region of second causes which is imperceptible, but also that, even could it be perceived, it would probably be unintelligible. And the easy corollary on the preceding is, that even that which is perceptible is not necessarily intelligible[1].

[1] This presentation contains and extends that of Sir W. Hamilton. "The relations of *knowledge* are those which arise from the reciprocal dependence of the subject and the object of thought" (*Lectures*, Vol. I. p. 146). "If the condition of *relativity* be not purified, there results *the impossible to thought*, that is what may exist but what we are unable to conceive as existing" (*Discussions*, pp. 178, 179).

For if the perceptible and the intelligible are determined with reference to our animal existence, it follows that the one need only coincide with the other in so far as the coincidence is necessary or desirable for that existence. And this *à priori* conclusion is supported by the indisputable couplet of facts before noticed, viz., that whether we trace scientific ideas to their source or to their termination, we are alike landed in the domain of the inconceivable. We have, therefore, no warrant for supposing that even what our senses are able to perceive, our intellectual faculties are able to appreciate. There may be ultimate scientific ideas of which our intelligence is unable to take cognizance; and there may be innumerable combinations amongst the ideas we have, of which, nevertheless, we are unable to conceive.

§ 17. Most of the foregoing considerations will, no doubt, appear to the man of science to be of little value because of so indefinite a character. He has been accustomed in his modes of thought to rigour and exactitude— to believe only so far as he can prove. But to carry this affection of mind into a province which confessedly transcends knowledge, is merely to take a dwarfed and narrow view of the case. No doubt conservatism of thought is most desirable when the subject investigated admits of precision; but where this is not the case, it becomes irrational to close our eyes to probabilities merely because they are not precise. In short, that mode of thought which is the only legitimate one to apply to the knowable, is just the mode of all others the most illegitimate when applied to the unknowable.

The general conclusions, then, which the foregoing considerations establish, may be thus briefly summarized. Our ignorance of second causes is not only certainly great, and great to an indefinite degree, but in all probability necessarily so—not only is there certainly an indefinitely large tract of second causes unknown, but in all probability there exist innumerable second causes in their nature unknowable. " The philosophy of the conditioned proves that things there are which *may*, nay *must*, be true of which the understanding is wholly unable to construe to itself the possibility[1]."

§ 18. To a mind acquainted with the *à priori* argument against miracles and the kindred subject we are now considering, the above conclusions will, no doubt, appear beside the question. Fully admitting that our ignorance of second causes is indefinitely great, such a mind will feel that we are, nevertheless, sufficiently acquainted with them to know that their action is determined by " adamantine Law." And to such an extent will such a mind be imbued with this conviction, that it will be irritably intolerant of any suggestion to the contrary. 'As well,' it will be said, 'might we believe with our grandfathers that the geological strata had been purposely interfered with by miraculous agency in order to deceive the impious, as brook the idea for a moment that the Reign of Law terminates with human experience. What then is the use of shewing how limited that experience is, so long as it is sufficient to indicate that Reign?'

All such statements as these have the appeal to analogy at their foundation. It therefore becomes imperative briefly to enunciate the character of analogical arguments. We have already seen that science in making this appeal to analogy has ceased to be scientific; if, therefore, men of science object to logical enunciations in this matter,

---

[1] Sir W. Hamilton's *Discussions*, p. 597.

they must remember that they have brought them upon themselves;—if they have quitted their own province, they must expect to encounter the forces of the province they invade.

§ 19. Analogy is strictly a Λόγων ὁμοιότης[1], or resemblance of relations. "There is no word, however, that is used more loosely or in a greater variety of senses[2]." "In ordinary language it has come to mean any resemblance between things which enables us to believe of one what we know of the other[3]." Further, there is no mode of argument which admits of such a variety in the degrees of its cogency: "it may amount to nothing, or it may be a perfect and conclusive induction[4]." But whatever the sense in which the word analogy may be used, or whatever degree of cogency arguments founded upon it may possess, the latter must all admit of being reduced (in accordance with the primary conception of the process) to a formula of proportion. "In every analogical argument there must be two ratios, and, of course, two terms in each ratio. The ratios must be distinct, but all four terms need not; one term may be repeated in each ratio, and so three distinct terms are sufficient. One ratio being better known than the other, serves to explain it[5]."

Thus much as to the essential nature of analogical arguments in general being premised, I think no logician will take exception to the following canon :—The argumentative value of any particular analogy, varies inversely as the difference between the ratio known and the ratio un-

---

[1] Aristotle. See Whately's *Rhetoric*, p. 58.
[2] Mill, *Logic*.
[3] Jevons, *Logic*, 226.
[4] Mill, *Logic*.
[5] Wilkinson.

known; whether this difference consists in the number or in the importance of the relations involved[1]. Now this is true of all cases, but it will, I think, be further conceded that there are two essentially distinct classes of the unknown ratio; one in which its limits are perceived, and the other in which they are not perceived. In cases where they are perceived, the exact value of the analogy can be determined: in cases where they are not perceived, the value of the analogy fails in direct proportion to the degree in which such perception fails. For any failure in such perception entails, not only a corresponding degree of ignorance as to the amount of difference between the two ratios in respect of their *extent;* but also an indefinite amount of possibility that the unknown ratio may present a difference from the known in respect of *likeness* or *kind*.

As these distinctions will subsequently be found of great importance in the general argument, it may be desirable to render them more evident by means of an illustration. Let us suppose that a geologist is exploring a newly discovered country, and finds in the first portion of it which he examines a certain complex superposition of strata, which he recognizes as identical with that of another country where he knows this order of superposition to be uninterrupted and universal. If the limits of the country he is exploring are known to him, he will be able to estimate the exact degree of analogical probability there is, as to whether the particular superposition of strata in question is likewise in this case universal. But

---

[1] When this Essay was almost completed, the Author's attention directed itself for the first time to Prof. Bain's canon (see *Inductive Logic*, page 143). The striking similarity between that canon and the above, is therefore purely unintentional.

if the limits of the country he is exploring are unknown to him, it is manifest that he is, proportionably to his ignorance upon this point, precluded from estimating this analogical probability. And his inability to make this estimation refers, not only to the probable *extent* of the observed superposition, relative to the size of the whole country; but also to the probable degree in which the rest of the strata differ from the observed portion in *character*.

§ 20. Applying then these considerations as to the nature and value of analogical arguments to the case of the scientific appeal to this method, we have first to observe that the analogy instituted is not unassailable even in its known ratio. In other words, we have no warrant to predicate of any Natural Law whatever that it is eternal and universal. For the only means we have of ascertaining the existence of any Law, is by observing its operation within the limits of experience. When, therefore, we pass beyond the jurisdiction, so to speak, of those limits, we are necessarily unable to bring any particular Law to the test of experience; and consequently we are unable to assert whether or not beyond these limits it is in operation. This view is upheld by Mr Mansel with great ability, who extends it even to the law of causation; asserting it to be quite possible that beyond experience the sequence of phænomena may be either independent of all Laws whatever, or be determined by Laws which are continually changing. "We cannot," he says, "*conceive* this state of things, but we can suppose it; and this very inability to conceive a phænomenon as taking place without a cause—in other words, this subjective necessity of the law of cause and effect—results merely from the conditions of our experience." "We cannot," he continues, "conceive a course of nature without uniform succession, as we cannot conceive a being who sees without eyes, or hears without ears; because we cannot, under existing circumstances, experience the necessary intuition. But such things may notwithstanding exist; and under other circumstances, they might become objects of possible conception, the laws of the process of conception remaining unaltered[1]."

It is so rare a thing to find the opinions of this author endorsed by Mr Mill, that the eulogy of the latter upon those just set forth is significant. He writes, "This exposition, I do not hesitate to say, contains more sound philosophy than is to be found on the same subject in all Sir W. Hamilton's writings." Again, in his system of logic, Mr Mill says: "It must be remarked that the reasons for this reliance [*i. e.*, even in the law of causation] do not hold in circumstances unknown to us, and beyond the possible range of our experience. In distant parts of the stellar regions, where the phænomena may be entirely unlike those with which we are acquainted, it would be folly to affirm confidently that this general law prevails, any more than those special ones which we have found to hold universally on our own planet[2]." Now it is evident that if we suppose any known Law to be of a merely local or relative application, the whole of the *à priori* objections which we are considering immediately disintegrate. For, if any one Natural Law is granted to be variable, either in respect of the extent or the manner of its operation; it becomes impossible to assign the diversity of the effects which may ensue upon its being

---

[1] *Prolegomena Logica*, p. 149.
[2] *Logic*, Vol. II. p. 108.

compounded with other and invariable Laws. To take a simple case, let us suppose that there are five invariable Laws which, by their mutual interoperation, are able to produce as many different effects as there are possible permutations amongst themselves; that is, 120[1]. Let us now suppose that a sixth Law is introduced, subject to the same conditions: the possible effects would now be 720. But if the sixth Law varied in only one direction— *i. e.*, with one alternative of action—the possible effects would be 1440. Now each of these new effects, viz., $1440 - 720 = 720$, would themselves become causes of other compounded effects, and so on.

No one will be more willing to admit the truth of these considerations than a man of science. They will, however, at first sight, appear to him beside the question; for, so long as it is admitted (as of course it is) that Natural Laws are *relatively* invariable, it appears at first sight as though the fact of any Law being variable or non-existent beyond experience, could not affect the operation of that Law within experience. That this, however, is not *necessarily* so, we can readily perceive. For, taking the case of variability of action, it is evident that a Law x which is invariably x within experience, but which is indifferently x or y beyond experience, if as x produces the effects abc... &c., in the one sphere, will also as x produce abc... &c., in the other. As y, however, it will produce the effects $\alpha \beta \gamma$... &c., and these themselves becoming causes in the remote sphere (whether of space

---

[1] It is to be observed that *Laws* differ from *Causes*. Five invariable Causes could only produce one effect, but five invariable Laws could produce an indefinite number of effects, the number depending upon the possible diversity of the material and mechanical agents through which the Laws operate.

or time), *may* propagate their influence to the sphere of experience—an influence which, although lost to cognizance amid the general intermixture of effects, would none the less produce its full measure of result.

I do not urge these considerations as being of much weight; and, indeed, should not have advanced them at all but for the sake of a symmetrical argument. At the same time, it must be added, we have no means of gauging the possibilities or the probabilities in this matter; so that while different minds are at full argumentative liberty to attach any degree of weight they choose to the italicized word *may*, no one is at liberty to deem his opinion of more value than an unsubstantiated hypothesis. This much, however, we may safely affirm—*if* such variability is ever propagated, from no matter how remote a point, into the sphere of experience—such variability must, as we have said, within that sphere produce its full measure of result; so that, *if* any Natural Law is not absolutely what it appears to be relatively, it is impossible for us to estimate the total relative effects of its operation.

§ 21. We now enter upon a more important and a less mystical portion of our argument, viz., the estimation of the second ratio in the analogy we are considering. It is for the purpose of this estimation that it has been necessary to enter at so great a length into the subject of our ignorance regarding the total operation of second causes. The application of that lengthy discussion to the subject now before us is sufficiently obvious. For, waiving the objection to the first ratio just adduced, and assuming that all Natural Laws with which we are acquainted are universal, and absolutely unconditional, it is evident from what has been said upon our ignorance of second causes, that the unknown ratio is in this case not only certainly of very great extent, but also that it has its limits wholly beyond perception. According then to the canon already laid down, the value of the analogy is not only certainly low, but low to an indefinite degree. And this degree of lowness (whatever it may be) is of the kind which necessitates the presence of an indefinite degree of possibility, that the unknown ratio may differ from the known in likeness or kind.

Now, in contradiction to these truths, the scientific appeal to analogy is made with the object of proving, not only that General Laws obtain throughout the entire series of second causes, but also that their *character* is throughout identical with that which we proximately observe,— that the whole domain of second causes, whatever its extent may be, is precisely the same as that with which we are partially acquainted, and in no wise understand,— that there cannot exist a class of second causes whose operation is (not only other than intelligible, but) other than that class with which experience is thus acquainted, —that the particular interactions among those second causes with which we are thus partially acquainted (and which constitute an indefinitely small portion of the whole), because we have observed them to be true relatively to this our limited knowledge, therefore must be true absolutely—cannot be modified by any changes or interactions taking place in the unknown domain of second causes. In other words, this analogy presumes to infer that the Almighty, Whose knowledge of second causes is conceded to be absolute, cannot, without violating their normal course, make them produce any particular effect He may desire; only because experience shews that we, whose ignorance of their nature and extent is confessed, are unable to perceive the mode in which He could so operate. It is of no avail for objectors to employ the *tu quoque* manner of argument, by pointing out that it is as impossible for us to prove that the Almighty does answer Prayer through Natural Law, as it is for them to prove that He does not; for this only leaves the matter in uncertainty, which is the only issue we are contending for. We are not engaged in proving that the Almighty does so answer Prayer, but merely in removing a presumption that He does not. Even, therefore, were we able dimly to perceive the manner in which He might so answer it—*i.e.*, the qualities in which the unknowable Laws might be conceived to differ from the knowable—this would not be the place to point them out[1]. "On the great Postulate of experience we are to accept uncontradicted experience as true. But where there has been no experience we can believe nothing. We are not obliged to show that a thing is not; the burden lies upon whoever maintains that the thing is[2]."

To sum up. If our knowledge of physical causation were absolute, we might be able to show some necessary reason why the Almighty does not answer Prayer through the normal course of Natural Law: as it is, the probability established is low in proportion to the degree in which our knowledge is removed from being absolute—*i.e.*, in proportion to the weakness of the analogy. Did we

[1] See chap. V.
[2] Prof. Bain no doubt intends this as a statement of the antecedent improbability attaching to the occurrence of miracles; and it is a beautifully concise and perfectly true statement of the case. Scientifically the fact of such occurrence is hopelessly uncertain; but it does not follow that this uncertainty cannot for this reason admit of being dispelled on other grounds. See chap. IV. § 19. Prof. Bain, *Inductive Logic*, p. 152.

know the precise distance by which it is thus removed—*i. e.*, the degree of that weakness—we might be able to measure the amount of the probability: as it is, our ability to institute this measurement decreases in proportion to our inability to estimate our ignorance.

§ 22. A candid opponent will here observe :— 'These arguments certainly establish the position that a class of unknowable second causes must in all likelihood be supposed to exist; and that as these must, to a greater or less extent, influence the known class, thus far it is not improbable that numerous, and necessarily unintelligible, though strictly normal changes, taking place in the imperceptible class, might produce effects in the perceptible, which would correctly be deemed miraculous. But this, after all, is not the real question at issue. Freely admitting that an unknowable class of second causes exists, we must yet believe that their inter-operations are governed by Laws as unconditional and as incapable of caprice, as are the Laws which preside over the known class. It is doubtless true that the analogy by which we infer that the Reign of Law beyond experience is precisely similar to the Reign of Law within experience, is essentially a case of 'enumeratio simplex ubi non reperitur instantia contradictoria,' and so perceptibly a very feeble one—more especially as it has been pointed out that if 'a lower rule of working' is ever 'superseded by a higher,' the fact must purposely be hidden from our cognizance;—and it is also doubtlessly true that this analogy is yet more feeble to an indefinite, because an imperceptible, degree. But it would be a great mistake to suppose that the analogy is really as weak as it is thus represented to be; for the strength of this analogy is derived, not from a mere observation of cases within experience, but from the transcendental probability that Nature is everywhere uniform. Although, therefore, as a mere analogy, it is a case of simple enumeration, it is at the same time a pledge assuring us of the mode of universal causation; and in the presence of this pledge thus afforded by experience, we must refuse to believe that 'strictly normal changes' taking place beyond experience, can 'produce miraculous effects' within experience, unless it can be shewn that the transcendental probability on which we rely is a delusion and a snare. All, therefore, that the foregoing considerations do is to remove the question a stage further back. This question is more ultimate, and admits of being briefly stated thus:—Is the Divine method of physical Government constant, whether conducted through the mediation of known, unknown, or unknowable Laws?'

This statement of the case serves to introduce us to the second division of our argument. It will be observed from what has been said in the last section, that the only meaning which can attach to the word "constant" in this statement is, constant in accordance with our ideas of constancy; so that the question may be more correctly presented thus:—Does our conception of Natural Law afford an infallible index of the method of Divine Government, taken as a whole? In entering upon this new division of our subject, it will not be forgotten that the conclusion to which the now closing division has, it would appear, unavoidably led, is, that in so far as any objection to miracles and the like is founded *only* upon the observed nature of known Laws, apart from any metaphysical considerations as to the method of the Divine Government considered as a whole, and the means we possess of estimating this, so far must such objections be deemed, to a certainly great, and a further indefinite degree, valueless.

The importance of this conclusion will not be undervalued by those conversant with the literature of this and kindred subjects. It practically nullifies the scientific objections to Prayer in the cruder forms of their presentation. No doubt all such forms of presentation are dimly supposed to refer to the more ultimate question, if, indeed, the subject of the former is not confusedly fancied, in some way or other, to include the latter. No two subjects, however, can be more widely distinct—the one forming but an indefinitely limited portion of the other; and it is for the sake of throwing this distinction into the strongest possible light, that the arrangement of the present Essay has been adopted.

All arguments, then, founded upon the bare ground of physical knowledge, however imposing their superficial aspect may appear, are in reality indefinitely unstable, since from the nature of the present case we must dig into the stiff soil of metaphysics, before an argument of any kind in support of the scientific proposition can be established. Let us then apply ourselves to this work, for the purpose of showing that the arguments in support of that proposition admit of a yet further reduction in the degree of their stability.

CHAPTER III.

§ 1. WHAT are the relations subsisting between the Almighty and His Creation? We have first the relation of cause to effect—a relation which in ordinary cases admits of no more ultimate reduction. In the present instance, however, we have as a datum something more than an ordinary cause; we have the First Cause. Now the idea of a First Cause, although necessary, is derivative. It is necessary, in order to terminate in a thinkable manner the sequence of cause and effect, which surrounds and permeates experience; but it is derived from that very sequence which it endeavours to end. I am aware that in making this assertion I am touching upon a moot point in philosophy, and one which it would be foreign to the purpose in hand to discuss. I have, however, merely given my view as to the origin of the idea in question, in order to shew that this view is not incompatible with the statement immediately to be adduced. To those who hold the opposite opinion, viz., that the idea of a First Cause is a primary intuition, the following statement will appear self-evident. This statement is, that prime causation differs from secondary in kind. That this must be so, even upon the derivation hypothesis, is manifest; for the mere fact of that hypothesis instituting a resting-place in the sequence at all, shews that it postulates a difference in kind between the influence of the First, and that of all other causes. Some writers have endeavoured to draw a distinction between causation as a necessary inference from action, and as a necessary inference from existence; alleging that the former is the true ground of the conception in question—existence "not requiring to be accounted for in the same way that material action is." Now, we have nothing to do with this question beyond stating that, even upon this view, the above statement remains unaffected; since, upon the one doctrine, action becomes as *essential* an instance of cause and effect, as existence is upon the other.

We may arrive at the same conclusion thus:—Did the two orders of causative influence differ from one another in degree only, they must differ in a practically infinite degree, (since the influence of the First Cause extends through all the lines of second causes, and these are practically infinite in number and direction,) and a practically infinite difference in degree is, to finite minds, identical with a difference in kind.

Lastly, it may be shewn that the very mention of the First Cause as an existence, is contingent upon the supposition that it is an influence *sui generis*. For this cause must be self-existent, while all other causes are derived: but the self-existent cause must differ from all originated causes, not in degree only, but in kind. "Between the creating and the created, there must be a distinction transcending any of the distinctions existing between different divisions of the created. That which is uncaused cannot be assimilated to that which is caused: the two being, in the very naming, antithetically opposed[1]."

Now these are no mere meaningless mysticisms—

[1] Spencer.

they belong to the very essence of the term we are considering:—*i.e.*, the term cannot be employed without carrying with it the conclusion they contain. We may, if we like, altogether refuse to think of the First Cause; but, if we think of it, in the very act of framing our idea, we of necessity assume that it differs from all else in character and kind.

§ 2. When we impose the limitation of intelligence upon the First Cause, we open up a field of numerous, complex, and indefinite relations; for these are not merely such as subsist generally between the conscious and the unconscious, the intelligent and the non-intelligent, the subject and the object. In this case the unconscious has no being apart from the conscious—the object exists within and is sustained by the subject. In short, when we impose this limitation and conceive of the Origin of Things, no longer in the aspect of a mindless Cause, but in that of a Deity; the relations between the causing and the caused become utterly inconceivable, although, as we must suppose, unutterably numerous.

§ 3. Philosophy no less than theology compels us to predicate infinity as an attribute of the Unconditioned. Now the genus infinity contains, when ascribed to the Deity, the species with which we are more intimately concerned,—the attribute of Omnipotence. The relations introduced by this further ascription are of great importance to the present argument.

The term Παντοκράτωρ is expounded by Barrow[1] as presenting five ideas, viz., that of authority over all things (omnipotestas), power to effect all things (omnipotentia), actual exercise of such authority and power (omnipotentatus), possession of all things (omnitenentia),

---

[1] Sermon XI.

and the upholding of all things (omnicontinentia). Pearson more concisely generalizes these meanings, in accordance with the etymology of the word, as containing two ideas, viz., that of universal power, and that of universal rule. The first of these establishes an unthinkable relationship, which, nevertheless, must be deemed an actual one, viz., that of potential Creator to the non-existent; "God's actual dominion being no otherwise necessary, than upon supposition of a precedent act of creation[1]."

Kant divides the conception of nothing into four parts[2]. The first of these is, "Empty conception without an object"—*i.e.*, an intelligibly possible, though non-existent entity: the second is, "Empty object of a conception"—*i.e.*, "a conception of the absence of an object:" the third is, "Empty intuition without object"—*i.e.*, a mere form of intuition, which is itself no object, such as space or time: the fourth is, "Empty object without conception"—*i.e.*, "the object of a conception which is self-contradictory," and therefore impossible. It is only with the first and last of these divisions that we are concerned:—with the first, because an Omnipotent Creator must be able at any moment to convert an "empty conception" into its corresponding "object:" with the last, because even an Omnipotent Creator cannot effect contradictories:—"Deus propterea quædam non potest, quia omnipotens est." In both cases, however, it must be observed that our faculties are inadequate to decide as to what is or is not possible or congruous to the Deity. "God cannot do things which are really contradictory, but He can reconcile things which may seem to us to be contradictory." We must,

[1] Pearson.
[2] See *Critique of Pure Reason*, Bohn's Trans. p. 208.

therefore, for the present exceptional purpose, add two other divisions, viz., Empty, and to our faculties inconceivable, object of a conception; and, Empty, and to our faculties inconceivable, object without conception. The former of these may be of great importance in the relation we are now considering: the latter can be of no importance whatever.

No doubt these considerations will appear of so abstract a character as scarcely to merit attention, and they would not have been adduced had they not lain so directly in our path. Nevertheless, it must appear that the relation of an Intelligent and Almighty Cause to an infinity of potential effects, may be of all relations the most profound.

We now turn to the other relation implied by the term Almighty, viz., that of Omnipotent Ruler to the Ruled. As this is the relation which the whole of the present Essay is more or less engaged in considering, it is needless in this place to do much more than mention it. It must be observed, however, that this relation includes the attributes ascribed to the Deity by Scripture,—not necessarily, indeed, *as* ascribed, for the ascription is confessedly adapted to human intelligence; but as presenting in the language of human ideas the most faithful possible designation of their symbolized realities.

§ 4. I have now briefly enumerated all the relations which are known to subsist between the Almighty and the Universe; or, more correctly, all such relations as are necessarily implied by the mention of the former. My object in doing so has been to render yet more conspicuous the immeasurable extent of our ignorance concerning those which remain. We are thus indeed shown to possess a knowledge of a few relations, as it were in the abstract; but, on examination, these will be found to serve only as torches to reveal the immensity of the surrounding darkness. None of these abstract relations supply us with any real knowledge concerning what may be termed the effective ones: they serve only, like the ideas of space and time, as the formal conditions of an endless number of possible concretes. "Lo, these are part of His ways; but how little a portion is heard of Him! Canst thou by searching find out God? Canst thou find out the Almighty unto perfection? It is as high as heaven; what canst thou do? deeper than hell; what canst thou know?"

Now this fact—the fact that our ignorance concerning these relations is inconceivably immeasurable—being of vital importance to the present argument, it is desirable clearly to understand the position which the objections we are considering occupy with regard to it.

§ 5. The scientific proposition asserts that a Being, Who is acknowledged to stand to the World in the relations just set forth, never produces a certain class of effects. Now such an assertion can only rest upon one or more of three grounds:—either, proximately, because experience shews that He does not; or, ultimately, because we have reason to believe that such is not His intention; or, intermediately, because we have reason to believe that some obstacle prevents Him. Now the first of these grounds must be excluded, unless the defenders of the proposition can show some reason why we should expect this causative influence to be taken cognizance of by our experience, supposing that influence to be exerted. That they cannot do this, while, on the contrary, it can be shewn that there is a necessary reason why such influence, if exerted, should be hidden from experience, we have already seen. Similarly we have seen that the second ground must be excluded, science having no voice in questions which involve the ultimate volitions of the Deity. We come then to the third ground as the sole and only one on which the scientific proposition is founded. And this is the issue which a thoughtful opponent will not hesitate to accept. He will perceive that the whole of the present question arises from the supposed existence of such an impediment—the existence of General Laws. He will further perceive that it does not signify, for the purposes of the present discussion, whether this impediment is ultimately supposed to exist independently of the Divine will, or in accordance with it; that is, whether or not this third ground of objection merges into the second one: for, whether in reality it does so or not, the proposition under consideration is, as we have seen, by its nature precluded from estimating the fact. We may therefore in this place, without any prejudice to that proposition, assume that its sense amounts to this:—The Government of the World by General Laws is to the Deity an obstacle, which effectually prevents his answering Prayer, supposing Him desirous of doing so.

Now in estimating the ability or inability of any agent to accomplish any definite action, it is surely a sound canon that the value of our estimation decreases in direct proportion to the decrease in the sufficiency of our knowledge, concerning the whole of the relations subsisting between the agent and the patient. Therefore, if our knowledge of these relations is such as to acquaint us with the existence of an apparent preventive to any course of action we may be considering, the probability that this *apparent* preventive is an *actual* one varies inversely as the difference between the number and importance of the relations known, and those of the relations unknown. And, just as in the case of analogical arguments, those instances in which the exact limits of the unknown relations are perceived, afford an opportunity for estimating the exact value of this probability; while, in cases where those limits are not perceived, the possibility of making this estimation—or, which is the same thing, the probability of its being accurate when made—varies directly as the possibility of perceiving those limits.

If it is not self-evident that this canon is valid, we shall most easily perceive it to be so by taking any case in which our ignorance of the relations involved is entailed by their futurity; for a little thought will then render it obvious, that it is only because of the truths set forth in this canon that prediction is more fallible than perception. A merchant, for instance, of the last generation might well have deemed it *a priori* incredible, that his firm in London should ever be able to purchase stock in New York in less time than it could then purchase it in Liverpool. It would so appear because he knew *all* the relations then subsisting between his firm and New York; and he knew that one of these relations was an intervening ocean, which it took six or seven weeks to cross; and he knew that other of these relations were such, that stock could only be purchased by communication conveyed in a material form. Yet the introduction of a single new relation has now rendered perceptible that which was previously incredible.

§ 6. Applying then this canon, the argument stands thus:—We have already seen that science has no voice in the question as to whether or not the First Cause has an intelligent regard for man, or a desire to answer his petitions : if we suppose such regard to exist, the effect of this canon is to prove that science, if it is to sustain its universal proposition, must shew some reason why the Almighty should not be able, without violating the course of Nature, to produce any particular physical effect in answer to Prayer, not, observe, as before pointed out, through the agency of unknown causes, but even through known or strictly analogous ones[1]. But, by the terms of the canon, science is necessarily unable to do this, in the same degree that it is unable to perceive the totality of relations subsisting between the Almighty and the Universe. In other words, as we previously saw that the probability established by the scientific objections, decreased in exact proportion to our ignorance of second causes ; so we now perceive that this probability yet further decreases, in exact proportion to our ignorance of the relations subsisting between the First and second causes—always supposing the former to act exclusively through the whole course of the latter.

§ 7. I have presented this second division of our argument in its most concrete form, in order that it may be clearly apprehended. It is to be observed that this presentation goes deeper, and includes that which is usually given in arguments to prove that the Deity may produce miraculous effects, &c., through the operation of known Laws. The usual presentation virtually amounts to drawing an analogy between human directive influence and the Supreme Directive Influence—in supposing the Deity to stand to Law in the same relation as we

[1] It will, of course, be observed that this argument throughout applies both to known and unknown causes; but the former alone are considered in order to shew the full strength of the argument.

might imagine an immensely advanced human intelligence to stand to it. Now this presentation, for reasons afterwards to be mentioned, is thoroughly valid, and has the advantage of being easily understood. The present, however, appears to me to be the fundamental statement of the case, since it is not legitimate to confine the possible relations of the Supreme Intelligence to Law by any known relations, however extended.

In giving this presentation it is unnecessary to burden it with details; for these would not only be incompatible with the reasonable limits of an Essay, but would carry us into an abstruseness that would be undesirable. It is, however, necessary to expand and explain the general presentation already given.

§ 8. At first sight, then, it may seem that the notion of "impediment" contained in that presentation is not strictly fair to the scientific position. "It is not for me," the supporter of this position may urge, "to limit the out-goings of Almighty power[1]:" 'I do not say what He can or cannot do; I merely assert that *if* He answers Prayer, He must do so in some other way than through the operation of known Laws.' This proposition, however, and every other possible proposition of the kind, is tantamount to saying that the Almighty *cannot* answer Prayer in the mode indicated—is merely another verbal form of asserting that, so far as this mode is concerned, an effectual *impediment* exists.

Now what is the warrant for this assertion? A man of science will doubtless answer:—'The warrant is conveyed by the very mention of the term "General Laws;" for the only meaning of that term is that the production of particular effects through their agency is impossible.'

[1] Tyndall.

Impossible, however, to whom? We cannot say to the Almighty, without assuming a complete knowledge regarding those very relations, of our total ignorance of which we are now treating. That the production of particular effects—particular, that is, as having a special reference to the petitioner—through General Laws is to *us* impossible; and that the production of such effects by the operation of second causes of any kind upon other second causes is perhaps likewise impossible—these are points which in this place, for the sake of perspicuity, we may readily concede. Their concession, however, does not help us one step towards deciding the wholly distinct question now in dispute. Our life-long familiarity with General Laws (let us suppose) renders it hard to imagine that there can be a Being, Whose relation to them is such that He produces indifferently special or general—or even, let us say, few or many—effects through their agency; but it is evident that we can only assert the contrary, by virtually if not avowedly instituting a supposed similarity between the relations of the Almighty to the Universe, and the relations of second causes to each other.

§ 9. We thus discover the presence of a new and totally distinct analogy, which, though less upon the surface, is no less essential to the maintenance of the scientific proposition, than is the one already examined. We have seen that the value of our estimation as to what the Almighty can or cannot effect through the agency of known or analogous Laws, varies inversely as our ignorance of the relations subsisting between the Almighty and the Universe; and we have seen that this ignorance is, as to positive information, worse than total. Therefore science, to have any pretence of a standing-ground at all, is compelled to fall back upon that from which all her ideas of causation are derived; and, first, considering the relations in which known second causes (ourselves included) stand to General Laws, she then assumes an identity, or a similarity of relations to subsist between these and the First Cause. Otherwise there would plainly be no room for argument at all; for, if no such analogy is supposed to exist, our ignorance of the last-named relations would then be avowedly total; and, General Laws being thus conceded to be in these relations a wholly undefinable entity, the question as to what the Deity could or could not effect through their agency, would become wholly beyond the power of reason to infer.

Therefore, even if science could prove to demonstration that Natural Law is throughout its extent such as we know it, it would still remain for science to prove that some likeness subsists between the mode in which the operation of the First and that of second causes is conducted,—so far at least as General Laws are concerned. Hence, as we previously saw that the value of the scientific proposition decreased in proportion to the weakness of the former analogy; so we now perceive that this proposition depends for its existence upon its success in establishing the present analogy. Let us estimate its value.

§ 10. We have already seen that, so far as we can argue upon such a subject at all, we have every reason to suppose that prime causation differs from secondary in kind. Now this fact is at the outset a serious objection to the present analogy, even were that analogy in other respects unexceptionable. It may be true that the arguments which substantiate this fact are of a mystical and merely logical nature; but, as they are the only arguments available, the conclusion to which they tend must in all reason be accepted. Hence it follows that we cannot reasonably institute any analogy between the causative action of the Deity and that of other causes—cannot, from our knowledge of the latter, frame a shadow of logical probability as to what the former can or cannot effect through their agency.

Laying this objection aside, however, and supposing that we are unable to shew that prime causation differs in any wise from secondary; supposing even that we are unable to infer this, and consequently that the analogy has been fairly and logically instituted; we shall see that even as an analogy it is intrinsically of the weakest possible kind.

When dealing with the nature of analogical arguments in general, it was pointed out that the greater the number of unknown relations in proportion to the known, the weaker these arguments were. More recently we have seen that of all relations concerning which it is possible for man to think, the most unknowable and the most inconceivable, both in their nature and their magnitude, are those relations which constitute the unknown ratio of the present analogy. And this *à posteriori* conclusion admits of easy confirmation *à priori*, since it is evident that these relations must ultimately embody all things whatever which are to man unknown or unknowable. Hence it is certainly not too much to say, that the present analogy is of the weakest possible kind.

It may serve to intensify our appreciation of this fact, if we look at the matter in another light. All causes with which we are acquainted, however much they may differ from one another, agree in this—their action is determined by General Laws. Now it is this fact, and this fact alone, it appears to me, which renders all analogical reasoning whatever, not only valid, but possible.

The savage who witnesses the daily recession and advance of the tide, and has heard from his fathers and forefathers that within their experience no exception to the phænomenon has ever been observed, does not dream of the possibility that to-morrow's tide will not occur. Why is this? Simply because his own experience and that of his forefathers has been formed within a region of General Laws. For whatever view we take as to the origin of human intelligence, the mere fact of its existing adaptation to surrounding conditions warrants us in assuming the truth of the evolution theory, as an illustration, if not an explanation, of the present point[1]. When, then, intelligence became nascent, it encountered in all its relations the influence of General Laws; and, throughout its development never escaping from that influence, became perfectly conformable to it. The rational faculty of the savage, then, having from its very origin been moulded by the operation of General Laws in external nature, and these General Laws having invariably brought about similar results in similar cases; it follows that all his rational faculty has to do in order to obtain a practically valid inference, is empirically to register the concomitants attending past phænomena, and to anticipate the reappearance of the same phænomena whenever the same concomitants arise. Thus it is that, although he may never have speculated upon the *cause* of the tide (and had he done so his conclusions would certainly have been erroneous), yet this makes no difference in the confidence with which he awaits its

[1] See note at end of this section.

recurrence; for his whole experience, and the whole experience of intelligence before him, has uninterruptedly gone to shew that the mere fact of previous occurrence warrants an expectation of future recurrence, in a degree proportionate to the number of observations—and this solely because throughout the history of intelligence the same General Laws have been uninterruptedly in operation. And, without examples, it is evident that these considerations apply equally to phænomena of co-existence, as to those of sequence.

When we ascend a stage higher in the intellectual scale, we perceive the spirit of methodical investigation into the causes of phænomena taking its rise. Civilized man is not content with a mere observation of facts; he aspires to know the Why, and this not (as satisfies the barbarous) a merely conceivably or apparently probable Why, but the only possible Why: he is satisfied with nothing short of *proof*. Now, when the intellect thus "climbs from the region of facts to that of laws[1]," the confidence with which it awaits the recurrence of the phænomena which it has explained is greatly intensified. In cases such as that of the tide, where the sequence is uninterrupted for an indefinite number of times, the expectation of its recurrence is, no doubt, for all practical purposes, as strong in the savage as in the civilized man: but not so theoretically; for although the latter in common with the former "shares the belief that summer will succeed spring, that winter will succeed autumn[2]," yet "he knows still further that this succession besides being permanent is, under the circumstances, *necessary;* that the gravitating force exerted between the sun and a revolving sphere with its axis inclined to the plane of

[1] Tyndall, *Fragments*, p. 56. [2] *Ibid.* p. 63.

its orbit, *must* produce the observed succession of the seasons[1]." But the only reason why in such cases the empirical expectation (so to speak) is, even for practical purposes, as strong as the rational one, is because the General Laws at work—either from the fact of their being uncompounded with other Laws, or from the fact that the observable effects of their operation are frequently recurrent—admit of the effects being empirically registered. In exact proportion, however, as the causes become complex, or the observable results rare or irregular, in that proportion does the empirical register fail, and consequently the strength of the expectation formed upon it. Not so, however, with the rational expectation; for this, being independent of empirical observations, is able to declare with certainty the effects which must follow from known causes: instance an astronomer who awaits the occurrence of an eclipse with the same certainty as he does the recurrence of the seasons. But now let us ask, how does civilized man attain to this superior knowledge? Assuredly in every case by analogical reasoning. He first observes, as the savage observes, the effects of unknown causes; and then by discovery of the latter, rises from a mere observation to an explanation of the former. But this process—the great process of induction—would be impossible were it not for the ubiquitous influence of General Laws. It is only because in every case we postulate their underlying presence, that it becomes possible for the mind to infer, that because the effects A and B resemble each other more or less, therefore there is a proportionable probability that a relation of common causality exists between them. And this inference would in every case be a certainty, were it not for the com-

---

[1] *Ibid.* p. 63.

plexity of the causes which are in most cases at work. We thus observe that, from its lowest to its highest development, the perception of the value of analogy ultimately rests upon that from which it is derived—the Government of the Universe by General Laws. It is not, of course, necessary to the validity of any analogical argument that this its ultimate derivation should be perceived; but it is none the less the real foundation of all[1].

It profits nothing to say, in opposition to this view, that the idea of analogy rests more ultimately upon that of the Unity of God; because the only means we have of forming that more ultimate idea is by our proximate experience of the action of General Laws; as is proved by the fact that primitive religions recognize no such unity.

The fallacy, therefore, of arguing from the action of General Laws to the action of that which transcends them, becomes thus strikingly apparent. For it is simply to apply a derivative mode of argument to that which transcends that from which it was derived. It would be sufficiently illogical, because "infinitely precarious[2]," to institute an analogy between the action of one Natural

[1] It will be observed that upon the evolution theory we have here, it seems to me, a full and adequate explanation of the fact that "the principle by which we are disposed to extend our inference beyond the limit of experience, is a natural or ultimate principle of intelligence." (Sir William Hamilton's *Lectures*, Vol. IV. page 166.) From this fact (whatever be its explanation) there arises the overpowering tendency in our intelligence—noticed somewhere by Bain —to believe that what exists here and now, exists everywhere and always. This tendency should constantly be borne in mind by those who reason upon such subjects as the present; for it must evidently be pernicious, and the yielding to it irrational, in proportion to our recedure from the experiential order of things.

[2] Butler.

Law and that of another—such, for instance, as that because the planets travel in orbital curves in obedience to the Law of gravitation, therefore the heat and light radiated from their surfaces, and which are independent of that Law, should also move in orbital curves. But illogical as this obviously is, because glaringly opposed to common sense, it is not so fundamentally illogical as endeavouring to institute an analogy between the action of Natural Law—a sphere of action from which the idea of analogy alone arises, and in which alone it must terminate[1]—and the action of that which in transcending Natural Law also transcends that sphere[2].

§ 11. Thus the value of this analogy is virtually *nil;* yet upon this analogy depends the whole weight of the probability we are estimating. 'But is it not simply unthinkable,' our imaginary opponent will urge, 'that

[1] That is, of course, only so far as General Laws are concerned. Analogies such as that on which Butler's treatise is founded—*i. e.*, analogies depending, not on the presupposition of invariable Laws, but on that of the unity of the Divine Nature—we are not now concerned with.

[2] It is to be observed that even the the supposition of the idea of analogy being intuitive to specially-created man, does not materially affect the above argument; for it is from that supposition impossible to infer that analogical arguments are of any validity when applied to a sphere transcending General Laws. It is so because all that the supposition can possibly entitle us to assert is, that in this particular our intelligence has been originally endowed with a method of thought relative to General Laws, which is exactly suited *to the sphere of existence in which it is placed;*—cannot entitle us to infer that *on this account* there is no sphere of existence possible in which this intuitive method would not apply. On either supposition, therefore, the fact of our adaptation to our environment is all that we are supplied with, and in neither case can this fact afford any shadow of inferential probability, that analogical reasoning of this kind is of any validity beyond the sphere of General Laws.

action of any kind should take place through General Laws without the production of general effects?' Let us suppose that it is so, and how does this affect the question? It merely shews that the matter has now been carried into an unthinkable province; and this through no fault of the analysis, but because the proposition which it examines refers directly to that province. All, therefore, that it is incumbent on the present argument to shew is, not that the action of the First Cause is thinkable, not even that it is not such as the scientific proposition assumes it to be; but merely, and on the contrary, that such action being altogether unthinkable, that proposition is for this very reason invalid, presuming as it does to limit that action by the measure of the thinkable. Hence, the supporter of that proposition only weakens his argument, by again pointing out the fact that one of the ratios of its essential analogy is not merely indefinite, but also inconceivable.

§ 12. But now let us ask parenthetically, Is it true that such action is altogether inconceivable? I say "parenthetically," because it would be no disparagement to the present argument if the case were an inconceivable one; since, as just observed, the very basis of that argument is, that the relation of the Almighty to General Laws is not conceivable. If then we can shew, in no matter how small a degree, that the proposition itself is not altogether true,—*i. e.*, that in this particular it is not altogether unthinkable that the action of the First Cause should be such as that proposition condemns as wholly unthinkable,—we shall have done more than the present argument requires.

If we endeavour to symbolize in thought a universal cause which includes all effects whatever—*i.e.,* all other causes as its effects,—and likewise the Laws according to which these causes act; it would seem that, unless we suppose this universal cause itself subject to a Law determining the channels, as it were, in which its causative activity is to flow, we must suppose that the production of one series of effects is as easy, so to speak, as the production of any other series,—confusion being in all cases equally avoided by the existence of General Laws, which prevent any effects—*i.e.*, any conditioned causes—from interfering with one another·so as to produce discord. Now, no series of effects can be considered infinite, without destroying the all-containing nature of their ultimate cause; for the Infinite cannot be itself contained[1]: but, if any series of effects is limited, there is no more reason against the existence of a special series, than of a series more general. Hence the only question that arises is, as to whether the Supreme Cause is subject to any Law such that it must of necessity act in certain directions, or not at all. The answer of pure logic to this question is clear and decided. "If it contains something which imposes such necessities or restraints, this something must be higher than the First Cause, which is absurd. Thus the First Cause must be in every sense perfect, complete, total: including within

[1] "'The inference of a First Cause assumes,' says Kant, 'the impossibility of an infinite ascending series of causes.' The manifest convergence of the various systems of causation which Science exhibits to us, seems to indicate that in the material world at least such a series does not exist. However far beyond anything that man can ever grasp, that centre lies in which all things meet, it is towards a centre that all his knowledge tends; and indefinitely vast as the stupendous scheme of Nature must be, Infinity is the property not of it, but of its cause."—*Burney Prize*, 1868, p. 34.

itself all power, and transcending all Law[1]." But, discarding logic, is it not as easy, or rather why is it more difficult, to symbolize in thought the origination of a special series of effects, than that of a general? "All change (*i.e.*, every effect) is possible only through a continuous action of the causality[2]:" hence, on the supposition of a First Cause, the origination and continuance of one series of changes, although these may be conceived as less usual, are not a whit more essentially unthinkable, than those of any other series whatever. But the objection that the answering of Prayer through known Laws is inconceivable, requires to its validity as an objection, not merely that the origination of any series of effects should be inconceivable, but that the origination of a special series should be *more* inconceivable than that of a general,—it being a necessary belief that "God is as universally the final as the efficient cause of His operations[3]."

The truth appears to be that the real place at which the inconceivable in this matter should be posited, is in the hypothesis of a Self-existing Cause producing all series of effects whatever; there being, as we have just seen, nothing more intrinsically unthinkable in the existence of a special series of effects than in that of a general; and the only difference is that that of the former at first sight *appears* to be more so, in consequence of the originating agency (which imparts to each alike its unthinkable nature) being here directly referred to, while in the other case it is but tacitly assumed. But the real difficulty is not so much to conceive of this or that class of effects originating, as it is to conceive of any class of

---

[1] Spencer, *First Principles*, p. 33.
[2] Kant.   [3] Pearson.

effects originating,—to conceive of an Intelligence standing in such relation to the Universe that all other causes whatever are but the effects of its Will.

§ 13. To conclude this division of our subject. It is a favourite argument against the credibility of miracles, etc., that "there is not the slightest analogy between an unknown or inexplicable phenomenon, and a supposed suspension of a known law.... Arbitrary interposition is wholly different in kind," etc.[1] Now, there is manifestly no argument in such statements at all, unless it is assumed that a miracle *does* entail the suspension of a known Law; and our warrant for this assumption is the subject at present in dispute. How do we know, how can we know that a miracle (supposing it to occur) "is wholly different in kind," with regard to its causation, from any other phænomenon, whether unknown, inexplicable, or otherwise[2]? All our knowledge and all our ideas of causation are only and can only be derived from the relation in which observed second causes stand to observed Laws; but once let us overstep the limits of second causes, and we must enter a province where we must suppose that General Laws encounter other and wholly new relations,—*i.e.*, relations of which not only can we have no direct knowledge, but which even analogical inference is unable to touch. Yet, once admit that our ignorance of these relations is absolute, and,

---

[1] *Essays and Reviews*, pp. 109, 110.

[2] It will of course be perceived that these remarks do not lend any countenance to the silly argument often met with, viz., that because some natural phænomena are inexplicable, therefore some analogy exists between them and miracles. I have even heard it stated under the dome of St Paul's, that the fact of Christ turning water into wine is no more difficult of acceptance, than the fact of water becoming grape-juice in the cells of the grape!

even were our knowledge of second causes no less absolute, and were the First Cause proved in all cases to act through the whole course of Natural Law; it follows that we should have no warrant whatever for supposing that the First Cause, in so acting, cannot in any case work a miracle, or produce effects having a special reference to Prayer. In the face of such ignorance as this, it is arbitrary assumption to speak of "arbitrary interpositions," if this term is meant to signify any difference in the Divine method of action absolutely considered; that is, considered in relation to the Deity as distinguished from ourselves. It is arbitrary assumption because, for ought we can know or even infer, the ultimate relations encountered by General Laws may be such that all effects whatever (including those we are specially considering), are finally due to the same method of the prime directive Power. "Since the monarchy of the universe is a dominion unlimited in extent, and everlasting in duration, the general system of it must necessarily be quite beyond comprehension. And, since there appears such a subordination and reference of the several parts to each other, as to constitute it properly one administration or government, we cannot have a thorough knowledge of any part without knowing the whole. This surely should convince us that we are much less competent judges of the very small part which comes under our notice in this world than we are apt to imagine[1]." In a word, once admit that our ignorance of the relations we are considering is total, and it becomes impossible for us to assign limits to the causative ability of the Supreme Intelligence, acting through the agency of Law.

[1] Butler, *Ignorance of Man*.

It is no doubt difficult, especially at first, and more difficult to some minds than others, to imagine that a miracle can really be precisely assimilated to other effects of the Divine influence; but we must all remember that this difficulty is only what we should in any case expect to encounter. For, whether or not the relations subsisting between the Deity and His creation are such that all effects whatever stand in the same relation to His superintendence; we should alike expect, from our total ignorance of these relations, to find ourselves unable, either to anticipate the possible number of apparently different kinds of effects, prior to observation; or, subsequent to observation, to conceive of the manner in which these relations can be similar. Thus it is manifestly absurd to declare that the Almighty cannot produce this and that effect through this and that agency, merely on the ground that we cannot ourselves so produce it, or conceive of the manner in which it could be so produced. *A priori* reasoning is a reasoning from cause to effect, and is assuredly a most powerful engine of thought, when we possess some reasonable amount of knowledge concerning the former in its relation to the latter: but when the cause is a free and inscrutable Intelligence, whose relation to its effects contains all that is to man unknown and unknowable, —then assuredly the substance of such reasoning evaporates; and we are left to supply the void with any belief, conceivable or inconceivable, which there may be independent and adequate reason to accept.

CHAPTER IV.

§ 1. Thus, the double appeal to analogy which is necessary for the very existence of the proposition we are considering, renders the probability we are estimating not only certainly very low, but low to an exceedingly indefinite degree. Yet low as we have seen that probability to be, we have not seen how low it is. For, the considerations recently adduced to shew our total ignorance concerning—nay, our utter inability even to conceive, the relations subsisting between the Almighty and the Universe,—these considerations clearly shew how completely unwarrantable is the supposition upon which we have hitherto been going, viz., that the Almighty in every case acts through the whole course of Natural Law. Even if Science could render the probability as high as we have seen it to be low, that the Almighty can only answer Prayer through Law by violating Law,—even if Science were able to prove this to demonstration, it would still remain for Science to shew that the Almighty is under some necessity to act in obedience to certain rules.

I am aware that in entering upon this division of our subject, I am taking up a position which many of the leading writers in support of miracles have abandoned.

The fact of their having done so, however, appears to me an error to be regretted, rather than an example to be followed. It is most certainly the first duty of an advocate for miracles, to shew that it is a gratuitous proposition, beyond proof and even inference, to assert that the Deity cannot produce such and such an effect through the agency of Law; but it is none the less clearly his duty not to concede even the outposts of his general argument, unless he has thoroughly examined the full intrinsic meaning and all the logical consequences of the adverse argument. I am far from denying that this adverse argument does, in this particular, at first sight appear overwhelming; but I conceive that this fact only renders a penetrating scrutiny into its essential value the more imperative. By way then of indicating the direction in which such scrutiny should lie, we shall continue our examination into the value of the scientific proposition.

§ 2. In accordance with the law of excluded middle, we may make the following exhaustive proposition:— Either the Almighty does or does not in all cases act through the whole course of Natural Law[1]. If we suppose that He does, our supposition, in so far as it is rational, must rest on one or both of two grounds;— either because universal experience testifies that He does, or because *à priori* considerations render it improbable that He does not. Now, as repeatedly shewn, the first of these grounds must be carefully excluded, because, whatever weight any arguments founded upon it may be supposed to possess in the case of miracles, such arguments are, in the present connection, absolutely

---

[1] The supposition that Law is self-acting is considered in § 11.

null[1]. Thus we may at once dismiss all considerations founded on the uniformity of experience.

§ 3. Nevertheless, it is desirable to notice in passing, that the essentially invalid nature of this class of objections is habitually disregarded by the majority of writers upon the present subject; arguments being adduced of great apparent plausibility, which are, nevertheless, wholly valueless, because resting upon this false foundation. As an example of this numerous and misleading class, we may notice the following, which is perhaps the most conspicuous. It is said,—" Religious men do not pray for eternal sunshine or for physical immortality. Why? Simply because they recognise that such would be *contrary to the will of God, as revealed in the laws of external nature*, and it rests with them to prove that one single physical event may validly be excluded from the list of the predetermined, before they call on us to pray with reference to it[2]." Again, "by degrees we learn to include all that seems at first sight anomalous within the majestic sweep of predetermined law. And is it not in exact proportion to our ignorance of what is fixed, that we make it the subject of our petitions[3]?" Evidently so, but not necessarily for the reason given in the former quotation. Our ignorance on this point is the measure of our inability to appreciate the causative action of God : the faith,

---

[1] The *à priori* argument against miracles is composed of two factors, 1st, the improbability that a Natural Law should be suspended, and 2dly, the improbability that an otherwise uniform experience should be interrupted. These two factors are far from identical; and it is with the former only that we are concerned.

[2] Rev. Mr Knight, *Contemp. Rev.* Jan. 1873.

[3] *Ibid.*

therefore, which sees independent reasons for the cessation of that action within the sphere of the miraculous, and yet believes that it is not on this account in total abeyance, can only be consistent with itself by making the degree of its ignorance the measure of the legitimacy of its petitions. "This argument is against common sense, and is obviously founded on the assumption that the reasonableness or unreasonableness of a petition has no bearing whatever upon the possibility of its being granted[1]." "It is our conviction as to God's will, not any doubt as to His power, or His willingness in itself, to listen to our petition, which sets the limit to what we ask of Him in prayer[2]." In short, we must "pray with the spirit," but "with the understanding also;" and in the "moral sphere," no less than in the "physical," there are numerous miraculous manifestations of Divine power, which, although conceivable and even desirable, a religious man would nevertheless rightly deem it impious to pray for.

Thus, so far as the objection refers to miracles only, it is manifestly absurd. There is, however, another subject touched upon by implication in the above extracts, and expanded by the anonymous writer in the *Contemporary Review*, with whose uncourteous jargon we must all regret to see Prof. Tyndall's name associated. This writer ironically divides "the realm" "of the natural and invariable order" from that of "the providential," and adds, "Thus it is that class I. grows larger day by day, while class II. diminishes in like proportion. Where shall this progress stop[3]?" etc., indicating through-

---

[1] Argyll, *Contemp. Rev.* Feb. 1873, p. 468.
[2] Karslake, *Theory of Prayer*, p. 32.
[3] *Contemp. Rev.* Oct. 1872.

out his argument that the objection we have just considered necessarily embodies, or is identical with, the wholly distinct question as to the value of Prayer ignorantly uttered, for things which are seen by a more advanced intelligence to be impossible or inexpedient. This question we shall subsequently have occasion to discuss, and it has only been mentioned here in order to eliminate it from the other with which it has been confused.

§ 4. We now revert to the *à priori* considerations in support of the supposition that the Almighty in every case operates mediately through the entire course of Natural Law. Now it does not devolve upon us to state these considerations, for the attitude we adopt towards them is, that the subject to which they refer is altogether beyond the range of philosophical discussion. All these *à priori* arguments must ultimately ground upon experience; and, no matter how elaborate or admirably constructed they may be, they are, as arguments, valueless; for they refer to a province which is *wholly* beyond experience. As, then, the present endeavour is to cut away the very ground on which alone all such arguments can rest—*i.e.*, to shew that experience is in this matter empty of authority—it would manifestly be a mere waste of time to refute these arguments separately.

§ 5. As this endeavour will, no doubt, be at the outset considered by opponents over-bold, I have the less compunction in presenting the strongest conceivable case. Before stating it, however, we may observe that throughout the coming argument we are not endeavouring to prove, or even to render it in the lowest degree probable, that the Almighty ever acts externally to Law;

but merely to shew that we have, and can have, no warrant to assert, or to infer, that He does not. Hence, the only position we are contending for, is, that the question is one which must ever remain in argumentative abeyance.

Turning now to the case referred to, there is probably no single proposition that can be propounded, which would appear to a man of science at first sight so extravagant or incredible, as that a physical effect can exist out of relation to other physical effects. Yet, if we allow that we have no right to assume the existence of any analogy between the causative influence of the First, and that of other causes; by what right can we assert that isolated effects do not exist? If no such analogy obtains, we have no means of even approximately conceiving of the manner in which the First Cause operates, and it becomes a gratuitous assumption to assert that this cause can only produce any single effect, by producing at the same time a variety of other effects. That the production of a multiplicity of effects is the condition of human activity, is axiomatic; and it is, perhaps, scarcely less so, that throughout the range of second causes, the production of a multiplicity of effects is the condition of all activity whatever. But when we have said this, we have said all we can—we are unable, in the absence of analogy, to assert anything farther, or to infer anything more.

A man of science will say:—'But it is simply incredible that physical effects can exist wholly out of relation to all other physical effects.' But is this true? Is this supposition as to the existence of isolated effects a supposition intrinsically incredible, or is it not rendered so only by the super-added belief in the operation of

General Laws? I think the answer is afforded without investigation, by the fact set forth in the opening section, viz., that prior to the belief in General Laws, all effects whatever were believed to be more or less independent of one another[1]. 'But now that we possess the additional belief,' it will be urged, 'the whole aspect of the case is altered: superior knowledge has shewn incredible that which superstition believed.' But the word "incredible[2]" here tacitly appeals to the analogy which, as we have seen, we have no right to institute. It may be *highly improbable* that General Laws in any of their relations admit of the existence of isolated effects— that is, effects out of relation to all other effects, and, consequently, out of relation to these Laws,—but we cannot assert that this is *incredible*, without assuming an inferential knowledge of all these relations. Indeed, the assumption amounts to more than this; for, as we have just seen, there is nothing intrinsically incredible in the supposition that the Almighty may produce isolated effects, were it not for the existence of General Laws. Before, then, this existence can be considered an *insuperable* obstacle to the production of effects out of relation to General Laws,—*i.e.*, before such production can be considered *incredible*—it is necessary to *prove* a

---

[1] By this is not, of course, meant that physical causation was not appreciated in ancient, or even in primitive times; but merely that all physical phænomena being referred more or less immediately to the Divine agency, the necessity on the one hand of a proximate cause, and on the other of a commensurate effect, was not recognized:—hence the easy belief in supernatural manifestations.

[2] This word is here, of course, used in the sense of "being fully persuaded that some opinion is not true," and not in the sense of "a mere absence of belief" from "the insufficiency of proof."—Mill.

knowledge of *all* the relations which are encountered by General Laws; and, by parity of reasoning, whatever degree of *improbability* that existence may be supposed to impart to the possibility of such production, that degree must be exactly equal to, because solely determined by, the strength of the *analogy* before mentioned —this being the only other source of knowledge available.

§ 6. We see, then, that there is nothing incredible in the supposition that isolated effects may exist in Nature. "But," it is retorted, "no physical fact can be conceived as unique, or without analogy and relation to others, and to the whole system of natural causes[1]." If by this statement is meant that we are unable to conceive of such effects, as it were in the concrete, I am perfectly willing to admit it; for it is a mere truism to say that we cannot correctly represent that which we have never seen. But, if the word "conceive" is here meant to imply conception of such entities, as it were in the abstract, I meet the assertion with a flat denial.

Mr Herbert Spencer devotes his chapter on the "multiplication of effects" chiefly to prove the proposition, that "universally the effect is more complex than the cause." Now this proposition is certainly true so far as it goes, but it is only one side of the truth; for the proposition would be equally true were its terms reversed. Every effect is the resultant, not of a single cause (although one cause may be more *conspicuous* than the others), but of an indefinite number of past causes, just as it will be a cause of an indefinite number of future effects. If we take any one of Mr Spencer's

[1] *Essays and Reviews*, p. 142.

illustrations we shall find that it applies equally well to the converse proposition—the burning of a candle, for instance, being quite as much the effect of innumerable causes, as it is the cause of innumerable effects. There is one case, however, in which the above-quoted formula is most true, viz., in that of the First Cause; for this includes all other causes as its effects. Now, why is it inconceivable that this all-containing and all-generating cause, can only produce effects which are conformable to rules, themselves ordained by that cause? We have already seen that there is nothing intrinsically beyond conception in the idea of isolated effects existing in Nature, were it not for the existence of General Laws: but if we look upon General Laws as themselves but the directive channels appointed by the Creator, in which *some* conditioned causes are invariably to flow, it does not follow that *all* conditional causes must invariably flow in such channels—that those causes which do thus flow exhaust the causative influence of the Being who originated both them and their channels. Suppose the First Cause had only produced one effect: it is manifest that this could never have become a cause, and so could never have been subject to a Law determining its causative action. Suppose now the effects to have been dual instead of singular: does it follow that these must necessarily have stood in any immediate relation of causality to one another—that they could not have co-existed without producing a miniature universe of inter-operating causes? If not, by what right do we assert that plural effects cannot co-exist without such immediate inter-relation: or, which is the same thing, by what right do we assert that in the Universe, as it at present exists, the First Cause cannot originate a single effect like its only effect just imagined—*i. e.*, an effect out of relation to all other effects? It appears to me that we have no right whatever, and that the only reason why the idea seems at first sight an inconceivable one, is because we confuse the notion of Cause with that of Law. To us, no doubt, every cause must exist under laws; but, unless we identify Law with Cause, we can establish no necessity why every cause whatever should so exist—*i. e.*, why the First Cause cannot produce any effects, without simultaneously framing rules under which they are to act as causes.

§ 7. I say we cannot establish any such necessity: I think another class of considerations will shew that we cannot even establish a probability. This conclusion has indeed been previously arrived at by implication in the closing sentence of section 5[1]; but the following confirmations are worth giving, for they arrive at the conclusion by wholly different routes.

We have already seen that it is only because of the existence of General Laws that the process of induction is possible. Now all knowledge, save the so-called intuitive, is ultimately derived from induction: hence, in the absence of General Laws, all such knowledge would be impossible. This fact alone is amply sufficient for our argument; but, more than this, even the so-called intuitive knowledge is, according to the evolution theory, ultimately derived from the action of General Laws—is but the stereotyped adaptation of the race's intelligence to its environment: hence, upon this theory, even intuitive knowledge would, in the absence of General Laws, have been impossible. But these two

[1] " The strength of the Analogy" having previously been shewn " virtually nil."

kinds of knowledge are together the sole factors of experience: hence, in the absence of General Laws, our experience itself would vanish.

I find that Kant has also arrived at this conclusion, although, of course, by a different route. He argues thus:—" Accordingly, when we know in experience that something happens, we always pre-suppose that something precedes, whereupon it follows in conformity with a rule. For otherwise I could not say of the object, that it follows; because the mere succession in my apprehension, if it be not determined by a rule in relation to something preceding, does not authorize succession in the object. Only, therefore, in reference to a rule, according to which phænomena are determined in their sequence, that is, as they happen, by the preceding state, can I make my subjective synthesis (of apprehension) objective, and it is only under this pre-supposition that even the experience of an event is possible[1]."

Lastly, psychological deduction warrants the same conclusion. For we are able to think only in relations: if, therefore, any effect exists out of relation to other effects, not only is it of necessity insensible (because standing out of relation to our sense organs), but it is also of necessity, as a concrete, unthinkable.

Now it has already been shewn that there is nothing essentially or abstractedly inconceivable in the supposition that isolated effects may exist; and we have just seen that if they do they must of necessity be imperceptible: we are hence deprived of all data for estimating the probability as to whether they do or do not. The relations in which General Laws stand to the Law-giver

[1] *Critique*, p. 146.

may or may not be such as to admit of effects standing altogether out of relation to all other effects; but whether these relations do or do not admit of such effects, and whether, if they do, such effects exist,— these are questions concerning which not only are we ignorant, but as to which we are of necessity unable to distinguish even a shadow of probability.

§ 8. Now the case of isolated effects is, as before observed, the strongest which it is possible to imagine. If then we admit, as the foregoing considerations appear to compel us, that the question as to whether or not such effects exist—or, which is much the same thing, whether or not they can exist,—is a question altogether beyond the jurisdiction of experience to decide; it necessarily follows that experience is wholly precluded from adjudicating upon the alternative proposition we are now considering. For, if any effect can exist out of relation to General Laws, it necessarily follows that, if at any point this insulation is broken, and the unrelated effect enters the domain of General Laws, at that point a new cause is introduced—the Almighty may not have operated through the whole course of Natural Law. And, if the existence of even an insulated effect—*i.e.*, an effect perpetually out of relation to all General Laws —cannot be shewn improbable; neither can an effect introduced, as it were, into the current of General Laws at any determinate point, be shewn improbable. For, until so introduced, it must be imperceptible; and, after being introduced, its influence must be normal. True it is that its introduction may be rendered conspicuous by giving rise to startling phænomena— *i.e.*, to a miracle; but we have no reason to suppose that this conspicuity would be a *necessary* attendant on such introduction. On the contrary, so far as we can argue upon such a transcendental subject at all, it appears that, if such introduction ever takes place, it would, according to the doctrine of chances, be more likely to be inconspicuous. For by far the greater number of sequences are, from the composition of causes at work, and the multiplicity of effects produced, obscured, within a very short distance from their perceptible outcome. Hence, the chances are that the introduction of a foreign cause would be imperceptible, not only on account of the fact just stated, but also because from this fact it follows, that a smaller degree of *potency* in the new cause would be required in a case where its operation is imperceptible, than in a case where it is perceptible; for, in most cases at least, according to the doctrine of chances, a smaller amount of potency properly directed would be required to occasion a given resultant in the case of a complex system of inter-operating effects, than in the case of a simple; for, not only would the number of points at which the new cause might be introduced be thus augmented, and so a corresponding number of additional chances afforded for a suitable coalescence with some member of the system; but also the proximity, which, in the case of a perceptible introduction, is a necessary condition, would, in the case we are considering, be unnecessary; and hence an indefinite amount of opportunity would be afforded for the new cause to acquire momentum, so to speak, by its accumulating influence in the system through which it would have to descend.

§ 9. A man of science will here exclaim, 'This is mere mysticism. Look for a moment at the other side, and behold the contrast! The grandest generalization which human intellect has ever achieved is the recognition of Law. This is the key that has unlocked the mysteries of Nature,—this is the doctrine which has infused harmony of action and unity of principle throughout the Universe. Shall we discard it merely for the sake of a few mystical conceptions, which would never have been seriously entertained but in support of a desperate cause? From the nature of the case it is impossible to demonstrate that the Almighty operates in every conceivable instance through the whole course of Law; but, if inferential reasoning has any weight in any case, surely in the present case that weight is full. If that which all experience, all science, and all philosophy, unite in declaring, not merely the only true, but the only really conceivable mode of action, does not constitute a sufficiently firm basis for an inductive inference, the sooner such argument is expunged from our logic, the better.'

Such representations may be multiplied indefinitely, as all who are acquainted with the literature of miracles must be aware. Such representations, however, can only, it seems to me, be made by those who have never honestly considered the whole bearing of the case. As already stated, I believe the question to be of such a character that opinions may legitimately vary concerning the degree in which it is improbable that the Almighty should ever suspend a Natural Law; but I think such variation is only legitimate within comparatively narrow limits—*i.e.*, is not warranted by the whole logical aspect of the case. Any man has a full argumentative right to say:—
'To me it seems more probable that the Almighty should never suspend a Law than that He ever should:' but no one has any argumentative right to use such

expressions as, "next to impossible," "almost incredible," and so forth. Why should the analogical method be expunged from our logic, merely because it is devoid of authority when applied to a transcendental doctrine, concerning which all argument whatever is no better than guess? We do not object to the *method*, but to its application in the present case; for the nature of this case nullifies the validity of the method. Although analogical reasoning is of prime authority when applied within the sphere of General Laws—a sphere by which, as we have seen, it is alone originated, and in which alone it must terminate,—it merely assumes the question it pretends to solve, when it is applied to a sphere which transcends these Laws. It does so because the argument then becomes a case of reasoning in a circle. It begins by assuming that the method, which is undoubtedly valid when applied within the Proximate, is likewise valid when extended from the Proximate to the Ultimate: but the sole condition of its validity in any case must be conceded to be the presupposition as to the existence of General Laws[1]: therefore, the conclusion is wholly contained in the assumption; and, the mere fact of applying the method at all being thus necessarily a begging of the whole question at issue, all arguments, however good and elaborate in themselves, are entirely superfluous; because the whole matter turns, not in the slightest degree upon the strength of these arguments, but entirely upon the validity of their method. If the latter is valid, these arguments are useless, because the question is decided by the fact: if not valid, these argu-

[1] The only other condition possible, viz., the transcendental probability as to the uniformity of the Divine method, is afterwards considered.

ments cannot strengthen the case by the minutest tittle. Hence, whenever the validity of the method is, in the smallest degree, assumed, in that precise degree is the whole question prejudicated.

If, then, the mere fact of applying this method assumes the whole question to be decided, its condemnation is contained in the very act of applying it. Apart, however, from this crushing refutation, it may be worth while to add, that even were the method in no wise affected by the fact that the case in dispute refers to General Laws, that method in this case would still be valueless. For the value of analogical reasoning varies inversely as the difference between the known and the unknown. Now, according to this canon, the method under examination would here be quite as illegitimate as we saw it to be in the two previous cases[1]. For, as the most eminent of recent logicians remarks,— "The uniformity in the succession of events, otherwise called the law of causation, must be received not as a law of the universe, but of that portion of it only which is within the range of our means of sure observation, with a *reasonable degree of extension to adjacent cases*. To extend it further is to make a supposition without evidence, and to which, in the absence of any ground from experience for estimating its degree of probability, it would be idle to attempt to assign any[2]."

The method, then, which we are considering, is only valid when applied within a reasonable distance from

[1] Viz., in arguing from known second causes to their entire range; and in arguing from the known relations of observed second causes to each other, to the relations between these and the First Cause.

[2] Mill.

the domain of experience, and cannot even found a probability as to whether or not General Laws obtain in other parts of the Universe. This is the conclusion previously arrived at in the second chapter, and is now reverted to in order to ground an argument *à fortiori*. For, if this is so in the case of second causes, much more must this method be invalid when applied to the First Cause. If analogical reasoning is impotent to raise, even to a low stage of probability, an inference as to the necessity of General Laws existing throughout the realm of the Conditioned; much more is such reasoning unable to render it probable that any such necessity influences the action of the Unconditioned.

Lastly, it is of the essence of inferential reasoning, that the "generalization of an observed fact from the mere absence of any known instance to the contrary, affords in general a precarious and unsafe ground of assurance[1]." Most of all then must a generalization be unsafe in a case where we can see from independent considerations, that *if* any instance to the contrary ever occurs, it must of necessity be unobservable. Yet, that this is so in the present instance, we have seen in sections 6 and 7 to be a fact beyond dispute.

We are hence irresistibly led to the conclusion that the only kind of reasoning available in the present case,—viz., inference from the observed method of Divine Government within experience, to the character of that method in its totality,—is a kind of reasoning utterly destitute of authority; firstly, because it cannot be applied at all without assuming the whole question at issue; secondly, because, even if it could, it would still be indefinitely valueless, since the unknown ratio

---

[1] Mill.

contains all that is to man unknowable; and thirdly, because, if in other respects unexceptionable, the inference would still be invalid, from the fact that it can never admit of verification. Even as an inference it is no better than a guess; because, if erroneous, we have no means of discovering the error.

§ 10. To this conclusion, it appears to me, there is only one objection which it is possible to urge. 'Fully admitting the truth of all that has been said,' an opponent will observe, 'I cannot deem the conclusion impartial, because no allowance has been made for the antecedent probability, that the method of Divine Government is everywhere uniform.'

I think an adequate consideration of this subject will be seen only to intensify the conclusion already attained. Before commencing it, however, it is necessary to point out that, even were it not so, any argument grounded on this "antecedent probability" is of a very meagre character. There is, no doubt, an antecedent probability of the kind mentioned; but who is to assert what constitutes the unity of the Divine method, absolutely considered? Who is to say that this unity *must* consist in the Almighty having laid down eternal rules for the guidance of His own directive influence? Or, supposing this granted, who is to declare what these rules are? "The Laws of Nature are nothing else than man's own expressions of the orderly sequence which he discerns in the phænomena of the Universe[1]," and we have just seen that *if* there is any other method of the Divine Government—or, more correctly, if the existence of *General* Laws is but a portion of that method[2]—we are of necessity precluded from perceiving the fact.

[1] Dr W. B. Carpenter. [2] See Section 13.

Further, granting even that General Laws constitute the whole of the Divine method, the existence of General Laws merely in relation to us, affords no pretext for supposing that these *same* Laws exist in any final relation, so to speak, to the Supreme Will. They are, indeed, the formal conditions of our experience; but it does not therefore follow that they are the formal conditions of absolute order. Again, even supposing that these relatively General Laws are absolutely General—*i. e.*, that " man's own expressions" are absolute truths—it is still quite conceivable that, were we able to see the Divine method in its totality, we should perceive that this absolute system of General Laws, which is likewise relative to us, constitutes an indefinitely small portion of the whole: for, were we able to soar above experience and to take perceptible cognizance of that which is now transcendental, it is not improbable, much less incredible, that we should be able to see why it is now unrealizable that action should take place externally to relative Law; for, by rising above an experience which is formed by and only possible under such Law, to an experience which transcends such Law, we might well perceive how orderly action could be possible without such Law—*i. e.*, through other and higher Laws. Lastly, even were this not so, who is to say which General Laws possess an absolute value, and which a relative? Even if we suppose that the Almighty is in some cases impeded by His own Laws—or, perhaps, more correctly, that *if* He should desire to effect some particular action, He could not do so and maintain the uniformity of His method—even upon this supposition, I say, we are still unable to distinguish these cases from others in which He is not thus impeded. It is manifest that each of these points invites development; but, as conviction is the main object in view, we shall proceed at once to the objection raised.

§ 11. This objection is evidently the most transcendental we have yet encountered. As such we are not responsible for the transcendental nature of the considerations necessitated by its discussion.

For the sake of perspicuity we have hitherto considered Law as being in all its relations a definite entity —as being at its distal extremity, so to speak, somewhat similar, if not identical, with that which we know it to be at its proximate—as being of such a character that it would persist, whether or not employed by the Almighty as the vehicle of His directive influence. Upon this view of Law we have seen—firstly, that even upon the assumption it embodies, our ignorance of Law is still so profound that it is quite conceivable that the Almighty could answer many if not all petitions strictly through its course,—secondly, that our ignorance of the relations subsisting between the Almighty and Natural Law further precludes us from imposing limits upon the Divine directive ability, even if restricted in its action to known or strictly analogous Laws,—and thirdly, that this same ignorance wholly invalidates all arguments adduced to shew that the Almighty is in any way restricted in His causative action.

It now remains to shew, that not only have we no data for asserting that Law is thus in all its relations a definite entity,—that not only have we no right to say that the Almighty can only act without Law by acting against Law, *i.e.*, by suspending Law,—that not only is it a mere assumption to suppose that Law is everywhere such as we know it—absolutely indestructible as we know it to be relatively so ; but that all these ideas are in direct antagonism with the hypothesis of an Intelligent First Cause.

For, upon this hypothesis, there are two and only two verbally intelligible suppositions as to the nature of the directive influence to which the order of the Universe is due. We may suppose that the Almighty sustains the activity of the Universe by a continual causative influence emanating from His own existence ; or we may suppose that such activity is maintained by a self-adjusting power inherent in the Universe itself. It devolves upon us to shew that these two suppositions, although apparently dissimilar, are really identical.

Just as we are by the laws of thought compelled to lodge the attribute of self-existence somewhere, so we are by the same laws precluded from lodging it in more than one substance. Hence, upon the supposition of a self-existing Deity, the Universe of necessity becomes dependent,—first as to its existence, and consequently as to its action. But if the action of the Universe is absolutely dependent on the Deity, it follows that whichever view we choose to adopt as to the character of that action, thus much is certain—it is the result solely of the Divine influence. If the Universe is self-adjusting and likewise dependent, its self-adjustment is but the mode of the directive influence of that on which it depends. Hence, whether we choose to speak of the Divine influence as everywhere in operation, or as eternally in abeyance, we are merely presenting the same idea in different words ; since, if we once deprive the Universe of its quality of self-existence, the absolute quiescence of the Deity becomes synonymous with His universal activity. And if this statement appears at first sight paradoxical, it is only because we have not succeeded in divesting ourselves of our anthropomorphic conceptions regarding the Divine action; for it is merely a statement of the truth that, upon the Theistic hypothesis, all activity whatever is ultimately due to the Divine influence.

It may here be objected that the institution of this paradox is tantamount to the obliteration of all the foregoing arguments; for, if we suppose a continual cycle of recurrent energy guided by Law to be the necessary mode of causation throughout the Universe, it is merely a quarrelling about words to prove that this cycle is but the expression of the Divine activity. 'Be it so,' it will be said, 'but so long as this mode is supposed general, so long is the objecting position tenable—is in fact supplied with all the data it requires.' Now, this difficulty would be perfectly valid, did it not embody the fallacy of lodging self-existence within Law, *i. e.*, making the operation of Law an *absolute* necessity—and this is the very fallacy we are throughout this chapter resisting. If, then, we expressly deprive Law of this attribute, the difficulty vanishes—Law, being then contained together with Matter and Energy within the Self-existing Substance, becomes but the regulative influence of that Substance—is but the mode of its directive activity, as the constant cycle of energy (supposing such to exist) is the mode of its dynamic activity[1].

Now this is a fact systematically overlooked by writers on this subject, and the ignoring of it gives undue

---

[1] Whether or not this mode of activity *actually is* general, is another question; the only point we are above concerned with being, that whether or not it is so, it cannot, on the Theistic hypothesis and in an absolute sense, be *necessarily* so.

apparent weight to their arguments. So long as we regard Law as a sort of independent deity, there remains a certain intellectual *vis inertiæ* to be overcome, in order to conceive of the Almighty as antagonizing its influence; but we thus perceive that this *vis inertiæ* only arises from the material nature of our symbols. Either let us altogether discard the notion of the Almighty, and believe in the self-existence of the Universe; or let us accept with that notion the only logical conclusions to which it leads.

§ 12. Upon the Theistic hypothesis, then, the term Natural Law becomes synonymous with that of the Final Directive Activity; so that whatever course this Activity assumes, such course is by this very fact constituted, in the full sense of the term, a Natural Law. Hence, the only question that arises is, as to whether or not the course of the Final Directive Activity is as invariable, and invariable *in the same particulars*, as it is tacitly assumed to be when spoken of as Natural Law. There is, no doubt, at first sight a strong analogical probability that it is so, from the presupposition as to the uniformity of the Divine method; and many writers of ability have, it seems to me, too hastily subscribed to it. For, referring again to section 10, if we had any means of estimating the extent of the Divine method known to us, relatively to that method as a whole, then, no doubt, the argument would be abundantly valid; provided, at least, that *in that case* its *perceived* value shewed it to be so. As it is, however, we are evidently unable either to make this estimation, or to perceive the distance, so to speak, by which we are removed from the possibility of making it; and so, if the canon on which we have throughout relied is valid, the argument collapses. Further, we have seen that experience is only possible under General Laws, or, which is the same thing, that if General Laws constitute only a portion of the Divine method—a portion no matter how comparatively small,—there is a necessary reason why we should be unable to perceive the fact. These considerations appear to shew conclusively that the question as to whether or not the course of the Final Directive Activity is invariable according to our ideas of invariability—ideas, be it always remembered, which are formed by and only possible under a certain class of General Laws,—is a question which cannot be answered one way or the other with any assignable degree of probability. "The most slight and superficial view of any human contrivance comes abundantly nearer to a thorough knowledge of it, than that part, which we know of the government of the world, does to the general scheme and system of it; to the whole set of laws by which it is governed[1]."

Something, therefore, will have been gained by presenting the question in this form, if it serves to render yet more intense the appreciation of our utter ignorance regarding the modes and the means of the Prime Directive Agency.

§ 13. More than this will have been gained; for it now becomes axiomatic that the uniformity of the Divine method of Government, or more plainly, the uniformity of Nature absolutely considered, is the synonym for the consistency of the Divine Will. So long as that Will remains consistent, so long must the perceptible sequences occurring in Nature be uniform, however small a portion of the whole we may suppose

[1] Butler.

such sequences to constitute; and when we speak of the uniformity of Nature in an absolute sense, we are tacitly referring to that consistency. The question, then, merges into this :—Can the Divine Will answer Prayer, and yet remain consistent?

It will be observed that the proposition we are examining undertakes to answer this question with an unequivocal negative, while we merely contend that it is unanswerable. For the purpose of ascertaining which position is the more tenable, let us ask, What is it that constitutes consistency of will? There is, it seems to me, only one answer possible, viz., a similarity or identity of desire under similar or identical conditions; and so, in the case of an unimpeded will, a similarity or identity of action. Now we have just seen that Natural Law is, on the Theistic hypothesis, synonymous with the Final Directive Activity; so that the Divine Will can in no case be impeded in the execution of its desires. The ultimate question, then, which arises, is :—Can the Almighty *desire* to answer Prayer, and yet remain consistent? This question at first sight appears again to merge into the more ultimate question as to the nature of the Divine attributes, but in reality this is not so; for, what the scientific proposition when regarded from our present standpoint necessarily affirms is, that the possession of attributes leading to the answer of Prayer would be incompatible with the consistency of the Divine Will. Without at present waiting to shew that the attributes postulated by the term "Almighty," to say the least, admit of no warrant for this assertion, or that the more detailed representation of the Divine character contained in Scripture appears to meet it with a direct negation; it is sufficient for the maintenance of the attitude adopted, to point out the truth already so often insisted upon, viz., that Science can have no voice in this most ultimate of questions. Apart from Revelation, all propositions referring to the Divine attributes are, in their very mention, contingent upon information which we do not possess. The question then as to the nature of the Divine attributes being, on philosophical grounds alone, in total abeyance, it is an indefensible position to assert that the Deity cannot desire to answer Prayer without violating His own attributes. If God is mindful of man, if He has a merciful and even a loving regard for his happiness, if He "hearkens to the voice of our petitions," and if He is able to see when the granting of any request would be for the benefit of the petitioner; then, assuredly, it becomes at least amply conceivable, that, to such a Prayer-hearing God, the element of Prayer occurring among other "conditions" should constitute a difference of occasion, even although such an occasion should in all other respects resemble some other one. If so, it follows from the definition recently given, that any corresponding diversity of action would not constitute any inconsistency of the Divine Will, and so would in no wise mar the uniformity of Nature[1].

[1] "The true immutability of God consists...in His never changing the principles of His administration. And He may, therefore, in perfect accordance with the immutability of His nature, purpose to do under certain circumstances, dependent on the free agency of man, what He will not do under others; and for this reason, that an immutable adherence to the principles of a wise, just, and gracious government requires it." (Dr Chalmers.) "It may be agreeable to perfect Wisdom to grant that to our prayers which it would not have been agreeable to the same Wisdom to have given us without our praying for it." (Dr Paley, quoted in Mr Karslake's *Efficacy of Prayer*, p. 18, [1874].) "The doctrine

§ 14. We are now drawing to the close of our principal argument. Before finishing, however, it is necessary to observe, that many of the considerations and arguments employed have been of the kind so happily designated by Mr Spencer, "symbolic conceptions of the illegitimate order." That is to say, we can conceive of no great magnitudes, durations, numbers, etc., *actually*, but only by a process of building up symbolic conceptions from conceptions of smaller though similar entities, which we can "realize in imagination"—that is, by imagining the smaller entities correspondingly extended. Now, although it is by this process alone that we are able to arrive at general propositions, and so at general conclusions, the legitimacy of the process evidently decreases, in proportion to our inability to "assure ourselves that our symbolic conceptions stand for actualities." Many of the preceding considerations, then, have been of this illegitimate order; but it would be a great mistake to suppose that on this account they are valueless to the general argument. On the contrary, the fact of their being of this character is but an intensification of that argument. For the latter has for its object, not the institution, but the destruction of a proposition; and the whole ground of its conduct has been, that the proposition is valueless *because* referring

---

of God's immutability, instead of being an objection to Prayer, is our chief encouragement to pray. God has appointed this mean to procure certain blessings; and it is only because of His unchangeable nature that we can have any assurance as to the success of this mean. The case thus resembles that of all other means,—all our labours in temporary things presupposing our knowledge that the laws of Nature—that is, the ordinances of God—are permanent." (Dr Romanes, MS. Sermon on Prayer, [1874].)

to a transcendental province. If then, in the course of rendering this manifest, we have employed this kind of symbolic conceptions, it has only been because, from the nature of the proposition, these were the only conceptions possible for the adequate conducting of its examination. Only if these considerations could be proved to have no bearing upon that proposition, would they be open to any objection on the score of transcendentalism. Otherwise, the fact of their transcendental character only increases the force of the general argument; for it shews, independently of discussion, that the proposition virtually contains at least as much transcendentalism as is contained in the argument against it.

§ 15. We have now finished that argument. It is not necessary to its validity as a whole, that every idea and every subordinate argument contained in it should be accepted, or even that every such idea and argument should be incapable of refutation; since their sum, it seems to me, cannot but be deemed sufficient to establish the only position we are contending for, viz., that the question raised is, on philosophical grounds alone, an uncertain one. This indeed is a conclusion which, to the majority of persons at least, will appear evident without discussion; but if it did so to all, there would have been no need of a Burney Prize for the subject of this Essay. Further, even although the question is thus deemed an uncertain one prior to its discussion, it then becomes one as to the *degree* of uncertainty; that is, the amount of probability contained in the scientific proposition. The impartial estimation of that amount has been the principal object of our analysis, and the out-come has been that this amount is not only to perception exceedingly small, but that it is yet smaller to an indefinite, because an unknowable, degree.

§ 16. It will be observed that this analysis has throughout been an elaborate exposition of the argument from ignorance—an argument which men of science are often too prone to neglect or despise, but an argument which a true philosopher cannot but deem of all arguments relating to subjects beyond the sphere of possible knowledge, the most weighty and the most profound.

It will also be observed that throughout this analysis I have abstained as much as possible from mingling with it the element of *feeling*. Yet I am persuaded that this is the element of all others which, in the present question, is the most potent in forming the decision of each individual mind. For this very reason, however, I deem its careful exclusion the more imperative ; and I cannot lose this opportunity of expressing my regret, that all writers upon this subject, with only one exception, mingle feeling and argument indiscriminately. As a question of feeling let it be decided by feeling, and as a question of intellect by intellect ; but let not the one contaminate the other. No doubt every one has an equal right to decide the question for himself, in accordance with the inclination of his own sentiments ; but no one has a right to project his sentiments into his argument, for by this means the latter acquires an unlawful increment of persuasive force. True it is that in most subjects, and in such as this one most of all, the platform of preconceived opinion is that on which discussion is but too stringently confined—that we all argue as advocates in support of a formed conclusion, rather than as judges on a question in dispute[1] : but although the ray

[1] Cf. Bacon, *Nov. Org*. Book I. pp. 46—9.

of truth is thus of necessity more or less differentially refracted in its passage through the many-faceted medium of diverse opinion, we should all be careful that the medium is *pure*—that the ray, although refracted, should not be coloured—although it may be decomposed, that its constituents at least should be left intact. Δεῖ δ' ἐλεύθερον εἶναι τῇ γνώμῃ τὸν μέλλοντα φιλοσοφεῖν.

A man of science, nevertheless, who has been accustomed to give the rein to his emotions, will deem the foregoing discussion unsatisfactory, even although he may not be able to overturn the argument as a whole. He will not be satisfied to have the subject decided by purely intellectual methods. It is a "case specially bearing on purely *physical* contemplations, and on which no common rules of evidence or logical technicalities can enable us to form a correct judgment. It is not a question which can be decided by a few trite and commonplace generalities as to the moral government of the world and the belief in the Divine Omnipotence— or as to the limits of human experience. It involves those grander conceptions of the order of Nature, those comprehensive primary elements of all physical knowledge, those ultimate ideas of universal causation, which can only be familiar to those thoroughly versed in cosmical philosophy in its widest sense[1]." And how splendid is the conception of Universal Law! Little as our minds may be, small as our opportunities undoubtedly are, we have yet at last obtained a glimpse of the Government of God, and we have found, that worthy of the immensity of the Universe, worthy of the infinity of its Author, is the majesty of His Reign. Shall we renounce our

---

[1] *Essays and Reviews*, p. 133.

hard-earned attainment of so magnificent a truth, merely for the sake of a few little, selfish, and absurdly presumptuous hopes; or shall we not rather embrace more firmly than ever the grand belief, that here we have revealed a truth which does not end within the narrow limits of our faculties—that here we possess a pledge of the one all-pervading, ever-enduring method of the Most High? And in the presence of so great a thought, shall we not cheerfully submit to take our place within this glorious system of unerring order,—an order which "knows no exception, is all-sufficient, and furnishes to us, its children, the highest type and model" of perfection? Nay, shall we not rather rejoice in such a system—"confide, hope, trust in it, know that our own place is a part of the grand whole, and do our work unquestioningly and unsuggestingly"?

> "All are but parts of one stupendous whole,
> Whose body Nature is, and God the soul:
> That chang'd thro' all, and yet in all the same,
> Great in the earth, as in th' etherial frame,
> Warms in the sun, refreshes in the breeze,
> Glows in the stars, and blossoms in the trees,
> Lives through all life, extends thro' all extent,
> Spreads undivided, operates unspent[1]."

But there is another side to this matter. While a man of Prayer will feel with the man of Science, that the recognition of Law magnifies his conceptions of the Government of God, as the discoveries of science magnify his conceptions of His Dominion; such a man will also feel that he cannot, without violating all that is to him most cherished, consent to believe that the morality of

[1] Pope.

God is swamped by His power. He has loved to believe that that power is infinitely great, and he hails the conception of Law as enabling him in some small measure to realize his belief; but he has loved yet more to think of that power as a watchful, guiding influence, to which the small is as the great, and without which no sparrow falls to the ground;—an influence which in human form and with human lips has declared, that man is to Him of all that is on earth immeasurably the dearest charge; that there is no word, no thought, of ours which escapes His loving care; that mindful through all our forgetfulness, constant through all our inconstancy, His earnest compassion is over us;—that we have but to ask and it shall be given us, to believe and we shall obtain. Are we to relinquish this great and hallowed creed, merely for the sake of an empty figment of intellect, which can have no substantially valid reason for its support? Call these hopes and these desires little, selfish, what you will, they are to us, and must be to all, the most momentous and important of all things in life. And how beautiful is the thought of our daily dependence upon God! Even had we no external evidence to support the belief—were it founded merely as the counter-hypothesis is founded, on the authority of our innate intelligence,—it would still appear to us the more congruous of the two; for surely it is *à priori* improbable that such a sense of dependence should be present in man, without something to correspond to it in God. But now when natural religion has been endorsed by revealed, all doubt is taken away, and in the light of that finished scheme we can exclaim with an intensified meaning—" I will praise thee with my whole heart; I will worship towards thy holy temple, and praise thy name for thy loving-kindness and for thy truth: for thou hast magnified thy *word* above all thy *name*[1]."

There is thus no doubt as to the side on which the pre-potency of feeling occurs, and the scientific disputant in prudence, if not in logic, should abstain from allowing this element any part in the controversy. But, as we have seen, it is wholly wrong in disputants on either side to allow their emotions to encroach upon their argument; it is but "making opinion the test of opinion[2]," and in whatever degree this is done, we really weaken our *argument* (although we may illegitimately increase its superficial gloss), for in that degree we virtually deny the presence of external facts or reasons to justify our belief.

§ 17. A man of science will yet object that, more or less apart from mere feeling, the foregoing discussion is unsatisfactory. Conclusions founded on dry logic alone are not enough for him; there appears to be a massive body of common sense to be removed, the inertia of which such flimsy considerations are unable appreciably to affect. But let us ask him, Whence this common sense? It is not common to us all, or your views would meet with no opposition. His answer would be given without hesitation, and it would be the true one. Men of science obtrude upon us that the speciality of their pursuits engenders in them a speciality of thought; and therefore that their antecedent conceptions regarding this and kindred questions differ from those of other men. But what is this favourite saying adduced to prove? It is little better than a truism to assert that modes of thought and feeling are affected by intellectual pursuits;

---

[1] Psalm cxxxviii. 1, 2. Cf. John ii. 21. Cf. John i. 14. Cf. Psalm lxxv. 1, and Rom. i. 20.

[2] Cf. Mill, *Logic*, I. 419.

but the only influence which these pursuits can be expected to have upon the thoughts and feelings of those not engaged in them—*i. e.*, the only extent in which they coincide with "the conditions of external reality,"—is strictly limited to the facts and the argumentative probabilities which these pursuits may be able to establish. Only if men of science were able to shew that their studies gave them a superior vantage-ground in perceiving or inferring the ultimate methods of the Deity, would there be any argumentative use in pointing to the influence of these studies upon their intelligence. As it is, their favourite maxim is a positive detriment to their cause. Substantially a man of science is in the same condition as other men in respect of knowledge, the only difference being that he has given more exclusive attention to a particular department of the Proximate. Naturally therefore his mind, by being in this department more persistently in contact with orderly sequences occurring within the Proximate, becomes more imbued than that of other men with the idea of Law: but, this conception being as a doctrine fully recognized by all educated persons, and so allowed its full *doctrinal* weight in all arguments, it is an infirmity to be overcome, rather than an advantage to be gloried in, that his intelligence is precluded more than other men's from taking a comprehensive view, in all its bearings, of the question before us. "Any one study, of whatever kind, exclusively pursued, deadens in the mind the interest, nay, the perception of any other ;" therefore, "when anything, which comes before us, is very unlike what we uniformly experience, we consider it on that account untrue[1]."

Thus the "common sense," which the man of science

[1] Dr Newman, *Lectures on University Subjects*, p. 322.

opposes to argument, is not merely a sense not common to educated persons; but, when traced to its origin, is found to arise from no valid principle—when analysed is shewn to contain no pledge of authority. Yet supporters of the proposition we have examined habitually ground their arguments, as well as their beliefs, upon this basis of pre-conceived opinion; avowedly refusing to come into the arena of fair and general discussion. There is a bigotry among men of religion, but it would be hard to find a bigotry surpassed by this, which confessedly turns away from the principles of reason and logic, merely because they cannot be pressed into the service of pre-conceived ideas. Opinion is here again made the test of opinion, and a careful observer cannot fail to see that such argument as may exist is weakened by its very discussion.

§ 18. Lest these observations should be deemed too strong, I shall, by way of illustration, briefly criticize the most recent presentation of the case by the eminent physicist, who may be said to have revived this discussion. I choose this illustration because of its brevity, its clear style, its temperate tone, and the authority of its writer. Prof. Tyndall begins his argument thus:—"I would simply ask any intelligent person to look the problem honestly and steadily in the face[1]," etc. If by this request is meant an honest investigation of the problem in all its bearings, we have endeavoured to answer the summons, and the result has been to confirm the words of Canon Liddon, "It dissolves into thin air, as we look hard at it, this fancied barrier of inexorable Law." That this, however, is not the Professor's meaning, he soon proceeds to shew. "To any person who deals sincerely with the subject, and *refuses* to *blur* his *moral* vision by *intellectual*

[1] *Contemporary Review*, Oct. 1872, p. 764.

subtleties, this, I think, will appear a true statement of the case." The words I have italicized speak for themselves.

As the result of "refusing to blur his moral vision," Dr Tyndall proceeds to make an extraordinary statement, to the effect that a scientific student "claims the right of subjecting" the influence of Prayer "to those methods of examination from which all our present knowledge of the physical universe is derived;" and so of deciding the question at issue "upon pure physical evidence." It is hard to believe that a man of Prof. Tyndall's attainments can here be in earnest, but if he is so (and those who are acquainted with the general tone of his other writings can scarcely think otherwise), there has probably never been a statement penned by a man of ability, which so well exemplifies the dwarfing influence of too exclusive an attention to a single class of studies. Only if "our present knowledge of the physical universe" included a complete knowledge of its ultimate source, of the relations of this source to it, and a further knowledge of its entire current, would this statement be true. Proximate manifestations of physical energy belong to a wholly different sphere from that to which Prayer refers, supposing it physically efficacious: how then, if it is thus efficacious, can a man in reason expect the methods which apply to one sphere, to be of equal value in the other? If we knew enough of the remote sphere to be deductively certain that no influence could be exerted by it on the observed sphere, without being to perception unusual; then, indeed, we might subject the whole question to experiment; only as there would then be no question, there would be no need of verification. As it is, the institution of experiment is merely an irreverent mode of asking the Deity to work any stated number of miracles, at a place and time appointed by ourselves.

Not to dwell longer on a proposal, which must appear self-evidently absurd to all who as yet have not "refused to blur their moral vision[1]," let us, for the encouragement of such, still further observe the effects of doing so. After shewing that there is no "inherent unreasonableness in the act of Prayer," since "from the analogy of an earthly father......it is no departure from scientific method to place behind natural phænomena a universal Father, who, in answer to the prayer of His children, alters the currents of phænomena," Dr. Tyndall argues,—" But without *verification* a theoretic conception is a mere figment of the intellect, and I am sorry to find us parting company at this point,—" and so on, explaining the process of verification. After so noble an admonition to abstain from "intellectual subtleties," it is a pity that the learned Professor should have himself ventured within the treacherous domain of Logic. It is, of course, perfectly true that a theory without verification has "little other value than that of a conjecture;" but the fallacy resides in tacitly assuming that verification is the synonym of experiment—that experiment is, in every case, the only means we have of verifying theory. What would a Lawyer or a Statesman say to this doctrine? Or, would Prof. Tyndall himself undertake to assert that Christianity, as a whole, has no more to say for itself than Fetishism? Again, even in physical science what would become of the statement? Prof. Tyndall, indeed, tells us elsewhere that he has "not even a theory of magnetism;" but we cannot suppose this to mean that he regards the impon-

[1] For a fuller refutation of this proposal, see M'Cosh in the same number of the *Contemporary Review*.

derable fluid with the same favour as did his forefathers. This, however, introduces us to another fallacy contained in the above presentation, viz., the implied doctrine that verification must either be absolute or *nil*—demonstrative or valueless. If Prof. Tyndall's beliefs do not admit of degrees—if he only begins to believe where he can prove, then of all men he must be the least practical, and the most irrational.

How does such philosophy contrast, on the one hand, with that of Mill[1],—"It is in the power of everyone to cultivate habits of thought which make him independent of them (*i.e.*, supposed instinctive beliefs). The habit of philosophical analysis (of which it is the surest effect to enable the mind to command, instead of being commanded by, the laws of the merely passive parts of its own nature), by shewing to us that things are not necessarily connected in fact because their ideas are connected in our minds, is able to loosen innumerable associations which reign despotically over the undisciplined or early-prejudiced mind," etc., etc. ; or, on the other hand, with that of "Butler of the 'Analogy' (who, if he were alive, would make short work of much of the current *à priori* 'infidelity')[2],"—"to us probability is the very guide of life."

§ 19. In closing this division of our subject we must ask, Whence this violent contrast between the feelings or the preconceived opinions of the disputants on either side? A mere difference of intellectual pursuits is not sufficient to account for it, since in no other subject does such difference engender so great a strength of opposite conviction. The answer is to be found in the fact already discussed, viz., that it is impossible to overrate the influence

---

[1] *Logic*, Vol. II. p. 98.
[2] Huxley, *Lay Sermons*, p. 69.

of our views as to the truth of Christianity, upon our views as to the antecedent probability of the more special question before us. "This fancied barrier of inexorable law" is, after all, in most cases a mere intellectual scapegoat, made (unconsciously I admit) to carry the weight of our unbelief in the authority of Revelation. "Once believe that there is a God, and miracles are not incredible[1]," is a maxim which must remain irrefutable, so long as our intelligence remains human[2]. I am aware that the substance of this maxim is contradicted by Hume, and where he has inadvertently stumbled, it is not surprising that others should have fallen. He says:—"Though the Being to whom the miracle is ascribed, be in this case Almighty, it does not upon that account become a whit more probable; since it is impossible for us to know the attributes or actions of such a Being, otherwise than from the experience which we have of His productions in the usual course of nature[3]." Now Hume himself elsewhere admits, what all supporters of the *à priori* objections must admit, viz., that the only ground on which these objections have to stand, is the fact that experience does not supply us with a cause adequate to

[1] Paley.

[2] In the course of an elaborate disquisition on Miracles, published while this Essay was in the press, the anonymous author truly observed that Paley's "argument culminates in the short statement" above quoted; but after the word "God" in that quotation, he adds in brackets, "*i.e.*, a Personal God, working miracles,"—thereby reducing the proposition to a comical truism. If this author requires punctilious exactitude at the expense of conciseness, the proposition may be thrown into this form :—To a Theist, as distinguished from a Deist or an Atheist, miracles are not incredible. (See *Supernatural Religion*, Vol. I. p. 209) [1874.]

[3] *Miracles*.

produce the alleged effect. Upon the premise, however, of an Almighty Agent, the adequacy of an assumed cause is granted; and the only legitimate conclusion is that a miracle is a *more* probable event than it would be in the absence of such an assumption. For, in the presence of this assumption, a miracle, as Brown in substance observes, is not a violation, but an instance of law of causality[1]; and this obvious truth is assented to by Mill, who adds—"Of the adequacy of the cause, if present, there can be no doubt; and the only antecedent improbability which can be ascribed to the miracle, is the improbability that any such cause existed[2]." The true statement of Hume's case is, that although the occurrence of a miracle is much more probable upon the supposition of an Intelligent and Almighty First Cause than it would be in the absence of such a supposition, yet a miracle is still highly improbable—or, more correctly, the fact of its having occurred is highly uncertain,—because we are ignorant as to the other attributes of that Agent[3]. When, however, these are supplied, as they are professed to be by Revelation, and when that profession is accepted as authoritative—when, that is, we believe in "*the* Almighty" —then the assumed Agent is supposed to possess not only the *ability* but also the *intention*, and a miracle ceases to be improbable, in exact proportion to the

---

[1] *Cause and Effect*, Notes A and F.

[2] *Logic*, II. p. 168.

[3] The anonymous author previously referred to, although very jealous of his logical reputation, has nevertheless failed to perceive this obvious inconsequence in Hume's reasoning. It would have appeared somewhat more impartial, if the writer had taken time to consider this point, before adducing the above quotation from Hume, as proof that Mill "apparently overlooked" it. (Vide *loc. cit.*) [1874.]

degree of belief entertained as to the existence of such an Agent. Thus, while Philosophy alone, even when supplied with the premise of an Intelligent and Almighty First Cause, is logically bound to pronounce the question, as to whether or not a miracle ever occurred, a hopelessly uncertain one; Philosophy supplemented by Revelation, and thus starting from a new premise, can have no hesitation in pronouncing the occurrence of a miracle credible, in the precise degree in which the premise is held so.

And it is evident that these remarks apply equally to the case of Prayer. On philosophical grounds alone no real presumption can be raised against it, and the whole question turns upon the truth of Christianity, and the statements of Scripture when accepted as Divine.

Thus Philosophy—even when expanded to its widest meaning, and understood as the unification of all our knowledge[1]—Philosophy must now, as in her early home, rear her altar to the Unknown God; but when she does so let her at least be consistent; and if an Apostle of another system has come to declare that God Whom she ignorantly worships[2], let her listen to His preaching with an impartial and unbiassed ear—let her decide upon the merits of that system, not by preconceived opinion, but in accordance with its own credentials. And, in any case, let her above all things abstain from the folly of asserting what the Unknown God can or cannot do— what He does or does not desire:—so shall she cease to stultify herself, and to mislead the less thoughtful of her children.

[1] Cf. Spencer, *First Principles*.
[2] Heb. iii. 1.

CHAPTER V.

§ 1. OUR examination thus far has already been characterized as "an elaborate exposition of the argument from ignorance." That examination, however, would be incomplete, were it allowed to end with this exposition. Our main argument has been, that the question at issue is a question entirely beyond the range of philosophical discussion; but a subordinate argument remains to be adduced. The scientific proposition rests entirely upon *à priori* considerations, which, when we shut our eyes to our ignorance, certainly tend to shew that the Almighty cannot answer Prayer through the normal course of Law. There are, however, antagonistic considerations of the same class,—that is, considerations shewing how the Almighty may be conceived to answer Prayer through the normal course of Law,—and the statement of these constitutes the subordinate argument.

Before commencing this statement, however, it is desirable definitely to understand the position which these *à priori* considerations are intended to occupy in the general argument. The scientific proposition asserts, that in no case does the Almighty answer Prayer with a physical equivalent: I have endeavoured to shew that the reasons by which this assertion is supported have very little authority; and this point is, as repeatedly observed, the principal one with which the present Essay is concerned. We have nothing whatever to do with the question, *How* does the Almighty answer Prayer? but merely with the examination of the reasons inducing us to suppose that He does not. Even were science able to shew that it transcends our faculties to conceive of any manner in which the Almighty could answer Prayer, our argument would still remain intact—the whole basis of that argument being, as just observed, that the question *is* one which transcends our faculties. Nevertheless, as men persist in applying reason to a sphere that transcends reason, and in supposing that their abstract symbolisms have a concrete value, it becomes desirable to adduce such kindred arguments as tend to support the opposite view; since the scientific objections to Prayer may thus, even upon their own ground, be neutralized to a greater or less extent—even apart from all considerations as to the essentially invalid nature of the scientific proposition, that proposition may thus itself be shewn not altogether true. From what has been said, however, it will be evident that in the case of no single method which it is possible to suggest, is it pretended that there is even so much as a probability that such method is really the one by which an answer to Prayer is secured. These suggestions are only made in order to shew, that, even to our present faculties, it is not inconceivable that the Almighty *may* answer Prayer: they in no wise presume to indicate the manner in which He *does*. Indeed, on philosophical grounds alone (we must in consistency observe) we have no more adequate data for supposing that the Almighty ever answers Prayer, than we have for supposing that He does not. Our business, however, throughout has been, not with the question as to whether or not He actually does, but merely with the question as to how far it is improbable that He should. It is hoped, therefore, that the following conceivable possibilities as to the manner in which, so far as we can see, He might, may yet further reduce the improbability which the scientific objections endeavour to establish[1].

These objections are, as already observed, entirely of an *à priori* character: the antagonistic considerations, therefore, about to be adduced, being of the same character, have the following advantages over these objections:—firstly, These objections endeavour to establish a negative proposition, while the antagonistic considerations endeavour to establish an affirmative; and it is "much more difficult to exhaust the field of negation [*i. e.*, to be sure that an apparent negative is an actual one], than that of affirmation[2]:"—secondly, The scientific pro-

---

[1] "A thousand possibilities do not warrant a specific or positive assertion on our side. But one possibility is of equivalent power to displace and nullify the objection on their side. We could not, without the transgression of sound philosophy, select the one which is certain out of the many which are conceivable. But it were a transgression greatly more violent, to affirm of the Eternal and Inscrutable Spirit, who operates unseen through the mazes of His own workmanship, that He could not in the infinity of His resources devise a method by which both to uphold the visible uniformities of nature, and yet to meet and satisfy our prayers."— *Select Works of Chalmers*, Vol. v. " Efficacy of Prayer," § 28. This author suggests several conceivable methods which it is unnecessary to adduce in the following discussion. One of these, however, deserves comment because of its boldness. This is that Prayer and its answer are connected as cause and effect;—a supposition which, it appears to me, would require to assume the truth of the philosophy embodied in the proposition, "all force is will-force." But as this proposition can never be disproved, the supposition founded upon it can never be nullified. Upon this supposition, human will in Prayer is acting centripetally, while in all other cases it is acting centrifugally.

[2] Mill.

position is universal—there is no method whatever conceivable or inconceivable by which the Almighty can answer Prayer,—while the propositions about to be adduced are particular:—thirdly, From this fact it follows that the latter propositions may legitimately be of any degree of vagueness and uncertainty, for the universal proposition lays itself open to any such; and these more definite possibilities, which are conceivable even by our very limited faculties, may well be supposed representative of numerous others to us inconceivable. And this supposition is considerably strengthened by the consideration which occurs in some part of Butler's *Analogy*, viz., that it is far from improbable that a veil is *purposely* drawn over some of the scenes of Divine power. To this we may add that the antagonistic considerations are not, as are the others, in logic bound to the tether of experience; and so on the one hand can never be proved wholly valueless, while on the other they are free to draw upon an indefinite number of possibilities.

From these observations it follows, that it is not open to objectors to repudiate the following or kindred arguments, on account of any transcendentalism which they may present. It is for the defenders of the universal proposition to combat each of the following and kindred particular ones in detail—they must be prepared to encounter all such particulars as it is possible to adduce. Hence it matters not to the validity of the following possibilities whether or not they are of a transcendental nature; for if it is admitted that a universal proposition is not sufficiently comprehensive to meet all possible adverse particulars, then it has ceased to be a universal proposition, and so, in the present case, to be a valid proposition at all. In short, as in the previous case, the primary effect of the transcendental nature of these particular propositions is not their own invalidation, but that of the universal proposition which, in effect, is framed to include them.

For the sake of brevity only two or three of the more definite among these propositions will be adduced. It is to be understood that throughout we shall give to the scientific proposition all the data it demands; we shall waive all those considerations of ignorance on which the main argument relies; we shall assume that Law is throughout its course a definite entity, and that the Almighty stands to it in practically the same relation as we ourselves do; we shall imagine that the Supreme Cause operates upon conditioned causes in the same manner as these operate upon one another; and we shall shew that, even upon this anthropomorphic conception of the Deity, there are several methods by which it is amply conceivable that He might produce any special physical effect, strictly through the mediation of Physical Law, and yet without in any way violating the cause of its action.

§ 2. "God," says Leibnitz, "has provided everything; he has remedied everything, beforehand. There is in his works a harmony, a beauty, already pre-established. This opinion does not at all exclude the providence or the government of God. A true providence on the part of God demands a perfect foreknowledge; but it demands not only that he has foreseen everything, but also that he has provided for everything—otherwise he is deficient either of the wisdom to foresee, or the power to provide." These views have been legitimately, because logically, extended by Dr M'Cosh, who shews that "the monadical theory of Leibnitz when carried out" denies the pre-established harmony of events which are causally connected—events not causally connected, but made by fore-ordination to concur, being thus supposed the only means by which special events can be wrought by General Laws. There is, however, no reason for this limitation—on the contrary, there is every reason against it; and "the true doctrine of pre-established harmony" comprises alike events which are causally connected and events which are not. But, even were this not so, the present argument would remain unaffected; for it is impossible to assign limits to the special events which might be wrought by pre-established concurrence alone.

This argument it seems impossible to refute, so long as we adhere to the Theistic hypothesis. "Magna dii curant, parva negligunt[1]," is a maxim philosophically absurd, if by "curant" is meant fore-ordination. "Those who suppose that there is a general, but that there cannot be a particular providence, are limiting God by ideas derived from human weakness." But not only so: they are of necessity propounding a contradiction in terms. All events must be known to the Deity by fore-knowledge; otherwise He would not be omniscient, and if He were not omniscient His Government could not be universal. If anything has been fore-ordained, all things must have been fore-ordained; otherwise those which had not been fore-ordained would not be included within the Divine Government.

Hence, upon the Theistic hypothesis (which, of course, alone affords a possible basis for our present discussion), the existence of General Laws affords no *logical* presumption against the efficacy of Prayer; for, if

---

[1] Balbus the Stoic, in Cicero *De Natura Deorum*.

every event occurring under those Laws has been foreordained, it follows that the distinction between general and special providence vanishes. If all things were prearranged, it matters not whether we regard any one of their number as a mediate or an immediate act of the Deity. "The only difference between the man of common sense and the studious, is concerning the time when the disposition was made, which one thinks a few days or a few minutes, another many ages ago; the one frequent and occasional, the other rare and universal: but both acknowledge that nothing ever happens without the permission of one Almighty and Ever-vigilant Governor[1]." "God works out His plans not merely in us but by us, and we may dare to say that that which is to us a free self-determination, may be not other than a foreseen element of His work[2]." "Prayer, too, is only a foreseen action of man, which, together with its results, is embraced in the eternal predestination of God[3]." "The fixed laws of nature might in all eternity have been adapted to our foreseen petition or neglect of petition[4]." "Some things Christ knew should come to pass and notwithstanding prayed for them, because He also knew that the necessary means to effect them were His prayers[5]."

This argument is, as we have said, on the Theistic hypothesis, incontrovertible. It may be vague and so unsatisfactory; but there can be no question that in strict reasoning it diametrically contradicts the scientific assertion, that to our faculties there is no conceivable method by which the Almighty could answer Prayer, without the violation of Natural Law.

[1] Tucker.
[2] Liddon, *Some Elements of Religion*, p. 193.   [3] *Ibid.*
[4] Pusey.   [5] Hooker.

There is, indeed, one objection which can be urged against this argument as it stands in this Essay, viz., that when the idea of fore-ordination was supposed to be advanced as an argument against the belief in the validity of Prayer, it was excluded because of so ultimate a character: how then, it may be asked, can it in consistency be admitted on the other side? In the first place, it will be observed, that if the present argument is valid, it destroys the counter-argument even if admitted— shews that the idea of fore-ordination is a support, instead of a detriment, to the belief in question. I have thought it best, however, because most accurate, to exclude that counter-argument altogether as inadmissible; and the reason why the present argument need not be similarly excluded is, because the idea of fore-ordination is not now, as before, a distinct question. In other words, the question as to fore-ordination, being more ultimate than that as to the efficacy of Prayer, includes the latter as a genus does a species: now it is a peculiarity of many of the species of this genus—*i. e.*, all those in which free-will is concerned—that they contradict their generic character: therefore it is no negation of the present specific question that it, in common with many other species of the genus, presents points which are not to our intelligence of generic character; for in the case of other such species the apparent negation is admitted not to be real. On the other hand, it is an affirmation of this specific question, if it can be shewn to present points which approximate it more than the other contradictory species to the generic type. In the one case the more ultimate question is excluded, because it has no more bearing upon this specific affirmation, than it has upon any other of the specific affirmations which it contradicts: in the other case it is legitimately admitted, because it is found to have a greater bearing upon this specific affirmation, than it has upon others of the specific affirmations which it contradicts—the argument being that in this case no such contradiction exists[1].

§ 3. We have now to elaborate a more definite argument, which, although an exceedingly obvious one, has never before been advanced. No one will be so willing as a man of science to admit, that if Force and Matter can be supposed capable of origination at any moment *de novo*, all possible *à priori* objections to the efficacy of Prayer, so far as General Laws are concerned, immediately vanish. It is important to observe that this supposition is enough to destroy these objections *in toto*, without the aid of the complementary supposition, viz., that Force and Matter can be at any instant annihilated. It is so because the application of originated Matter in sufficient quantity, and of originated Force in sufficient intensity, would be efficient proximate causes of the removal of pre-existing Matter, and the neutralization of pre-existing Force. These parallel axioms clearly shew that any miracle might be occasioned (so far at least as we can see) by a creation of Force, of Matter, or of both; but not necessarily by an annihilation of either; or, in other words, upon the assumption that Force and Matter were upon any occasion created by an Intelligent Cause, no miracle, however startling, need lack a full and adequate physical explanation.

The only objection which can be made to this con-

---

[1] It will be observed that those who altogether deny the freedom of the will, recognise no such contradiction in any case: to those, however, the objection to Prayer, which the above considerations are adduced to exclude, is not open.

clusion, were the hypothesis granted, is that it would be more difficult (so to speak) for the creative energy to originate Matter in one state than in another. Taking, for instance, one of the best authenticated of the Christian miracles, and the only one in which creative power was sensibly exerted, it may be objected that it is, for the latter reason, of all the Christian miracles the most incredible. For it must surely require a greater exertion of creative energy to originate *de novo* an organic product, than an inorganic; and most of all, an organized structure so high in the scale of being as one of the examples referred to. This objection, however, requires to its validity the truth of two assumptions. In the first place, it requires to assume that the creative energy admits of degrees; and in the next, that we are competent judges of the cases in which a high or a low degree would be required. These two assumptions, however, it is obviously impossible to raise even to the lowest stage of probability, and therefore the objection goes for nothing.

Returning now to our argument. We need not pause to consider the probabilities as to whether or not Force and Matter are identical, although these probabilities are neither few nor small. We need not do so because, even if we suppose them fundamentally dissimilar, no man of science will hesitate to admit that most, if not all, petitions would require for their answer but the creation of Force alone. We can see plainly enough that there is no prayer which may not receive a physical equivalent, provided that the Being to whom it is offered is able and willing to originate the adequate physical conditions; and we can see with equal clearness that these conditions need never be more than dual, and in the vast majority, if not in all cases, need only be singular. The whole objection, then, which is raised to Prayer on scientific grounds, depends, in this particular, upon the difficulty experienced by those who raise it, when they endeavour to conceive of an alteration—whether by way of addition or subtraction—being made at any specified time to the energy inherent in the Universe. Could this difficulty be removed, the entire objection would vanish : could it be lessened, the objection would be proportionably diminished. Let us then carefully examine the real magnitude of this difficulty.

§ 4. To begin with a quotation :—"No one can examine the conclusions at which Sir William Thomson arrives in his remarkable treatise *On a Universal Tendency in Nature to the dissipation of Mechanical Energy*, without being struck with their bearing upon the question we are here considering. In this treatise, as also in his unpublished *Rede Lecture* and in parts of the *Treatise on Natural Philosophy*, it is shewn that the tendency to the conversion of motion into the form of heat is not counterbalanced by any adequate tendency to re-conversion. Both by tidal friction, and by the resistance of the medium through which they move, the planets of our system are shewn to tend to a slower and slower movement, the result of which must be 'the falling together of all into one mass, which, although rotating for a time, must in the end come to rest—relatively to the surrounding medium[1].' This loss of energy is due to the radiation of the heat produced by friction, and the same must hold good therefore of all motion throughout the Universe. It appears from this that Force tends everywhere, however slowly, to become transmuted from molar into molecular, to lose the form of motion and to assume

[1] Tait and Thomson's *Nat. Phil.* I. 277.

that of heat; and this heat diffused through space will cease to give birth to energy in any form whatever. If these conclusions be correct, the notion of an ever-repeating cycle must be given up. When the solar system, and after it slowly but surely the vast aggregate of the material universe has reached the end to which it is thus shewn to tend, nothing short of a change in the existing laws of nature will produce any new genesis of motion. Energy will exist potentially, but the circumstances necessary to give it actuality can never arise[1]."

I do not make this quotation to endorse it, for a man of science will answer:—' It is assuredly true that, so far as we have means of ascertaining, molar motion, cosmically considered, exhibits a preponderant tendency to become converted into molecular; but it by no means follows that "Force tends *everywhere*, however slowly," to undergo this conversion. For, on the one hand (as Mr Scott himself points out), the condition of the existence of molar motion is the generation of molecular; and, on the other, the last-named form of Energy is unlike the first-named in that, when finally liberated from masses which are held together by gravity, it passes beyond the range of experience, because it is not, like the other form, (practically) itself subject to that restraining influence. From this, and from the fact of our own bodies being also subject to the influence of gravity, it follows that the motion of masses is the only kind which we are able to observe for any length of time—the resulting molecular motion sooner or later eluding our cognizance. As, then, the motion of masses is the only kind which we can, from the nature of our opportunities, consecutively study, it is

[1] *Burney Prize Essay*, 1868, pp. 43, 44.

not legitimate to conclude that molecular motion is never destined to reassume the form of molar, merely because if it is ever so destined, the transmutation must of necessity take place in a region without our ken. But not only is the conclusion illegitimate because thus embodying an illicit process of the minor term; it is further illegitimate from being opposed to an inductive inference of the strongest, because the most universal, kind. We have seen that when molecular motion becomes finally dissipated into space, we must of necessity lose cognizance of it. So long, however, as motion in this form remains within our grasp, we can take cognizance of it in as objective a manner as we can of motion in its other form. Now the great truth which the study of motion in this, to us, its evanescent form has established is, that it is re-transmutable into molar motion, and molar motion into it, for an indefinite number of times,—*i.e.*, so long as molecular motion remains within our cognizance, it is as definite and as indestructible an entity as is molar motion. The fact therefore of its dissipation into space is in no wise equivalent to the destruction of Energy, unless it could be shewn that the medium in which it travels is more extensive than the propagation of the Energy through it. When, therefore, the motion of molecules passes from the range of our experience, are we justified in the inference that it has ceased to be? Are we not rather justified in the belief, that its disappearance from our cognizance is merely due to our inability to trace its further history—an inability arising from the necessary confinement of our intelligence in its relation to space? But the inference does not stop here. It can be shewn that all scientific inductions whatever are ultimately grounded upon the doctrine that Force is persistent: hence, if we deny this attribute to Force, we must of necessity conclude that the entire range of Physical Law with which we are acquainted is but of local significance,—that other parts of the Universe are either Lawless, or governed, not merely by Laws that differ from those which obtain in this portion, but by a whole system of Laws which must differ fundamentally from that which here we study. This is a conclusion which we cannot accept without evidence, more especially as it is founded on a mere negative, and this a negative of the weakest possible sort. It is a negative of the weakest possible sort, because we can see the reason why it is a negative—we can see, as already explained, a good, because a necessary, reason why we should not be able to perceive the transmutation of molecular into molar motion, if it ever takes place upon a cosmical scale, as we can and do perceive it upon a local scale.'

I have thought it desirable to state thus fully the objections to which the quotation above made is liable, lest the use I intend to make of that quotation might be impaired by the suspicion that I am not sensible of their force. It would, however, be foreign to the present subject to discuss the point raised, because the only object with which I made the extract is to indicate in a concise form that the question is a dubious one. Lest, however, even this statement should be considered by some persons unwarranted, I shall fortify it with some remarks of Mr Spencer, whose mode of presenting the case cannot be improved upon. After dealing at length with the question as to the dissipation of Energy on a universal scale, and subscribing to the opinion that eventually all the heavenly bodies must come into mutual collision, and that in every such successive case "if stars, concentrating to a common centre of gravity, eventually reach it, then the quantities of motion they have acquired must suffice to carry them away again to those remote regions whence they started......in the shape of diffused masses[1];" Mr Spencer adds as follows :—"One condition, however, essential to the literal fulfilment of this result must be specified; namely, that the quantity of molecular motion radiated into space by each star in the course of its formation from diffused matter, shall either not escape from our sidereal system, or shall be compensated by an equal quantity of molecular motion radiated from other parts of space into our sidereal system......Here, indeed, we arrive at a barrier to our reasonings; since we cannot know whether this condition is or is not fulfilled......If throughout boundless space filled with ether, there exist no other sidereal systems subject to like changes, or if such other sidereal systems exist at more than a certain average distance from one another; it seems an unavoidable conclusion that the quantity of motion possessed must diminish by radiation; and so that on each successive resumption of the nebulous form, the matter of our sidereal system will occupy a less space, until it reaches either a state in which its concentrations and diffusions are relatively small, or a state of complete aggregation and rest. Since, however, we have no evidence shewing the existence or non-existence of sidereal systems throughout remote space; and since, even had we such evidence, a legitimate conclusion could not be drawn from premises of which one element (unlimited space) is inconceivable; we must be for ever without answer to this transcendent question[2]."

[1] *First Principles*, p. 534.
[2] *Ibid.* pp. 535—36.

§ 5. The question, then, is one which we are quite justified in declaring dubious. To this fact we must now add the consideration of the truly inconceivable magnitude of the Energy, sensible and insensible, that is inherent in the visible Universe. The momentum of the earth's motion is such, that were it suddenly arrested, its resulting equivalent in the form of heat would be "equal to that produced by the combustion of fourteen such earths of solid coal.. ...If then the earth......should fall into the sun......the quantity of heat developed by the shock would be 400 times greater[1]." Yet the earth is but one of the smaller planets: what must be the momentum of their sum?—The size of the sun is 1,400,000 times that of the earth, and, in addition to his axial motion, he is, together with all his planets, travelling at a rate which must be at least much more than 300 miles per minute. What must be the momentum of the entire system?—Further, nelecting the planetary heat as being indefinite, and fixing our attention only upon that of the sun: the energy received by the earth from him in the form of light and heat constitutes only $\frac{1}{2,300,000,000}$ of the entire amount he radiates into space: yet the energy, in the form of heat alone, so received by the earth in one year, is such, that "if distributed uniformly over the earth's surface, it would be sufficient to liquefy a layer of ice 100 feet thick, and covering the whole earth. It would also heat an ocean of fresh water 66 miles deep, from the temperature of melting ice to the temperature of ebullition[2]." What must be the Energy inherent in the solar system?—Yet

---

[1] Prof. Helmholtz, *Essay on the Interaction of the Natural Forces.*

[2] Tyndall, *Heat a mode of Motion*, p. 477.

this system is but a drop in the sidereal ocean! Never does the mind feel itself so utterly baffled, as when it endeavours to symbolize in thought the actual power of Omnipotence.

§ 6. It will then on all hands be admitted, that the foregoing facts have fully established two positions:—first, that the Energy inherent in the Universe is virtually if not actually infinite; and secondly, that even the finite portion of it which we are able to appreciate is continually radiating into infinity, and this in quantities of utterly unthinkable magnitude. When this is the acknowledged state of our ignorance regarding the disposition of the Energy inherent in the Universe, does not the whole *à priori* objection to Prayer assume an almost childish aspect? Far from grounding an *à priori* objection against the validity of Prayer, the doctrine of the Conservation of Energy, when regarded otherwise than superficially, affords a positive presumption in its favour. For, whether or not the amount of Energy inherent in the entire Universe is invariable in quantity, the foregoing considerations render it obvious that *if* it is ever added to or subtracted from, we can have no means of ascertaining the fact. An alteration in the total sum of Energy requisite to produce any physical result in answer to Prayer, might, in comparison with that sum, be inadequately represented by the difference between the mass of a chyle molecule, which is indefinable by the highest powers of the microscope, and the mass of the solar system. To this must be added the important consideration that, apart from all comparisons, if the sum of Energy is ever altered, such alteration must in all cases, excepting that of miracles, be unobservable; for, as Kant concisely observes, "creation cannot be admitted among phænomena, because the very possibility of it would annihilate the unity of experience;" and it is no less evident that destruction would do the same. In connection with this point also we may notice the fact so repeatedly insisted on by Comte—and this is highly important—viz., that those physical phænomena which are most simple as to the composition of their causes, are the phænomena which, being likewise of the most extensive significance, are therefore the "farthest removed from humanity;" and, counterwise, that those phænomena which most affect humanity are the most complex and the least extensive. The latter, therefore, being naturally the objects of petition, it follows that, if Energy is ever created or destroyed in order to accomplish such phænomena, the amount affected would be quantitatively of the smallest, while the greatest latitude of possibility would be allowed for the introduction of the external change being imperceptible. All, therefore, that, in its bearing on the present question, Science has done by establishing the doctrine of Force being, in its relation to us, persistent, is to indicate an amply conceivable *manner* in which the Deity *may* produce any special effect, and yet so produce it without in any wise altering the operation of Natural Laws. Taking the word "cause" in its widest, and, to science at least, most unobjectionable sense, as the collocation of all the antecedents which unconditionally produce the consequent; it is evident that it is only because Force is persistent, that the consequent is thus unconditional. In other words, were not Force present in a definite and indestructible amount in all the antecedents, the consequent would not be a necessity. We are hence constrained to admit, that the smallest accession or diminution in the amount of Force forming a condition of any one of the antecedents (no matter how numerous these might be), would of necessity give rise to an entirely different set of inter-relations among the antecedents, and so to an entirely different cause. The very rigidity of the relations by which the first set of conditions were held together, would now become the best conceivable guarantee for a new result. However small a change there might have been made in the amount of Force at any point in the total physical nexus which constituted the original cause, its discovery, so to speak, would be most certainly secured by the very unconditional nature of the Laws in operation. The sum of the conditions having been altered, in no matter how slight a degree, the same Laws, which by their invariability in the one case would have wrought out a (to adequate intelligence) foreseen result; would in the other, and in virtue of their same invariability, work out a wholly different though equally foreseen result.

§ 7. It will, no doubt, seem strange to those who have been accustomed to employ the doctrine of the Conservation of Energy, as one of their most trusty weapons against the doctrine of the physical validity of Prayer, to find it thus turned against themselves; and being long accustomed to consider their argument irrefutable, they will no doubt think there must be some fallacy in the reasoning which tends, not merely to ignore, but to reverse it. Hence it is desirable to estimate the comparative value of our respective arguments.

The following may be taken as a concise expression of the objection to Prayer, so far as it is grounded upon the doctrine in question. "It is supposed that the destination of a physical force can be arrested, and the otherwise inevitable result prevented, by an act of Divine volition. But the antecedent force *must* spend itself, and determine some consequent. It simply cannot be arrested, or lifted out of its place amongst the links of physical causation, without the whole chain falling to pieces. Its efficiency in giving rise to a new sequence *is involved in its very existence;* while the discovery of the correlation and transmutation of the forces proves that the prior agent is still present, and operative under an altered form[1]." These assertions may, of course, be elaborated; but they contain, as I think a man of science will admit, the full force of his objections. Now in the first place they are mere assertions[2]; and in the next they do not follow as necessary conclusions from the premise, that the sum of Energy existing in the Universe is undiminishable; for, as we have seen, the supposition of a neutralizing force being originated *de novo*, *i.e.*, that the sum of the Energy inherent in the Universe is not unaugmentable, is sufficient to annihilate these objections. Mr Knight himself recognises the force of this converse supposition. He says:—"But it is said that while the chain of physical sequence remains unbroken, the local *incidence* (if we may so speak) of each link may be determined by some etherial wave of hyper-physical energy, transmitted along the entire line from its fountain-head, in delicately subtle undulations, resembling the waves of light and sound, or the flash of electricity through a telegraph wire; and that the course of this hyper-physical energy may be determined in answer to the prayers of man[3]." Mr Knight adduces a series of objections to this view, but the only ones bearing upon the question (and

[1] Rev. Mr Knight, *Contem. Rev.* Jan. 1873, p. 186.
[2] Cf. Argyll, *Contem. Rev.* Feb. 1873, p. 463.
[3] *Ibid.* p. 186.

indeed the only ones that can bear upon it in so far as the persistence of force is concerned), are as follow :— "Again, suppose that there be no physical 'fountain-head' but an endless cycle of recurrent energy; and what becomes of the hypothesis?......For, though hyper-physical in its origin and character, the effect it is said to produce is not hyper-physical (in that case we should have no controversy with its advocates), but physical; and it is believed to give rise to an interminable series of fresh physical results[1]." Now it is to be observed that such terms as "hyper-physical waves," etc., can only be legitimately employed as thinkable illustrations of the manner in which the Deity operates when creating Energy—a question altogether distinct from the hypothesis that He does so operate, and a question which it is in no wise incumbent on that hypothesis to entertain. Turning, then, to the real point at issue ;—the whole of this class of objections, and so, as we have seen, the entire *à priori* objection to Prayer, is founded upon the supposition "that there is no physical fountain-head," but "an endless cycle of recurrent energy." This supposition has, as we have seen, a basis of inferential probability for its support, but it is, as we have also seen, a supposition which has never, and can never, be rendered other than dubious. The syllogism which supports the present inference contains, and must contain, the very same fallacy which we have previously supposed the man of science to have pointed out in the contradictory syllogism, viz., the fallacy of a term—to wit, experience—distributed in the conclusion, which cannot be distributed in the minor. For ought that science has shewn, or from the nature of things can ever shew, the supposition that

[1] *Contem. Rev.* p. 187.

all Energy whatever is, in its ultimate origin, a continually emanating influence from the All-sustaining "fountain-head," is just as probable a supposition as that of a "continual cycle of recurrent energy." The mere fact that we observe on an indefinitely small scale that Energy is recurrent, affords no manner of presumption that it is likewise so upon a universal scale, unless the quantitative relation of experience to actuality—of unity to infinity —were known. In short, we here return to the kind of reasoning which has been already refuted at length. The inference is, that because the doctrine of the persistence of Force is true with reference to the Proximate, therefore it is likewise true with reference to the Ultimate—an analogy which is certainly invalid, since one of its ratios is not only indefinite, but also inconceivable.

§ 8. Passing on, however, let us suppose, for the sake of argument, that the Cycle theory is the correct one, and that Force once generated, in no matter how small a quantity, can never become entirely dissipated in space, "without the whole chain of physical causation falling to pieces;" and yet the proposition on which the entire *à priori* objection to Prayer is founded, has only been supplied with one of its two data. The other datum is that the Energy inherent in the Universe is unaugmentable. Now we have seen that the inference which established the former premise was indefinitely weak, in that the thing inferred contained an infinite term; yet this much might be said for that premise—vaguely weak as it was, it was yet founded for what it was worth upon a positive basis. We are able to take cognizance of Force so long as it remains within the sphere of our senses, and during that time we perceive that it has, in its relation to us, the property of persistence. Our inference, therefore, that it is in all its relations persistent, however unwarrantable, is at least founded, for what it is worth, upon positive knowledge. Even this much, however, cannot be said for the other premise. The inference that the Force inherent in the Universe is absolutely unaugmentable can only be drawn from a knowledge of negation—we can only argue, Because we do not know that it is so, therefore we infer that it is not so. Now there is thus shewn to be an important distinction between the inferential value of the premise that Force is indestructible, and the premise that Force is unaugmentable. For the argument from the *à priori* probability that Nature is everywhere uniform, coupled with the indisputable fact that in the portion of the Universe falling within the range of experience, the persistence of Force is the most ultimate, because the most inclusive, of Natural Truths, certainly establish a valid, though, as we have seen for other reasons, a highly dubious inference, that Force is everywhere persistent. The other inference, however, and one which is equally necessary for the scientific position, has no shadow of *à priori* probability for its support[1]. Freely admitting that Force once generated is permanent, we may still argue :—If Force is ever added to, we should not expect to be cognizant of the fact: on the other hand, we are ignorant concerning the origin of all existing Force; how then can we found an *à priori* argument in favour of the belief that Force is unaugmenta-

[1] "That impious maxim of the ancient philosophy, *Ex nihilo nihil fit*, by which the creation of matter was excluded, ceases to be a maxim, according to this philosophy. Not only the will of the Supreme Being may create matter, but, for aught we know *à priori*, the will of any other being might create it, or any other cause that the most whimsical imagination can assign." Hume, *Inquiry concerning Human Understanding*, Section XII. Part III. note.

ble? It cannot be done. And this is a fact habitually overlooked by those who have touched upon this subject.

There is, indeed, one consideration of a negative character, which seems at first sight to invalidate the conclusion thus arrived at, viz., that the idea of Force being created is unthinkable[1]. Let us suppose, in the first instance, that it is so, and what follows? Surely not that Force is uncreatable, for this would be to limit the ontological order of things by the intelligible. As Mill observes, when dealing with this very question, "It does not follow that this is really the fact, for there are many things, inconceivable to us, which not only may, but must, be true[2]." Besides, upon the Theistic theory, all existing Force was once created; and it is no more easy to conceive of this primordial act than of others similar in kind. Further, as we have seen, the primary conception attaching to the word "Almighty" is "Omnipotentia,"—power, that is, to create without limit; and we hence saw that the relation of the Almighty Creator to an infinite potentiality of existence may be of all relations the most profound.

[1] Mr Knight advances two arguments on the same side, but they are not worth stating in the text. He says, "That it should be in the power of any creature thus to launch a new agency into the pre-arranged system of nature, and thereby to begin a new series of changes which are absolutely interminable in their effect, is simply incredible." It is evident, however, on the one hand, that the power is not under any view believed to reside in the creature; and on the other, that the doctrine of fore-ordination here introduced has no bearing whatever upon the subject; since it is no more difficult to believe that any fresh increment of force should have its functions for all time assigned to it, than that any equal quantity of previously existing force should originally have had its eternal cycle of transformation foreordained.

[2] *Examination*, p. 290.

Whether or not, therefore, the idea of Force being originated is unthinkable, the argument that it *may* be is alike unaffected. But now let us enquire, Is it true that the idea is unthinkable? Have men in all ages and in all conditions of culture failed to think of creation? Is the doctrine conspicuous by its absence from all religions? If not, then assuredly creation is not unthinkable[1]. What is unthinkable is Self-existence; and it has been to stave off this impossible conception one degree further, that all religions have agreed in teaching the doctrine in question. It is the Being and not the Action of the Creator that is to man unthinkable. Granted the existence of the Unconditioned, and the mystery of the Conditioned is absorbed.

This question, however, has, as we have seen, only an indirect bearing upon the present argument; since whether or not creation is deemed unthinkable, we must

[1] Compare Bain, *Inductive Logic*, p. 37, and for obverse aspect, Mill, *loc. cit.* Also the admirable remarks of Mr Scott, *Burney Prize* 1868, pp. 41—2. Mr Spencer uses the word "unthinkable" in a very loose manner. If asked for a definition to cover all the cases to which he applies it, his answer would probably be :—That concerning which it is impossible to establish relations in thought. But this genus includes two widely different species,—as different, says Clarke, as light is from darkness—viz., the case where the correlatives are, as such, incomprehensible ; and the case where they are, as such, contradictory. In the former sense, all things, or any thing, may be said, in the last resort, to be unthinkable ; for all our ultimate ideas are incomprehensible. To this category belongs the idea of creation, which can only be said to be unthinkable, not because something and nothing are contradictory, but because something and nothing are incomprehensible. Primitive man, on seeing the formation of a cloud, has no more difficulty in *thinking* of its creation, than he has in *thinking* of its existence after it is formed ;—the correlatives in each case being the same.

alike, upon the Theistic theory, believe that it is possible.

§ 9. Let us now turn to the question, How far, from *à priori* considerations, is it probable? We have just seen that the only argument *against* this probability utterly fails for two reasons: firstly, because the proposition itself admits of grave dispute; and secondly, because, even if established, would be immaterial. There is therefore no argument in support of the belief that the Creative Energy is spent or suspended. Have we any *à priori* argument in support of the belief that it is not? I think we have. If the Physical Sciences have been successful in establishing any one doctrine rather than another with reference to the method of Divine Government, such doctrine is certainly that as to the existence of an all-extending principle in Nature, the principle of gradual progression[1]. The ancient aphorism, "Natura nihil facit per saltum," has in recent years in every branch of enquiry been almost indefinitely extended, till now, from the evolution of a sidereal system to the growth and decay of the smallest physiological cell, we here behold a unity of method. Can we suppose that it was not always so? Must we not rather infer that this most universal of all the principles observable in Nature, is but the present manifestation of that according to which the procedure of the Unchangeable has ever been conducted? We have here at least a valid analogy, for although one ratio is finite and the other infinite, yet the term common to the two ratios—viz., the method of Divine action—is admitted to be immutable, all-pervading, and everlasting. Further, in the present case we cannot (as in those previously examined) see any probable,

[1] Compare Spencer, *Princ. of Biology*, Vol. I. pp. 347—8.

much less any necessary, reason why we should be unacquainted with habitual deviations from this method, supposing such deviations to occur. Lastly, even if we could see any such reason, we might still oppose this analogy to the scientific objection, because it depends upon one of the most incontestible doctrines established by science; and so would, even in that case, be exactly equal in value to the analogies on which these objections themselves are founded. If then we have so valid a reason to suppose that throughout the Physical Universe the principle of gradual change, rather than that of violent cataclasm, characterizes the method of the Final *Directive* Power, are we not thus led to infer that the same principle may also characterize the method of the *Originating* Power, residing as this confessedly does within the same Intelligent and Immutable Agency? As we see the principle of Evolution everywhere exhibited in things that are, does it not become natural to suppose that the same principle was manifested in the causing them to be;—that as everywhere we see *growth* to be the essential condition of *form*, so the *substance* should itself have primordially been subject to *increment;*—in short, that the act of creating should resemble in character the guiding influence shewn in creation?

And even were it not for this analogy, I think no one will hesitate to admit that it is easier to conceive of creation upon this view than upon any other. Mr Darwin towards the end of his great work asks the supporters of the Special Creation theory,—" Do they really believe that at innumerable periods of the Earth's history certain elemental atoms have been commanded suddenly to flash into living tissues?" It is as though the bare attempt to realize so inconceivable a proposition should, apart from all the previous arguments against it, induce a man to pause and think whether he had ever really meant what he professed to believe. Yet this question of Mr Darwin refers only to a special and comparatively very limited department of existing Creation. What must we think of the time (if we can here speak of time) when the entire Universe sprang, with momentary suddenness, from nothing into being? The idea is not only to us inconceivable, but it seems as though it would require to be, to any order of faculties, incredible. This much at least we may safely say: so far as any probability upon pure *à priori* grounds exists at all, it wholly tends towards the belief that Creation has been progressive[1]. And this is more than our argument requires; for all that it is properly incumbent upon that argument to shew is, that Science has failed to prove or to render probable the hypothesis that the Energy inherent in the Universe is an unalterable sum.

§ 10. We now enter upon another *à priori* argument. What is it that most distinguishes human intelligence in its relation to Natural Law? Most assuredly its utilizing ability—its power to direct the natural forces to the accomplishment of special ends. Indeed, objectively considered, Intelligence may be defined as an agency which combines the operations of Natural Law, in such a manner as to produce varied and highly complex physical results, which without such agency would never

---

[1] I find that Mr Todhunter goes further than this,—his argument leading to the following results: "We may thus, perhaps, be disposed to conclude that the Omnipotence and Omniscience which were exerted in creation, will *necessarily* continue active, and will not decline into merely potential faculties."—*Burney Prize*, 1848, p. 37 [1874].

have occurred. The mind of man, considered thus as a natural cause, is certainly of all single natural causes the most influential; not, of course, in respect of the *magnitude* of its effects, but in respect of their number and diversity. Thus it is that, even in common parlance, Art is habitually named in a sort of antithesis to Nature. Not to dwell too long upon this point, we may perhaps best realize the enormous influence of human intellect in Nature, by confining our attention to its influence upon the production of organic forms. We might well at first sight suppose that the subtle Laws which determine the reproduction of organisms—Laws of all others in Biology the least understood—should be especially without the domain of man's directive influence. Yet by guiding the operation of these Laws—the very existence of which is unknown to him—into definite channels, how marvellous are the results he has obtained! Compare an English race-horse with a prize English dray-horse,—an English greyhound—"that perfect image of grace, symmetry and vigour[1]"—with an English bull-dog,—a pouter pigeon with a tumbler, a carrier or a fan-tail,—a cabbage-rose with a moss-rose,—a peach with a nectarine or an almond; and, remembering that each comparison is instituted within the limits of a single species[2], how astounding is the influence of human intelligence over organic life thus shewn to be! If, again, each of the above-named indi-

---

[1] Darwin, *Variation of Animals and Plants*, Vol. II. p. 221. This great naturalist continues:—"No natural species can boast of a more admirably co-ordinated structure, with its tapering head, slim body, deep chest, tucked-up abdomen, rat-like tail, and long muscular limbs, all adapted for extreme fleetness, and for running down weak prey."

[2] This may not be the case with the dog, and almond.

viduals (and many other, though less conspicuous, examples might be added) be compared with its wild parent-form, it is not too much to say that, in respect of its influence over *type*, human intelligence has manifested a power, which in character may be deemed almost creative.

Or let us briefly contemplate, in the words of Mr Wallace, the influence of human intelligence over organic life upon a cosmical scale. "Man has not only escaped 'natural selection' himself, but he is actually able to take away some of that power from Nature which before his appearance she universally exercised. We can anticipate the time when the earth will produce only cultivated plants and domestic animals; when man's selection shall have supplanted 'natural selection;' and when the ocean will be the only domain in which that power can be exerted, which for countless cycles of ages ruled supreme over all the earth[1]."

§ 11. Now the application of this indisputable fact— the fact that our intelligence is above all things characterized by its influence over the natural forces—to the construction of an argument in favour of Prayer, is sufficiently obvious. When we ascribe the attribute of intelligence to the First Cause, we of necessity imply that the quality is similar in kind to our own—otherwise our ascription can possess no meaning. If then our finite intelligence, objectively considered, is pre-eminently characterized by its combining influence over Natural Law, much more must the Infinite Intelligence be so characterized. If the mind of man is able through the agency of mindless Law to produce such vast and varied effects, how inconceivably great and diverse must be the possible effects similarly producible by the Mind of God,

[1] *Natural Selection*, p. 326.

supposing this so to operate. We have already seen, when treating of our profound ignorance regarding second causes, how necessarily confined our faculties are in their appreciation of cause and effect. We saw that this confinement is necessitated for two reasons;—first, because all experience is derived through the senses, and secondly, because the intellectual faculties are, in their appreciation of physical phænomena, wholly dependent upon experience. We can, however, readily imagine that an intelligence similar in kind to our own, but differing immeasurably in degree, and in no wise subject to these limitations, could, were it so disposed, produce upon a practically illimitable scale special results, in a manner strictly analogous to that by which man produces similar results upon a comparatively limited scale. And not only can we infer this upon general *à priori* grounds; it seems to follow as a necessary corollary from the hypothesis of an unlimited advance upon human intelligence. For, in accordance with our previously adduced definition of intelligence considered objectively, we perceive that it must be in direct proportion as intelligence increases that its compounding or utilizing influence over Natural Law increases: consequently, so far as experience goes we find this to be strictly true. What is it that essentially distinguishes the actions of the higher animals (both instinctive and rational) from those of the lower, save that the former exhibit a greater variety and complexity in their adaptations to their environment; and an intellectual adaptation to external forces is, objectively considered, a guidance of these forces[1]. Again, what is it

---

[1] *e.g.*, the dam of a Beaver is a case of an intellectual adaptation by that animal to its environment, but obversely it is a utilization of the gravitating force of the stream, etc.

that distinguishes the intellectual operations of man, objectively considered, from those of the higher animals, similarly considered, save that those of the former display higher artistic powers than those of the latter? Lastly, the progress of human intellect, whether of the individual or of the species, is, objectively considered, but the increase of its ability to combine the natural forces with ever-advancing degrees of number and complexity.

To these considerations, founded upon the limited nature of our intellectual faculties, we must now add, that so far as our own *directive* as distinguished from our *appreciative* ability is concerned, we are limited not only by a want of knowledge, but also by a want of power. Our intelligence can only act upon Natural Laws through the medium of our corporeal substance, and this being, proportionably to the masses and magnitudes of the matter and forces in Nature, infinitesimal in quantity, human agency, cosmically considered, is utterly swamped. Yet this is the result, not so much of a deficiency in the intellectual or appreciative power—*i. e.*, the power of perceiving what ought to be done in order to produce a desired result,—as of a deficiency in the operative power, arising from the inadequacy of the material agent through which that power must of necessity be conducted.

Human intelligence then, in its influence over Law, is limited in two directions—by a deficiency in knowledge, and by a deficiency in power. In neither of these directions can we suppose any limitation to obtain in the Supreme Intelligence. Consequently, it becomes impossible for human intelligence to predicate the number and kinds of the special results which it is possible for the Final Directive Influence to produce, through the purposive combination of Natural Laws.

§ 12. There are only two objections to which the present argument is liable[1]. It may be said: 'It is unfair to institute an analogy between the directive influence of the mind of man and the directive influence of the Mind of God, for while that of the former is itself comprised within the domain of Nature, that of the latter transcends it.' We here touch upon the question as to the freedom of the will; a question which is not only altogether extraneous to our present subject, but one which, even were it included, we should not require to consider. For even if we fully admit that the human will is not and cannot be free, in the sense of being exempt from Law, and so at liberty to frame its own desires,—this does not make any difference in the nature of the will's activity. Whatever we may suppose the origin of our desires to be, this does not affect the character of the results to which they give rise, and it is these results with which alone we are

---

[1] For the sake of brevity I abstain from discussing a confirmation of this argument, which is deducible from Metaphysics. It may, however, be mentioned. Metaphysicians are agreed that the idea of cause is derived from the sense of effort—whether of body or mind is immaterial—which we experience when we originate any series of effects; so that, were it not for such originating power in man, he could have no conception either of Cause or of Law. But, on the Theistic hypothesis, all causation is due to the Divine Will. Hence, on this hypothesis, the very idea of Cause and of Law is "derived from the agency of man, as the representative of God in this part of the universe......Instead of there being a fixed unalterable order of cause and effect in the world, with which nothing can be supposed to interfere, it is from the very fact of there being such interference that the idea of causation as pervading the world of nature is derived." (Rev. W. Karslake, *Theory of Prayer*, p. 22) [1874].

concerned[1]. Indeed this objection is but an intensification of the present argument. If man's intelligence is not free, and he is yet able to direct the physical forces to so great an extent, how much more must an intelligence which is absolutely free, possess a similar directive ability!—If human intelligence, *although* forming "a part of Cosmos[2]," is able thus to react upon it, much more must the External Intelligence be able so to act. In short, this objection would only be valid if the freedom of the Divine Intelligence could be proved to make it differ from human in kind, and in such kind as to affect its directive influence. As it is, the attribute of freedom only serves to endow that Intelligence with an additional advantage in this respect, because rendering it independent of *all* and *every* Law.

It may be further objected that, as the analogy we have instituted between the Divine and human intelligence is illegitimate, therefore the conclusion founded upon it must be unfair. But this objection, again, is really an intensification of the present argument. No doubt the analogy referred to would be highly illegitimate, if by it we presumed to infer the whole character of the Divine Intelligence. Far from this, however, the analogy is only framed to include a single attribute of intelligence, which must exist as the condition of any intelligence—or, more correctly, which must form an essential part of that which alone we can conceive as intelligence,—

---

[1] Prof. Tyndall has failed to perceive this obvious distinction. (See his letter to the *Pall Mall Gazette*, Oct. 11, 1865.) His other objections to this argument—which he allows to be "a strong one,"—have no more application to it than to the Theistic theory in general.

[2] Mr Knight.

and which, under any view as to the nature of the Supreme Intelligence, we are bound to think the latter possesses in the most pre-eminent degree. Further than this the analogy is confessedly absurd[1], and the fact of its being so constitutes the strength of the present argument. If the human mind can do so much as it does in the way of directing the natural forces, how inconceivably immense must be the ability of the Final Directive Intelligence, transcending as it does so immeasurably its mere human analogue, and depending as all things do upon its Prime Directive Influence!

[1] So far, that is, as *degrees* are concerned. Compare Mr Scott's Essay "*Intellectual Character of the First Cause*," Part II. § 11. Also Sir W. Hamilton's *Lectures*, Vol. II. p. 29.

CHAPTER VI.

§ 1. WE have now finished our examination of the scientific proposition. The title of this Essay, however, requires that the discussion of our subject should not end with this examination. We have hitherto been engaged in considering the question as to how far it is antecedently improbable that the Almighty should answer Prayer; and we have seen that this antecedent improbability, although to superficial appearance of startling magnitude, is really without substance or solidity. It now devolves upon us to investigate the distinct question, as to whether or not He does answer Prayer; for, waiving all arguments drawn from antecedent improbability together with their refutation, this subject still remains untouched. The question, Can we believe in the efficacy of Prayer? has been answered in the affirmative, by destroying the supposition that we cannot: but the question, Ought we to believe in such efficacy? remains to be discussed [1].

§ 2. If the argument from ignorance on which we have throughout relied possesses any validity, it is evident that there is only one source to which we can look for an answer to the question propounded: only

[1] G. Warington, *Can we believe in Miracles?* p. 227.

from a Revelation can we define the utility of Prayer. Nevertheless, there are at least two *à priori* arguments which, independently of any doctrinal authority, tend to answer this question in the affirmative. Although these arguments are confessedly feeble, they are worth rendering because of their independent character.

We have already seen that fore-ordination may be pointed to as an amply conceivable manner in which the Almighty could answer Prayer without violating Law. I think that this argument admits at once of intensification and of extension thus:—By our fundamental postulate, the Almighty is the Author both of Nature and Morality; and as on the one hand Christianity is His scheme, and on the other the order of Nature but the expression of His Will, it is from these data *à priori* probable that in the framing, as it were, of the great conjoint scheme of Nature and Morality, the one should have been fore-ordained to harmonize with the other. "There must not only be a correlation of physical forces and a correlation of moral forces, but the physical and moral forces must be also mutually correlated[1]." Now every petition for physical benefits must be deemed acceptable to the Author of Christianity, for, as we shall subsequently see, whatever view we take on Biblical grounds as to the efficacy of such petitions, there can be no doubt that they are not unchristian. But the consideration, that every really Christian Prayer of this kind is acceptable to God, surely intensifies the argument from fore-ordination; for it carries that argument further than is required—it not only shews that we have a conceivable manner in which the Almighty may answer Prayer, but it also establishes an *à priori* probability

[1] Dr Littledale, *On the Rationale of Prayer.*

that He does. We have already seen that we cannot suppose the Divine activity to be impeded by its own methods; consequently in the fore-ordination of all things that Will must (so far as we can see) have provided, that every petition acceptable to itself should be so related to the co-existing physical conditions, that the latter should coincide with the former.

§ 3. The other independent argument alluded to is as follows:—We have already seen that, Natural Law being on the Theistic hypothesis but the synonym of the Divine Will, it follows that so long as this Will remains consistent, so long must the sequences occuring in Nature be necessary—otherwise such sequences would cease to be included within the domain of second causes, and so would require, either to become independent entities, or cease altogether to exist. But it is evident that this necessity of sequence obtains only *because* the Divine Will is consistent—that we cannot argue from this conditioned necessity (so to speak), that the Unconditioned Cause is itself under any external necessity to produce any one series of effects rather than another. The question, however, remains—Is it under any subjective necessity?—How far is it congruous in the Divine Nature to answer Prayer with physical equivalents? This question merges into that as to the nature of the Divine attributes; for on the one hand, it is a contradiction in terms to say that a free will can act in opposition to itself; and on the other, we are precluded from thinking of the Divine Will in this matter as we do of human. For while the attributes of human intelligence are frequently in mutual opposition, to suppose the possibility of a corresponding conflict among the Divine attributes, would be to mar the perfection of the Divinity, if not to destroy the unity of the First Cause.

From these considerations it follows that, so far as Natural Theology supplies any evidence of the Divine Beneficence, so far have we *à priori* reason for thinking it probable, that the Deity is not indifferent to the petitions of His sentient and intelligent creatures; and therefore not inactive in granting physical equivalents, whenever such equivalents would really be for the benefit of the petitioner. And the obvious rejoinder that the *maximum* degree of our physical happiness is in every case enjoyed independently of Prayer, is not merely a refined mode of begging the whole question in dispute; but is an assumption, for making which we can have no warrant whatever.

This argument, supplied on *à priori* grounds by Natural Theology, is greatly intensified when Revelation is accepted as authoritative; for the general and undefined indications of the Divine Beneficence, afforded by Nature, are immensely extended and particularized by Revelation; so that the present argument is correspondingly strengthened when supplied with this additional standing-ground.

§ 4. The principal bearing of Revelation, however, upon our present subject, is not that of affording *à priori* deductions from the character of the Deity as there declared, but that of supplying didactic information with expressed reference to this subject. It now devolves upon us briefly to investigate this information.

The question we are now considering, viz., Ought we to believe in the physical validity of Prayer? manifestly involves the more ultimate one as to the authority of Revelation. This more ultimate question, however, is no less manifestly much too extensive for us even cursorily to enter upon. We are then in this position :—If we reject Revelation, the specific question we are considering lapses: if we accept Revelation, this question remains open for discussion : we are unable to enter upon the argumentative merits presented respectively by the two aspects of this alternative : we must therefore for the purposes of our subsequent, as of our previous argument, assume without reserve the truth of Revelation. As we have hitherto been groping our way in the dim obscurity or utter darkness of philosophical speculation, concerning a subject transcending philosophical enquiry; we now "give heed" to Revelation as "to a light shining in a dark place :" as we have hitherto been endeavouring to ascertain the probability regarding the method of the Divine Government in a certain particular from experience alone, we now come for express information to the "oracles of God." Given then a belief in the Divine authority of Scripture, and the field of enquiry now opening to us is one of greater promise than that which we are leaving.

§ 5. Indeed at first sight it appears as though under this division there were nothing to discuss. To an ordinary reader, the voice of the Bible upon this subject appears so uniform and explicit as not to admit of evasion. Again, the Fathers are unanimous in not even being conscious that it is possible to urge any rational or plausible objection to the physical efficacy of Prayer. Lastly, the present authoritative expounders of Scripture, viz., the Christian Churches, are no less unanimous upon this subject than were the Fathers. It appears then, at first sight, as though there were no possibility of raising an objection to Prayer on theological grounds. Yet this has already been done to some extent, and no doubt will be done yet further by subsequent writers. Let us then here make an exhaustive statement of all such objections as it seems possible to raise, with the view of shewing their futility.

The argument open to those who feel to conviction the force of the objections raised by Science to Christian Prayer, and who wish to compromise their conviction in this respect with their Christian Faith, runs thus :—'We must altogether neglect the opinion of the Fathers, because the difficulty was not extant in their time. Similarly, the teaching of the Churches must by Protestants be neglected, because, in consequence of the time of their foundation, this teaching is but the reflection of that of the Fathers—so far, at least, as ignorance regarding this particular difficulty is concerned. We must, therefore, derive our opinions solely from the Scriptures, in accordance with the belief that these are of perennial adaptation to human intelligence.

'Now the objections raised by Science to Prayer are, in their essential nature, identical with those raised by Science to Miracles. But we Protestants all admit that the age of miracles is past; and, although we believe that they, or their equivalents, took place, yet the fact of their having now ceased shews that practically (whether *really* or not is here immaterial) there is some force in these *à priori* objections. In other words, it may be doubtful whether or not genuine miracles ever occurred, but there can be no doubt that they never occur now. But the Bible speaks of the physical validity of Prayer in precisely the same terms as it does of miracles, that is, as being among the things which are "not impossible to him that believeth." Nay, the two are expressly identified by Christ in at least two passages, viz., "For verily I say unto you, That whosoever shall say unto this mountain, Be thou removed, and be thou cast into the sea; and shall not doubt in his heart, but shall believe that those things which he saith shall come to pass, he shall have whatsoever he saith[1]." Again, "The Lord said, If ye had faith as a grain of mustard seed, ye might say unto this sycamine tree, Be thou plucked up by the root, and be thou planted in the sea, and it shall obey you[2]." Now the fact that miracles, supposing them to have been previously wrought, have now ceased, coupled with the fact that Scripture nowhere predicts their cessation, seems to form on mere Scriptural grounds a strong *primâ facie* case against the efficacy of Prayer. For the hypothetical case is strictly parallel with the demonstrable: in both physical results are involved, and in the same manner; both are spoken of in Scripture in exactly the same tone; and the cessation of neither is predicted. The fact, then, that the one class of physical results is at present nonexistent, affords a strong indication that the other is likewise so. For the only objection which can be urged against this commentary on Scripture is, that the one class had a special function to serve which the other had not—viz., attestation to Divine authority. But this has not much force, seeing that it is founded on no Scriptural warrant whatever—is merely a somewhat subtly-devised loop-hole to escape from an unpleasant conclusion. Further, nearly all the Apostolic miracles were wrought *in answer to Prayer:* hence it is but natural that a confusion should have arisen in the minds of believing writers—they supposing the miracles wrought by them-

---

[1] Mark xii. 23, 24. [2] Luke xvii. 6.

selves to be the result of their petitions; which at best they can only have been in a very subordinate sense, as shewing the power of a righteous man,—and even this subordinate sense would accord with the function of a miracle. In short, it is easy to see that there was, at the first institution of Christianity, a necessary reason for the success of Apostolic Prayer. But now that the object of a miracle has confessedly disappeared, it would be gratuitous to suppose that Prayer is still effectual; for not only, as we have seen, is there no Scriptural warrant for this supposition; but even against the objection from function it is easily answered, that this confusion which naturally arose in the Apostles' mind between the function of Prayer and that of a succeeding miracle, is perfectly intelligible; and, as the occurrence of miracle was the only means they had of estimating the validity of Prayer, not only is their method of identifying the one with the other just what we should have expected, but it thus affords us no Scriptural warrant for supposing that Prayer is of any validity apart from the object of a miracle.'

§ 6. Before commenting on these objections to Prayer, we may notice that they do not refer to any vital feature of the Christian Faith; and so, if it be true that "there are tens of thousands in Christendom[1]" who feel these objections an impediment to their faith, such minds may rest satisfied with the above arguments, and find in them a reconciliation between their religious and their scientific beliefs. On us, however, it is incumbent to examine such arguments critically.

In the first place it is evident, that the argument as to

[1] Mr Knight's Defence before the Presbytery of Dundee. Newspaper reports.

the confusion arising in the Apostle's mind between the function of Prayer and that of a succeeding miracle, effectually rejects all proof as to the physical validity of Prayer, so far as this can be deduced from the Apostolic teaching. It would therefore be a needless waste of time to shew the unanimity which pervades the teaching upon this subject, for the fact is not denied by the argument in question. It thus becomes necessary for us to take our stand upon the gospels alone. Before doing so, however, it should be noticed, that the objection which thus excludes Apostolic doctrine embodies a canon of interpreting Scripture in the highest degree dangerous. The epistles contain more of Christian doctrine than do the gospels, so that were the teaching of the former accepted only in so far as it was covered by that of the latter, Christianity would be to a large extent transformed. In making, therefore, this concession to the adverse argument, it must be understood that I do so under protest, and only because I believe that the gospels alone contain its sufficient refutation[1].

§ 7. Before beginning with the words of Christ, we may point out a strong negative argument from the fact of His supposed silence. If it is true that the gospels leave the matter in uncertainty, this very fact constitutes a strong *primâ facie* case in favour of the belief that answers to Prayer are given. For the question in dispute is a question of great practical importance to all Christians, and more especially so to the primitive ones: it materially affects our conceptions as to the relation in

[1] For an enumeration of the physically-availing prayers mentioned in the Old Testament, see Dr Hessey's *Recent Difficulties on Prayer*, pp. 14—32. Exclusive of actual miracles, they amount to thirty cases.

which the Deity stands to us; and has therefore a very direct bearing upon our spiritual culture. For these reasons we should certainly expect a finished Revelation to inform us concerning the uselessness of Prayer for temporal benefits, if such Prayer is really ineffectual. And this reasonable expectation is intensified by the fact, that the subject of Prayer occupies a prominent place in the teaching of Christ—numerous points connected with it, of much less interest and importance than the present one, being minutely developed. Further, Prayer for temporal benefits is certainly natural to man, being the necessary consequence of his belief in special providences. If this belief is erroneous—or, which is much the same thing, although this belief be well-founded, yet if the superadded belief in the efficacy of Prayer is unwarranted and false—we should expect a finished Revelation to tell us of such falsehood. Instead of this, however, Christ expressly teaches the duty of faith in special providence; and declares such faith to be a test specially distinguishing His followers from the heathen. "Therefore take no thought, saying, What shall we eat? or, What shall we drink? or, Wherewithal shall we be clothed? (For after these things do the Gentiles ($\tau\grave{a}$ $\check{\epsilon}\theta\nu\eta$) seek:) for your heavenly Father knoweth that ye have need of all these things." There are numerous other passages to the same effect, but this one has been chosen because there here seems to be an implied reference to Prayer; for, shortly before and in the same discourse, the concluding phrase of the above quoted passage is employed with an expressed reference to Prayer, and it occurs nowhere else. Also, shortly afterwards the subject of Prayer in connection with special providences is resumed.

§ 8. We now turn to the positive aspect of the case:—

Christian Prayer and General Laws. 179

Is it true that the gospels leave the matter in uncertainty? The first duty devolving upon us is clearly to meet the supposed difficulty, which arises from Christ identifying answers to Prayer with miraculous manifestations. To begin with an examination of the passages relied on, there are three and only three interpretations open to us of their sense—we may consider them hyberbolical, figurative, or literal. The first of these must in fairness be excluded; for it appears to me, as I think it must appear to all when their attention is directed to the subject, that the language of Christ is preëminently remarkable for the absence of hyperbole. There is likewise no reason to deem these words figurative; for the context certainly refers to physical results, which, in one case at least, were expressly declared to have been wrought in virtue of Prayer[1]. We are forced therefore to fall back upon the literal interpretation, as being the only fair rendering of these passages. In doing so, however, it must be observed that, although the assurance be taken as literally true, the reservation it contains effectually ensures that the specified examples shall never be literally accomplished. For the very purpose with which these examples were adduced, was to shew that the faith of the Apostles was inadequate to perform miracles requiring (as the implication certainly is) a smaller amount of efficient power, than would be required for the accomplishment of these supposed examples. Much less then can the faith of ordinary men aspire to the accomplishment of such results. To this should be added Alford's commentary on these passages, viz., that "such a state of mind entirely precludes the idea of *arbitrary* exercise of power[2];" so that even an adequate faith would probably never have oc-

[1] Matt. xvii. 21.   [2] Greek Test. Matt. xxi. 21.

casion to exert its influence—the presence of the requisite condition to such exertion being thus of all causes the most certain to prevent it. Why then, it may be asked, were such examples adduced? The answer is supplied by Alford :—"Though we cannot reach this faith in its fulness, yet every approach to it (ver. 21) shall be endued with some of its wonderful power—in obtaining requests from God[1]." These examples were given in order to shew that there is nothing too difficult for faith to accomplish, if present in sufficient amount—they are but theoretically possible results, which there is no reason to suppose need ever or will ever be performed. Far, therefore, from grounding any presumption against the efficacy of Prayer, these passages afford it the strongest possible support—they expressly declare that the only reason why Prayer is ever anything other than *wholly* effectual, is because it does not contain a sufficient amount of the prayerful element; and they clearly imply that the physical results attainable by Prayer are *commensurate* with the faith of the petitioner. We shall immediately see that both these points are in undisturbed harmony with the rest of Christ's teaching.

§ 9. It will be sufficient, for the substantiation of the last-mentioned doctrine, to give one or two references. To the centurion, at whose faith "Jesus marvelled," He said, "Go thy way; and as thou hast believed, so be it done unto thee." Again, after asking the blind men whether they believed that He was able to restore their sight, Jesus "touched their eyes, saying, According to your faith be it unto you." Lastly, to the woman of Canaan, "Jesus answered and said, O woman great is thy faith: be it unto thee even as thou wilt."

[1] *Loc. cit.*

Turning now to the other doctrine we have to substantiate, we first observe that further on in the discourse from which we deduced both doctrines, the promise occurs :—"Ask, and it shall be given you ; seek, and ye shall find; knock, and it shall be opened unto you." Now it is highly important to observe that "the only *limitation* to this promise, which, under various forms, is several times repeated by our Lord, is furnished in vv. 9—11, and in James iv. 3, αἰτεῖτε καὶ οὐ λαμβάνετε· διότι κακῶς αἰτεῖσθε[1]." The meaning of κακῶς in this passage is, from the context, evidently subjective—does not refer to the ignorant asking for things inexpedient, but, as in the case of the mountain and the sycamore-tree, to a deficiency of Faith. Coming now to the other passage alluded to by Alford, and which follows immediately upon the promise we are considering :—"Or what man is there of you, who if his son ask bread, will he give him a stone ? or if he ask a fish, will he give him a serpent? If ye then being evil, know how to give good gifts unto your children, how much more shall your Father which is in heaven give good things to them that ask him?" On this passage Bishop Hopkins remarks :—"Or is it temporal mercies thou wantest? Why he is thy Father: and why shouldst thou go so disconsolate who hast a Father so able and so willing to relieve and supply thee? Only beware that thou askest not stones for bread, nor scorpions for fish, and then ask what thou wilt for thy good, and thou shalt receive it[2]." Now this is certainly a fair commentary : can it then be shewn—can it be inferred from any other part of Scripture, that by stones and scorpions are here meant physical benefits? Does not the context as above expounded prove the very con-

[1] Alford, Matt. vii. 7.   [2] *Works*, p. 8.

trary? Bread and fish are the cheapest articles of diet, and are evidently here chosen in order to shew that we are dependent upon our heavenly Father for the very necessaries of physical well-being—that even "in the breaking of bread" we should "give Him thanks;" seeing that we should previously have looked to Him for our sustenance, Who feedeth the very ravens, and from Whom even the lions, in a sense, do seek their meat.

But this introduces us to another point. The mention of Bread in this passage in close juxtaposition with "your Father which is in heaven," seems plainly to refer us to the Lord's Prayer itself. Here, if anywhere, we must accept the teaching as authoritative; for this formula of Prayer is not merely a specimen but also a pattern of all Prayers, in so far as they are "*Christian*[1]." Now the clause with which we are concerned, viz., "Give us the bread which is this day requisite for our sustenance[2]," must in all fairness be taken to refer, primarily at all events, to actual bread; for there is no qualification attached to signify that the term is to be understood in a metaphorical sense; and some such qualification we should certainly have expected, if such were the meaning intended. Prayer for the necessaries of life is, as before observed, natural to man; and it had for its justification the precedent of innumerable such petitions in the Old Testament: if therefore such petitions are useless, it is almost impious to imagine that Christ should not have guarded this one from the plain meaning of its words. Not to dwell longer upon a point

---

[1] Παραδίδωσι τύπον εὐχῆς, οὐχ ἵνα ταύτην μόνην τὴν εὐχὴν εὐχώμεθα, ἀλλ' ἵνα ταύτην ἔχοντες πηγὴν εὐχῆς ἐκ ταύτης ἀρυώμεθα τὰς ἐννοίας τῶν εὐχῶν.—Euthymius.

[2] Alford.

which most adversaries will concede, the request we are considering is remarkable from its position in the Prayer. "The first three clauses refer exclusively to the Glory of God, after which we proceed to make requests for ourselves;" and the first of these is the one with which we are concerned. It is as though our physical well-being were recognized as the condition of our spiritual life; and that in looking to God for the latter, we are to remember that we can only hope for it, upon the presupposition of our recognized dependence upon Him for the former. This argument is important, because the sequence in which the other petitions occur in this Prayer is evidently throughout of doctrinal significance. Regarding the petition itself there is not much to say. The $\dot{\eta}\mu\hat{\omega}\nu$ must be understood as implying $\tau\grave{o}\nu$ $\delta\iota$' $\dot{\eta}\mu\hat{a}s$ $\gamma\epsilon\nu\acute{o}\mu\epsilon\nu o\nu$,—that petition in this, as in other cases, has an influence in the providential disposition of things—is the condition of receiving that which has been provided. $\tau\grave{o}\nu$ $\check{a}\rho\tau o\nu$ has ever been understood in a synecdochical sense, as meaning "all temporal and earthly blessings, that contribute either to our being, or to our well-being in this life;" and this interpretation is in full accordance with the use of the term in other parts of Scripture. But even if this interpretation be rejected, our warrant for believing in the efficacy of Prayer, so far as it is deduced from this great exemplar, would remain unaffected; since, if it can be shewn that we have the Divine sanction to pray for any one physical benefit, all the present objections to Prayer for other such benefits at once disappear.

The teaching of this passage seems to me so conclusive, that I think it is needless to occupy more space in commenting upon any other of the sayings of our Lord, which have a direct or an indirect bearing upon the subject before us. It must be noticed, however, that these contain no shadow of insinuation in support of views different from those here set forth; and to this we may safely add, that there is no single passage either in the Old or the New Testament from which any warrant for the former can be deduced or inferred[1].

§ 10. It will be observed, that while commenting upon the passages mainly relied on by those who object to Prayer on Theological grounds, no allusion was made to the supposed difficulty which arises from Christ having there identified answers to Prayer with miraculous manifestations, and having nowhere else predicted the cessation of either. Now, even if this difficulty were conceded insuperable, it would surely be a matter of grave responsibility for any commentator deliberately to expunge the plain and only meaning of these and numerous other passages, merely on the ground that they vaguely embody an intellectual difficulty of a highly

[1] Prof. Tyndall quotes James iv. 3, and takes advantage of the ambiguous nature of the English translation "ask amiss," to insinuate that the only allusion is to praying ignorantly for things inexpedient. Worse than this, Dr Tyndall further quotes Matthew v. 45, "He maketh his sun to rise on the evil and on the good, and sendeth rain on the just and on the unjust," as though these words "enfolded the philosophy" the Professor is contending for. A more outrageous commentary can scarcely be imagined. The words in question were spoken to exemplify the Divine beneficence and long-suffering, without the least shadow of implication that they were intended to cover the entirely distinct question, as to whether or not the children of God are a greater care to Him than the impious. Indeed, so far as this passage bears upon the subject at all, it clearly tends to the inference that they are so; for if the Lord is merciful even to the impious, much more will He give good gifts to His children who ask Him.

transcendental nature. On the same principle might we—nay, in consistency ought we, to expunge many of the chief among Christian doctrines. But now, Is this difficulty insuperable? Is it even serious? Let us suppose, for the sake of argument, that the identification relied on is very much clearer than it really is; and further, that we can see no reason why miracles should have ceased:—even in the presence of these suppositions it would surely still be an extravagant inference, that because miracles have ceased, therefore answers to Prayer have likewise ceased. It would be an extravagant inference, because unconditionally founded upon a gratuitous hypothesis, to wit, that answers to Prayer have no object to serve apart from some connection with miracles. We assume that the Divine superintendence of the World is such, that in no case does our " Almighty and most merciful Father" "save those out of their distresses," who "cry unto the Lord in their trouble;" we assume that because "the Lord is merciful" in making "his sun to rise on the evil and on the good," and "in sending rain on the just and on the unjust;" therefore the complement cannot be true, viz., that we " have not seen the righteous forsaken, nor his seed begging their bread," and that " in the days of famine the upright shall be satisfied." But not only do we assume that the " Hearer of Prayer" does not "attend unto our cry:" we also assume that in no case does He see fit to improve the moral nature of man through physical agency. We assume that all the numerous instances recorded in Scripture of Faith strengthened, Hope sustained, Thanksgiving occasioned, "Rejoicing in spirit" increased, and Praise evoked, in virtue of the perceived influence of God in Nature, are so many misconceptions worse than delusions. We further assume that all lessons such as the discipline of unanswered Prayer from the case of the Syrophœnician woman, the benefit of Faith from that of the centurion, and the duty of Obedience from that of the man born blind ;—we assume that these and many similar lessons are utterly fallacious, in so far as they are drawn from their illustrating examples. And we assume all this, not only without any shadow of warrant from the teaching of Christ, but, as we have seen, against His express declaration.

To this must be added, that, on the one hand, we *can* see a perfectly satisfactory reason why miracles should have ceased—the Christian system no longer requiring their support,—while, on the other, we can see no corresponding reason why answers to Prayer should have ceased. True it is that Scripture nowhere expressly predicts the cessation of miracles ; but before this fact can be raised to a presumption against the validity of Prayer, it must be shewn that we should antecedently expect such a prediction, if Prayer is of any validity apart from the function of a miracle. How this can be shewn, however, it is hard to see. Scripture nowhere warrants the inference that the validity of Prayer depends upon the function of a miracle—on the contrary, the warrant is, as we have seen, altogether the other way. If then such validity exists apart from such function, we can have no reason to expect that *on this account* the cessation of miracles should have been predicted. The inference which, it is said, we should expect Scripture to rectify if erroneous, is an inference which is really drawn, not from Scripture but from Science ; as we may readily perceive by asking the simple question :—Even if Scripture had predicted the cessation of miracles, will any one undertake to say this fact would materially have altered the case?

Now it is simply childish to assert that this obvious distinction between the function of a miracle and the efficacy of Prayer, is "a subtly-devised loop-hole of escape from an unpleasant conclusion." Such subtlety as there is resides with those who would so amalgamate answers to Prayer with miracles, as to deduce the cessation of the former from that of the latter. To those who do not endeavour to twist every available fact into their argument, it must appear that the only bearing which miracles have upon the question before us, is that of demonstrating the existence of a Power adequate to produce any physical effect in answer to Prayer. And this bearing is highly important. As Christians we must all believe in the occurrence of miracles, since the system we accept is inextricably bound up with them. Any antecedent objections, therefore, which on Scientific grounds we may feel to the belief in the efficacy of Prayer, are thus, on Scriptural grounds, removed; for in the presence of the fact that inscrutable causation is sometimes employed by the Deity, all theoretical objections to the belief in the possibility of such employment must disappear. To this it should be added, that the fact of Christ having performed most of His miracles in answer to Prayer ought to be taken as of doctrinal import; for, as the learned and gifted author of *Ecce Homo* observes, the teaching of Christ was remarkable from the significance which he attached to symbolical action.

Lastly, it must be observed that the doctrine as to the physical efficacy of Prayer is in perfect accordance with the general spirit of the New Testament. I will not, however, pause to develop this point, because I conceive that the difficulties raised upon Scriptural grounds have already been thoroughly quashed. Nevertheless, it must be mentioned that this point is one of great importance, not only because Christ habitually attached more doctrinal weight to the general spirit of His system than to any particular words or deeds of His own or of His followers; but also because in the case of a genuine Revelation, which appeals largely to the emotional and æsthetical parts of our nature, we should antecedently expect that the feelings should have been endowed with a considerable degree of authority in deciding such questions as the present.

§ 11. There is still one question which is covered by the title of this Treatise, and which remains to be discussed. Those who have previously considered Christian Prayer in the relation there expressed, and have arrived at conclusions opposed to the foregoing, do not restrict their contemplations to the *efficacy* of Prayer, but extend them to the raising of a question as to its *duty*. Without a single exception do these writers contend, that the doubt which they think their arguments have thrown over the benefit of Prayer, proves its obligation a nullity; and when even a Christian minister has written, "Such stammering becomes irreverence in mental manhood; and in this matter emphatically, when 'we become men, we must put away childish things[1];'" it is no longer in our choice to abstain from discussing this subject—briefly to demonstrate that, even if Scripture had left the question as to the efficacy of Prayer in as great uncertainty as we have seen it to be left by Philosophy; and even if the

[1] Mr Knight, *Contem. Rev.* p. 193.

writers against such efficacy had established a probability as high as we have seen that probability to be low; even then the duty of Prayer for physical benefits would have remained above suspicion.

§ 12. The Theory of Prayer, whether Christian or otherwise, is that of a petitioner recognizing his dependence upon a higher intelligence. Now in the Christian system, Prayer, which is thus by the act of offering a confession of dependence, is expressly declared to be *for this reason* a mean, not only to benefit man, but also to glorify God. And in harmony with this doctrine we find, that while the first sentence of the Lord's Prayer expresses our dependence upon God, the second refers to His glory. Prayer then no less, if not more than Praise, is a duty which we owe to a Prayer-hearing God, quite apart from all hopes of receiving that for which we pray. Thus the more truly "Christian" any petition is, the more intense will be the appreciation of this its two-fold character; and the more ardently we pray for any result, the more truly are we, in virtue of the act, praising God.

Now the recognition of this two-fold character of Prayer is highly important in estimating the duty of Prayer for physical benefits. It is not in the nature of man to be indifferent concerning such benefits; so that the fact of wilfully excluding their mention from our petitions, would be tantamount to refusing to "give unto the Lord the glory due unto His name." Only if Revelation had expressly prohibited such prayers, or if Philosophy could demonstrate their futility, would we be justified in abstaining from their expression. "For of Prayer there are two uses. It serveth as a mean to procure those things which God hath promised to grant when we ask; and it serveth as a mean to express our lawful desires also towards that, which whether we shall have or no we know not till we see the event. Things in themselves unholy or unseemly we may not ask; we may whatsoever being not forbidden either nature or grace shall reasonably move us to wish as imparting the good of men, albeit God himself have nowhere by promise assured us of that particular which our prayer craveth. To pray for that which is in itself and of its own nature apparently a thing impossible, were not convenient......Whereas contrariwise when things of their own nature contingent and mutable are by the secret determination of God appointed one way, though we the other way make our prayers, and consequently ask those things of God which are *by this supposition* impossible, we notwithstanding do not hereby in prayer transgress our lawful bounds[1]."

The closing sentence of this quotation introduces us to another point. It is no doubt perfectly true (as so often insisted by writers on the other side), that from the nature of the case, religious men are much more liable to pray for things inexpedient or impossible within the physical sphere, than within the moral. Yet, if it be true that *although* in ignorance thus asking for impossibilities, "we notwithstanding do not transgress our lawful bounds;" it appears to follow that such Prayer is, so to speak, wasted. There is thus at first sight an awkward doctrinal difficulty, which writers upon the other side have, without exception, draughted into their service. The difficulty, however, is only apparent, for common sense and Scripture alike furnish an obvious solution.

Every Prayer, in so far as it is "Christian," may be considered as composed of three factors relating to our-

[1] Hooker, *Eccl. Polit.* Book V. ch. XLVIII. § 4.

selves, and one relating to God. ' The last-named factor is our desire for the Divine glory; but it is with those relating to ourselves that we are now concerned, viz., Self-love, Trust in God, and sense of dependence upon Him. Now the former of these, in its relation to the other two, clearly ensures that, apart from all considerations for the Divine glory, every Prayer shall be conditional upon the desired result being in accordance with the Divine Will. For, in proportion to our trust in the goodness of God, and to our sense of dependence upon Him, will be our persuasion and our prayer, that He will vouchsafe His answers only "as may be most expedient for us;" and consequently Self-love will dictate that the most ardent of all our requests shall be the one which throws all the others into this conditional form. "Thy will be done" is therefore the implied or expressed foundation of every Christian Prayer. Hence, although it is certainly our duty "in all things to make known our requests unto God," it is no less certainly our wisdom to request most fervently of all, that the disposition of *results* shall be left in the hands of a merciful Providence—even in our punishment to say, "It is the Lord: let Him do what seemeth Him good." But now, are we to believe *for this reason*, that those prayers only are valid, in which the results designated express a coincidence between "the particular subjective will and the universal objective will?" To admit such a doctrine would be to violate both Scripture and common sense. If prayers uttered in ignorance for impossibilities are supposed to be but vain beatings of the air, it must be either because the fact of the thing being impossible proves that it was not our duty to ask for it, or that, although it was our duty, yet because the thing asked for happened to be impossible, therefore a fulfilled duty is not recognized by God. The former of these suppositions is conspicuously illogical, for, if Prayer is a duty *because* a recognition of our dependence upon God, the mere fact of the element of ignorance occurring in it cannot affect the duty of offering it; for the petitioner is, by the supposition, recognizing that dependence as fully in this as in any other case.

The latter of the above suppositions is as unscriptural as the former is illogical; so that, the dilemma being thus complete, we are free to fall back upon the deliverance which accords alike with Reason and with Scripture. When we pray for any particular benefit, we pray for it *because* we deem it conducive to our own or other's good. But if the Deity sees that the granting of our request would really be to our injury, the same spirit which prompts the request secures its denial—provided that the prayer is answered according to the spirit of its utterance[1]. But the petitioner is conscious that the Deity, to whom "all hearts are open, all desires known, and from whom no secrets are hid," knows of innumerable other benefits we require, for which notwithstanding "in our blindness we cannot ask." The same spirit therefore which prompts the original, and as to its expressed result, ineffectual petition, is really pleading, not for that result, but for some unknown equivalent. The fundamental clause "Thy will be done," refers not only to the granting or the non-granting of the particular results expressed, but likewise to the disposition of all results whatever. "Sed hoc devotionis debemus Domino Deo nostro, ut si ea (*i.e.*, dura, molesta etc.) non abstulerit, non ideo nos ab

---

[1] "Nonnullis impatientibus Dominus Deus quod petebant concessit iratus, sicut contra Apostolos negavit propitius." Compare also Hooker, *Eccl. Polit.* Book V. ch. XLVIII. § 3.

eo negligi existimemus, sed potius pia patientia malorum bona speremus ampliora; sic enim virtus in infirmitate perficitur." And not only in things physical do we ask that our prayers if ineffectual may "return unto our own bosom;" in things affecting our moral and religious welfare our supplications are no less contingent—nay, our ignorance in this life is such, that "we dare not ask" for any benefits unconditionally, save two; those, namely, which close the service of our Church. But in all cases we rest confident that the God who remembers even a cup of cold water given in the name of a disciple, and who cannot forget one even of our "idle words," is not a God who fails to be "attentive unto the voice of our supplications"—that even though the agony be not removed, He will send us His angels of blessing—that, cast upon the waters of His boundless Providence, Prayer shall return, although it may be after many days.

§ 13. We have said that it is as much our interest to pray thus conditionally, as it is our duty to pray at all. It remains in conclusion to observe, that it is as clearly our duty as it is our interest thus to pray. The most important factor of Christian Prayer is desire for the glory of God; because, in so far as Prayer is a duty, it depends exclusively upon this factor—the whole of such duty being contained in that of such desire. " Hallowed be thy Name" is therefore the most essentially "Christian" of all petitions—the petition which should occupy the first place in our desires as it does in our formulæ, and thus be carried through all the others. But how can the name of God be hallowed by us? Assuredly in the first place by recognising it as such—by the feeling and the utterance of Praise; and in the next by desiring it to be such—by desiring the fulfilment of the Divine Purpose:—we are free to glorify God by our submission to His Will. The first three petitions of the Lord's Prayer are thus seen to be virtually one; and when we ask that His Will be done towards us—that He grant us only such equivalents as may be most conducive to our ultimate good,—we not only consult our own interests, but we fulfil the main duty of Prayer. "'Father, glorify thy name.' As if He had said, Though life be naturally dear, and the cup which I am to drink very bitter, and the wrath that I am to undergo heavy and infinite, yet all these things are not so considerable to me as thy glory; and therefore, though it be by agonies, by death, by the cross, yet, Father, glorify thy name. The same mind should dwell in us likewise, and we should hereby be instructed to desire and pray for other things with limitations and restrictions, but for the glory of God absolutely and simply. 'Father, glorify thy name;' and if in the counsel of thy will, and the course of thy providence, it cannot be otherwise than by my suffering or sorrow, yea, or death itself; yet, Father, even in this glorify thy name; and out of my very ruins erect thou a trophy and monument to thy praise; be thou hallowed and sanctified, although at my cost, and with the loss of all[1]."

§ 14. The discussion of our subject is now completed. Throughout the pages in which it is contained, there has been much that will appear unsatisfactory to a man of Science; and much likewise that will appear so to a man of Prayer: this, however, is but the penalty which attaches to most writings whose aim is at impartiality rather than eclecticism. To him who has read

[1] Bishop Hopkins on the Lord's Prayer.

these pages in this the spirit in which they have been written, it cannot but appear, that amid much that is argumentative, much that is uncertain, and much that is obscure; one truth has been rendered as clear as it is cardinal,—the truth that the scientific proposition is virtually valueless. On each of three successive platforms of argument we have shewn in a cumulative manner, that the probability upon which this proposition depends, is not only to perception exceeding low, but is yet lower to an indefinite, because an imperceptible degree : and we have further shewn that, apart from all considerations as to the lowness and the vagueness of such probability, the scientific proposition itself is not altogether true—there are several methods by which it is amply apparent, even to our limited faculties, that the Almighty may answer Prayer, without in any way violating the course of Natural Law.

And some such conclusion is only what must have been anticipated by a man who believes in the authority of his religion. If it is true that the voice of Revelation upon this subject is explicit, a man who accepts its teaching as Divine can only be consistent in his beliefs, by maintaining a serene confidence that his persuasions concerning this subject are founded upon a basis which Science must ever remain powerless to subvert. For, as we saw at the commencement, this is certainly a subject in connection with which the purifying influence of Science upon Religion can never be exerted; and we may now add, that those votaries of the former who are thoughtless enough to confuse this subject with others in which the exercise of such influence is possible, are not only failing in their endeavours to purify Religion, but even were these endeavours capable in any way of affecting the latter, their influence would be to its detriment. For, on the one hand, each of the analogical arguments upon which the scientific proposition has been seen to depend, is in truth but an inference, from the nature of our own existence and the conditions of our own activity, to the nature of the Deity and the method of His Government; while, on the other hand, as before pointed out, the purifying influence of Science upon Religion has ever been exclusively confined to increasing our perception of these ultimate mysteries. When men of old could look upon the starry heavens, and feel that they were created by the breath of God—that He led out their hosts by the right hand of His power, and called them all by their names; they acknowledged a mystery, but it was proximate; His action was immediate, and His presence was near. To us how changed! But if the great mission of Science has been to render the Mystery of Things more inscrutable and sublime, let not her own disciples try to oppose that mission : let them not seek to penetrate the mystery she has intensified, or to substitute an Anthropomorphism more unworthy than that which she has dethroned.

The real interests of Science and Religion are therefore not "antagonistic but complementary;" and the present is most emphatically a subject in which the true character of each can only be maintained, by their meeting on the common ground of that Philosophy, at once the oldest, wisest, and most beautiful :—" The things which are hidden belong unto the Lord our God, but those things which are revealed belong unto us and to our children for ever."

POSTSCRIPT.

THE following Essay was originally intended to appear in a separate form; but, as the previous one was longer in passing through the press than I had anticipated, I have taken the opportunity afforded by this delay of publishing the two Essays in one volume. It is desirable to insert this statement, partly in order to shew why the one Essay is always alluded to in the other as a distinct publication, but chiefly in order to explain why the two Essays differ so much from one another in style.

It must be added that the Adjudicators of the Burney Prize are in no way responsible for any part of the following Examination.

October, 1874.

THE
PHYSICAL EFFICACY OF PRAYER,

DEDUCTIVELY AND INDUCTIVELY CONSIDERED:

BEING AN EXAMINATION OF THE ARGUMENTS SET FORTH BY
MESSRS. KNIGHT, ROBERTSON, BROOKS, TYNDALL,
AND GALTON.

AN ESSAY

BY

GEORGE J. ROMANES, M.A.

PREFACE.

THE subject discussed in the following pages was first prominently brought under my notice in February 1873, in consequence of its being then set for the Burney Competition of that year. As the Thesis proposed on that occasion, however, was expressly limited to Prayer in its relation to General Laws, and as the numerous objections which have been urged against the doctrine of the physical efficacy of Prayer have not been so limited; I felt that the resulting exclusion from that Thesis of a large portion of the adverse argument, might be deemed unsatisfactory by those who may read the former with a view of settling their opinions upon the question as a whole. As soon, therefore, as the decision of the Adjudicators was given—viz., in May 1874,—I undertook the following examination of such among the adverse arguments as remained; so that the present Essay is to be regarded merely as a supplement to that which obtained the Burney Prize of 1873.

I may take this opportunity of stating that my investigations from the first have been conducted with a strictly unprejudiced mind, notwithstanding I regard the question as one of great importance. There are, at the present time, thousands of religiously-disposed persons "painfully perplexed" concerning this question; and such a fact alone is sufficient to justify a Writer in taking more pains over his analysis, than has been taken by any of those who have hitherto dealt with the subject. Lest, however, the pains I have taken may be thought to indicate an anxiety to uphold a cherished conviction, I deem it desirable to state that such is not the case. If those whose arguments I examine are able, either to shew that some misunderstanding exists on my part regarding the arguments already adduced, or, on their own part, to adduce others of a less objectionable character; and if they are then able to shew that their case, as thus re-argued, presents enough of logical cogency and common-sense sufficiency, to cause a preponderance of rational probability on their side; then no one will be more ready than I am to disbelieve in the Physical Efficacy of Prayer. Until this is done, however, I cannot but argue on the side of conservatism. It devolves upon those who attack a well-founded belief of any kind, to make out a reasonably strong case against it; so that, in the present instance, only if I disbelieved in the Christian system as a whole, should I feel that time was ill spent in refuting erroneous arguments against one of its leading doctrines.

July, 1874.

THE PHYSICAL EFFICACY OF PRAYER,

DEDUCTIVELY AND INDUCTIVELY CONSIDERED.

THE writers who of late years have challenged the doctrine[1] as to the physical efficacy of Prayer, may primarily be divided into two classes. Those who form the one class approach the subject on its *à priori* aspect: they argue, Seeing the constitution of the world to be what it is; seeing that the Divine government is everywhere conducted through the mediation of natural law; seeing that, even if the Deity has any special regard for man, yet it is almost impious to imagine that He should alter his administration at the suggestion of man; seeing the impossibility of answering contradictory petitions; seeing, in short, a vast number of such antecedent objections attaching to the belief in question; we cannot but consider that belief as in a high degree irrational. Those who form the other class approach the subject on its *à posteriori* aspect: they argue, Without troubling ourselves about the metaphysics of the subject, or the antecedent improbability of this and that opinion, we consider the question simply as a matter of fact; for to say that Prayer is physically efficacious, is to say that Prayer is able to accomplish definite physical results, and so by implication to say that in this respect the value of

Prayer is determinable by the scientific methods: we therefore appeal to these methods, and, apart from all theory, with unbiassed judgment are content to abide by the result. Now of these two classes, the former admits of being again divided into two sub-classes—or, more correctly, the arguments employed by writers of this class admit of being so subdivided. One section of these arguments rests upon, or is deduced from, the now well-established belief in the universal operation of natural laws: the other section is deduced from the various antecedent opinions of the different writers, as to the nature and attributes of the Supreme Being, the position of man in this world with reference to the rest of the Divine works, the relation of the Deity to these same works, and in particular to man. Now it is clear that there is a great difference between the argumentative weight of propositions, logically deducible from the admitted fact that our lot is cast under a Reign of Law, and propositions resting merely on the individual opinions of different writers regarding questions of a highly transcendental nature. It is desirable always to bear this distinction in mind, when reading discussions upon such subjects as the present; but it is not only for this reason that I have drawn so sharp a line between the two sub-divisions of the *à priori* school. In order to make the following pages as concise as possible, I intend altogether to avoid the discussion of the Prayer-question, in so far as this rests upon our belief in the existence of natural law; for I feel that, if I did not make this limitation, either the following criticism would require to expand to a length that would be tedious to the general reader, or I should be compelled to mar the argument by its undue condensation. It is so easy for writers on the other side to take up the ordinary or scientific conception of natural law as a weapon ready fashioned to their hand, and then to wield it to the easy apparent destruction of our belief in the physical validity of Prayer, that it becomes difficult to impress upon the impartial reader how lengthy an examination of such views must necessarily be. Of course, if natural law is everywhere and always such as we know it; if we are quite sure, or reasonably satisfied, that it is absolutely what we see it to be relatively; if there is no rational probability that in its relation to the Deity, it differs widely from that which we perceive it to be in its relation to us; if it is but a confused mysticism to argue that natural law is after all but a merely human conception;—then, assuredly, it becomes an easy matter to overturn any belief, which is confessedly in direct antagonism with such truths. But the whole question turns upon that as to whether or not these statements *are* truths; so that those who take up the ordinary, or physical, conception of natural law, and carry it without modification into their metaphysical discussions, are really begging the whole question in dispute; and can therefore well afford to be at once brief and convincing. When, however, it devolves upon another writer to examine such arguments, the task is of necessity a more laborious one; seeing that he is in no wise concerned with their obvious conclusion except through the validity of their premise, and that the adequate examination of this premise is one of the most difficult which it can possibly fall to the lot of metaphysical analysis to conduct. For these reasons I can make no apology for omitting to entertain this aspect of the controversy, even though I know that by so doing I tacitly deprive my adversaries' position of its principal support. As, however, this aspect of the controversy has been already exhaustively treated elsewhere, I have no compunction in now depriving that position of this support.

The following examination, then, while it entertains all the *à posteriori* objections, is restricted to such of the *à priori* ones as are independent of our belief in the ubiquitous operation of natural law. Let us begin with the latter.

Of the writers who have treated of the Prayer-question according to the deductive method, the most prominent is the Rev. Mr Knight—not on account of the cogency of his arguments, but because his articles in the *Contemporary Review* have occasioned more popular excitement than has any of the other Essays upon the same side. For this reason I shall examine his views at greater length than those which have been advanced by the other writers named in the Title; and, presuming that the reader is already acquainted with the doctrine of "The Two Spheres," we may most fitly begin by observing that Mr Knight himself strangely eviscerates his argument, by virtually abstracting from it the scientific doctrine as to the unalterable rigidity of natural law. That is to say, Mr Knight himself in effect observes the distinction recently drawn between the two sections of the *à priori* class of arguments, and altogether abandons that section which is based upon the physical dogma, that the Reign of Law is universal. As this representation of Mr Knight's opinions will probably be somewhat startling to those who may have read his Essays, and would perhaps appear to Mr Knight himself entirely erroneous; I shall adduce and comment upon some of the passages which occur in those Essays, and which seem to me incontestably to justify such representation. But, if Mr Knight or his adherents can point to other passages occurring in the same Essays, and possessing a directly opposite signification, still the case will not be much bettered; for it will then become necessary to reconcile the one set of statements with the other. Natural law must be either alterable or unalterable in a human sense—it cannot consistently be assumed to oscillate between these two characters, according as the exigencies of an argument require.

To take, then, a single passage among several that might be quoted:—"The plasticity of nature is conceded the moment you admit the agency of a living Spirit within the whole [which, of course, Mr Knight does admit], and interpret its laws as the mere indices of his activity. But this theistic axiom......" etc. (p. 31). Now the language here is unequivocal, so that if Mr Knight's adherents point to others of his expressions, such as "the absolute fixity of physical law," "the rigour of adamantine law," etc.; they can only save their Author from the charge of inconsistency, by supposing that in such phrases as the last-quoted, the term "law" is intended merely to signify law in its relation to man. But if natural law is "conceded" to be everywhere "plastic" in its relation to the Deity—or, as we are elsewhere told, the mere expression of His will—it brooks nothing to argue that it is of adamantine rigour in its relation to us; for it is the former relation alone which, in any case, is supposed to be the effective one. Whether or not the Deity *chooses* to answer Prayer for physical benefits, is another question: that if He does so, the existence of general laws affords no obstacle to such execution of His will, is here plainly conceded. And if the fact of natural law being of adamantine rigour in its relation to us, establishes no probability that it is likewise of adamantine rigour in its relation to the Deity, we may as well discard the notion of law altogether; and the argument, so far as it rests upon a foundation of physical truth, is at an end. Once let us discard this relative notion, and we shall then come face to face with the real difficulties of the subject. What these difficulties are (according to Mr Knight), we shall presently have occasion to observe : meanwhile we have only to notice, that this concession to theism deprives Mr Knight's case of all the force it obtains from the terse antithesis of Prof. Tyndall—" Prayer and Natural Law."

I have said that Mr Knight can only be saved from the charge of inconsistency, by the supposition that he uses the word "law" in two different senses ; and that if we suppose this to be his usage, the argument, so far as it depends upon the conception of "law," entirely collapses. Mr Knight himself feels his liability to this charge, and likewise perceives the futility of the deliverance here suggested. He therefore affirms that his "theistic axiom carries with it a consequence which makes the assertion of flexibility barren and useless. For if the existing order be changed, the changed and the previous order being equally the outcome of the same governing Intelligence immanent everywhere in the whole, they would together afford but a slightly varying evidence of one and the same Supernaturalism" (p. 31). It is evident, however, that there is here no argument at all— the latter proposition being no proof of the former. Indeed it is worse than no proof, for it tends to a contradiction. If the previous order and the changed order are equally the outcome of the same Intelligence, and therefore equally and in the same sense supernatural, far from making "the assertion of flexibility barren and useless," this fact only serves to remove any presumption against the probability of a change. Consequently, we find the writer in the next sentences observing :—"There is no difficulty in supposing a change to occur in the common order of events, which we may call 'miraculous;' but the events preceding it and those which follow would be equally the result of divine preadjustment, as the particular change which arrested and elicited the wonder or the admiration of men. The speciality in some, which we call 'extraordinary,' to distinguish them from others which we term 'ordinary,' is due, not to a superabundance of divine agency within them, but to *such a significant display of it* as rivets and awakens us by its unwontedness. Were our vision perfect, we should discern speciality in all." Thus we again see that the position of the Physicist is distinctly resigned; but in order that there may be no doubt whatever upon this head, it may be well to quote another passage in which miracles are alluded to. "It is a simple contradiction in terms to suppose that, with a perfect foresight of the whole process of evolution, the divine Evolver should alter that which His omniprescience predetermined, and bring about an equally perfect result. Doubtless the phases which that perfection assumes may be very various; and a new manifestation wholly different from the old, may be equally perfect, being the outcome of the same animating and directing Intelligence. It is on this ground that the occurrence of a miracle can be vindicated before the tribunal of reason. But a miracle involves neither the violation of natural order nor the uprooting of existing agencies." (p. 26.) Now, we are not at present engaged with Mr Knight's views upon "omniprescience," and so may pass over the first period without comment. But how about the others? If it is admitted that the phases of the Divine operation admit of being "very various" in the direction of miraculous manifestations, why may they not be equally various (so far as natural law is concerned) in the direction of answers to Prayer? If "it is on this ground that the occurrence of a miracle can be vindicated before the tribunal of reason," why may not an answer to Prayer (so far as natural law is concerned) be vindicated on the same ground? The concluding sentence, perhaps, appears to imply a reason, viz., that an answer to Prayer *would* "involve the violation of natural order," etc. But if such implication is intended, it is clearly no answer whatever; for (so far as natural law is concerned) we can see no more reason why a miracle should be less a "violation of natural order," than an answer to Prayer would be, if granted. Perhaps it is so, but if it is so, we can have no means of distinguishing between the two cases; and to say that there is any distinction is merely to make an arbitrary assertion, not only incapable of proof, but destitute of any assignable degree of likelihood. In short, once admit the possibility of miracle, and all difficulties attaching to the belief in the physical efficacy of Prayer, (so far as natural law is concerned,) immediately vanish; for no one who asks the Deity to effect any physical change, expects to receive more than a miracle in reply.

Mr Knight will perhaps point to the unverifiable nature of physical answers to Prayer, in antithesis to the conspicuous nature of a miracle, but this is clearly quite beside the question; for, while it is evident that the element of conspicuity is a mere accident of the one case—*i.e.*, necessitated only by the *purpose* of the miracle, —it is no less evident that the absence of this element in the other can be no proof (so far as natural law is concerned), that a physical change has not been wrought. There may be other objections to our believing in the physical efficacy of Prayer, which do not apply to our believing in the occurrence of miracles; but in so far as the common objection urged by the Physicist applies to the one case, so far, most assuredly, it applies to the other; and if this objection is negatived in the case of miracles by the assumption of a "theistic axiom," it is idle to suppose that both the objection and the axiom are in force in the case of physical answers to Prayer. And this, I think, is a conclusion which Mr Knight cannot refuse to accept. So far as an attentive reading of his two articles has made me acquainted with his meaning, this appears to be the point at which he diverges from those who have founded objections to Prayer upon the conception of natural law. Mr Knight concedes the abstract possibility of the occurrence of any physical change, however unusual; and even goes so far as to maintain that this abstract possibility has been realized in the case of miracles: but the very possibility of such unusual changes in any case is denied by the thoroughgoing Physicist, as being tantamount, if realized, to the entire destruction of existing order. No doubt, in speaking against answers to Prayer, Mr Knight's articles are full of such expressions as, "It is blasphemous to imagine that God ever violates a law;" but in such expressions the writer must intend us to understand the word "law" in some transcendental sense; for if he means by it the merely human every-day conception, not only would most of us feel that it is yet more "blasphemous" to assume so intimate an acquaintance with the Divine *modus operandi* as would be required for the logical support of such assertions; but these assertions could not, by any amount of paring, be made to square with, for instance, the following statement :—" In both cases (*i.e.*, ordinary events and miracles) we come to believe in the constancy of law, by a closer scrutiny of what is apparently inconsistent, or has broken away from its ordinary course; the seemingly irregular giving us the hint of a deeper regularity underlying it, while the monotone of nature is broken by the momentary flash of its sleeping powers" (p. 27). Without enquiring why a monotone should be broken by a *flash*, it is evidently a mere juggling with words to speak of "constancy of law" in the case of miracles, and of "violation of law" in that of answers to Prayer, if the word "law" is intended to be understood in some different sense in the two cases. On the other hand, if this is not intended, it is no less evident, as before remarked, that, so far as man can see and natural law is concerned, the one case shews as much "constancy" or "violation" (whichever alternative we like to adopt) as the other; and that any endeavour to distinguish between the two can amount to nothing more than unwarrantable assertion. We see then, plainly enough, that Mr Knight has no objections to urge against Prayer on account of the existence of general laws. We may therefore leave this topic altogether, and, as though no question had ever been entertained with regard to it, proceed to his real objections.

So far as these admit of being condensed into a single proposition, they are as follow :—" We cannot even conceive a single occurrence undirected, if the universe be indeed pervaded by an infinite mind, and an omnipresent

Will. The error consists in the isolation of any one phenomenon or class of phenomena from the rest, and predicating a special direction of these, while others are left out of the reckoning" (p. 25). Now, to meet this abstract with equal brevity, it may be asked, if "*all* phenomena are invariably under the guidance of a supreme Intelligence," in what sense can the guidance of any phenomenon—whether or not effected in answer to Prayer—be said to be "*special*"? The only answer supplied to this obvious question is drawn from the doctrine of Fore-ordination. We must, therefore, next address ourselves to Mr Knight's views upon this subject.

He says:—"The notion of a pre-established harmony between our petitions for physical blessings and their reception, is a widely different one" from "the popular notion that prayer for physical changes can *then and there* determine the course of the event" (pp. 34 and 33). This, however, is only a piece of transcendentalism, and even in a transcendental sense it is easy to see that the two opinions merely refer to obverse aspects of the same truth[1]. Indeed, that there is no absolute difference between them, Mr Knight virtually asserts lower down upon the same page;—"I remember also that there is no 'before' or 'after' with God." "Time is 'an eternal present' to the eternal mind," etc. Passing over this point, however, as immaterial, we shall begin with a quotation. "Why should we draw a line, and exclude *any* physical phenomenon whatever from the category of the fixed and predetermined. By degrees we learn to include all that seems at first anomalous within the majestic sweep of predetermined law......and it rests with them to prove that one single physical event may validly be excluded from the list of the predetermined, before

[1] Cf. p. 140.

they call on us to pray with reference to it. We are bound to reply to this appeal of the naturalist" (p. 189). In these and similar passages the writer assumes, that if a physical change were effected in answer to Prayer, it must *for this reason* be of such a kind that it could not have been foreseen by the Deity, and therefore that such changes can never be permitted to take place. Now, the conclusion here is undoubtedly valid, were the premise so; but as no reasons are (or can be) given in support of the latter, we must deem the former valueless. If "we are bound to reply to this appeal of the naturalist," we are at least entitled to be shewn what there is to answer. It may appear axiomatic to Mr Knight that the wants and desires of a sentient creature cannot have been foreseen by the Deity, although the most minute of physical changes have been accurately preadjusted; but he must bear with those who fail to perceive this self-evident truth. If it seems to him clear beyond the possibility of dispute that a physical change, differing in no respect from others, must yet of necessity be "excluded from the list of the predetermined," only because it is brought about in answer to Prayer; he must pardon those who, perhaps with less insight, but certainly with more argument, have arrived at an opposite conclusion. If, again, to Mr Knight "it is the shallowest of solutions to imagine that the condition of the petitioner and his request were uniquely pre-adjusted to the precise physical occurrences which ensure a reply to his request" (p. 35); he should endeavour to be patient with those who, having perhaps thought less upon the subject, feel inclined to observe, "Why more '*uniquely*' in this than in any other case? Are the desires of humanity of less concern to the Deity than mindless physical sequences? And even if they

are so, must they not still have their place in the general scheme? Once admit fore-ordination in any case, and does it not become silly to attempt to throw discredit upon the same doctrine in other cases, by the mere use of abusive epithets? If Prayer for physical benefits is ever answered (as we believe to be the case), the Prayer and the answer *must* have been fore-ordained to coincide: the question is, what objection can there be found to the possibility of such coincidence?" The only answers I can find to the latter question are as follow:—
"Are not all the antecedent phenomena, both of the material and the spiritual spheres, adjusted with minutest correlation to *all* their subsequent issues? every thought and feeling in the spiritual adjusted to every turning of the wheel of the physical?...In short, the adjustment is either universal, or is non-existent; it is either everywhere or it is nowhere" (p. 36). All this most certainly, but where is the difficulty? Fore-ordination in any case postulates the fitting of all particulars into the general scheme; and if there is any difficulty in believing the system of pre-adjustments to have been thus perfect in the case of physical answers to Prayer—perfect, that is, because including the desire, the petition, and the answer, together with their "minutest correlations to all their subsequent issues,"—this difficulty is of precisely the same degree in the case of any other physical sequence; for the complexity of nature is already so great, that the introduction of so small an item as physically-availing Prayers makes no appreciable difference in our conceptions as to the immensity of the fore-ordaining scheme. In short, it is quite impossible for Mr Knight to escape from the conclusion (abuse it as he may), that if he admits fore-ordination in any case, he thereby opens

a gateway to his whole position—he affords, by way of necessary consequence, a possible and quite conceivable solution of all his other difficulties.

True, he has some objections to the belief that the abstract possibility of fore-ordination being exercised in the case of Prayer is ever realized; and these objections we shall now proceed to examine,—observing only that this question is distinct from the one we are now leaving. 1st, "The supposition reduces Prayer to the sphere of mechanical agency" (p. 33). If by "mechanical agency" is here meant the production (through the Divine Will) of mechanical effects, this, of course, is precisely the point contended for by Mr Knight's opponents, and so cannot be any difficulty in the way of their belief: but if the term is meant to signify *physical force*, the statement is manifestly untrue. 2nd, "It cuts away the freedom of the petitioner, and interferes with the spontaneousness of his request" (p. 33). To this it will be sufficient to reply in the words of the Duke of Argyll's criticism, although these were written in another connection:—"Can any one suppose that the difficulty here set forth can be confined to the sphere of the physical? And can any of us put these difficulties into words without a perfect consciousness that we must be talking nonsense—talking about things which we do not in the least understand?" etc. (p. 472). 3rd, "Results do not prove the existence of any such pre-arrangements. The thousand, the million of unanswered petitions touching external nature effectually negative it. While were it a matter of predetermination that there should be a coincidence between the petition and the reception of the benefit, the former automatically performed would invariably coincide with the latter, like the beat of two pendulums," etc. (p. 34).

This, however, is a very erroneous way of stating the case. Those who believe that some petitions have been fore-ordained to be answered according to the letter, are not therefore bound to believe that all have been similarly fore-ordained. In the case of Leibnitz's doctrine of pre-established harmony between the mind of every man and its environment, invariable coincidence is, of course, essential to the theory; for otherwise the latter would be negatived by facts. But the present case is in no wise parallel, seeing that it is in no wise necessary for the Prayer-theory of pre-adjustment, that every petition should be literally complied with. Because Prayer is supposed to be but one factor determining physical sequences in some cases, it does not therefore follow that it must be physically effectual in all cases—more especially as those who practise it believe that other purposes, besides the accomplishment of physical results, are effected by it.

Mr Knight continues:—" This idea then, of pre-adjustment between the Prayer (say, for the recovery of the sick), and the physical sequences that tend to the result, helps us no way towards a solution. What we wish to know is, whether the one is to any extent causal of the other." There is a little ambiguity about the word "causal" here. Of course if it means causal in the sense in which the term is applied to physical antecedents—*i. e.*, invariable, unconditional, etc.,—there can be no doubt that it is not so. But if by "causal" is meant the validity of means—if it is asked, Is Prayer a mean (together with innumerable others) by which man is enabled in some cases to obtain physical changes?—then the question is correctly stated. Mr Knight proceeds:—
" Suppose the petitioner knew the entire course which

the disease was *certain* to take, his request would simply be, 'Thy will be done:' but, inasmuch as he cannot know its course with certainty, he is tempted to ask that it may be as he wishes it to be, hoping that his request may be helpful toward the desired result." Now this is a perfectly accurate statement of the case. If we are able to foresee the result with *certainty*, then we *know* that nothing short of a visible manifestation of Divine power could alter it; and feeling that we have no right to expect miraculous interference, we accept the inevitable result as the expression of the Divine Will[1]. The case thus resembles, as Mr Knight points out, that of an event already past,—we perceive that it has been thus foreordained. But when the result is *uncertain*, who is to know the Divine Will *before the event?* To assume that Prayer in this case can be of no avail, is merely to assume that Prayer has had no place assigned to it in the prearrangement of all things,—that is, to assume the whole question in dispute. Such an assumption, whether or not it represents the truth, is, of course, as an argument, fallacious; but Mr Knight, in the next sentence, strangely concedes that it is itself untrue :—" I have already indicated how it may be so in the subjective region of our own personality; how a suggestion darted into the mind of a physician may be the direct cause of the use of a remedy which results in the preservation of life." Now, this "suggestion" must in all its relations have been foreordained; otherwise the physical results to which it gave rise would escape altogether from the domain of the preestablished. But if all the relations of this "suggestion" were thus fore-ordained, its relation to the "request" that "darted it into the mind of the physician" must also have been fore-ordained; and this is all that is required

[1] Cf. pp. 95, 6.

by the Prayer-theory. In other words, once admit that a petition to the Deity is capable of "darting a suggestion" into a human mind—whether of the petitioner himself or of another,—which suggestion is in turn capable of effecting a physical change, and any theory of fore-ordination we can rationally frame, must suppose the influence of Prayer to have been so pre-related to the physical forces, that its exercise by man is a mean to the accomplishment of physical results.

This curious admission is repeated in another passage:—" By pre-established harmony they [*i. e.*, spiritual antecedents and physical consequents, and *vice versa*] act and react continually. But it is not, for example, the morality or the immorality of an act (a spiritual antecedent) that determines the physical consequences that result from the act. It is the physical habit (say intemperance) that alone produces the physical detriment, injury to the frame; while that which is spiritual in the act (*i. e.*, its character as moral or immoral) always has its own spiritual consequences within the moral sphere," (p. 24). Now, this admits not only the abstract possibility, but the "continually" realized fact of events not, in a physical sense, causally connected, yet, in consequence of pre-established harmony, following one another in a determinate manner. If this is so in the case of intemperance, why may it not be so in the case of Prayer[1]?

Having now examined the two chief peculiarities of Mr Knight's views, we may descend to others; and these we shall take in the order in which they appear in his second article.

He first gives us his ideas upon the subject of free-will. I confess, however, that I am wholly unable to

[1] Cf. p. 139.

comprehend them; and if Mr Knight should ever favour us with a more lucid exposition of his views, this is certainly one of the points upon which his readers will expect some enlightenment. For example, immediately after the last extract we made, occurs the following:—
"Next, I am told that I 'give up the doctrine of free-will altogether,' by the statement that it is vain to reply to the physicist who maintains the invariability of law, that 'we are continually interfering with the seemingly fixed laws of the universe, and altering their destination,' etc. And I am asked what other answer I have to give? I reply, The only answer that is possible, viz., the conscious fact of freedom. It *is* 'a vain reply' to allege that we can ever escape from the domain of law; because the laws of the physical system always encircle, and invariably rule us in the phenomenal sphere. It is not in *that* region that we are free. It is only in the possession of a transcendental or noumenal freedom, the autocratic power of self-determination." I suppose this "autocratic power" in a man is that which determines whether or not, to take Mr Knight's own example, he will follow a course of dissipation: otherwise I cannot see in what this autocratic power consists. I for one am not conscious of possessing any such "power of self-determination," excepting in so far as I feel myself able to express this power by pursuing some definite line of conduct; and if Mr Knight tells me that my consciousness of this ability is an illusion on my part, I can only tell him in return, not merely what he says he has been told already, viz., that he thus "gives up the doctrine of free-will altogether," but also that he thus deprives me of my existence as an intelligent being. Whether or not the will is free, we can only know of its existence at all by

its enabling us to direct our thoughts and actions; and if anyone supposes that he is "in the possession of a transcendental or noumenal freedom," which is yet incapable of expressing itself in action of any kind whatever, we can only leave him with this strange and unintelligible "possession," hoping that time and quiet may some day restore him to his right mind. I repeat, then, by "autocratic power of self-determination," can only be meant that which determines a course of *action*,—*e.g.*, whether or not a man will commence and continue a course of dissipation. Yet, if this is what the writer means, I cannot see the aim of his discussion. If it is a man's will that brings about the physical results of dissipation, then so far has his will been the agent in directing a highly complex series of physical changes: therefore "in that region" (*i.e.*, the 'phenomenal sphere'), we *are* free, in the sense of being able to direct the physical forces; and this is the only sense for which the Duke of Argyll (whom Mr Knight is here answering) contends.

When, therefore, upon the next page, the doctrine of the Conservation of Energy is referred to in connection with the Divine Will, the difficulty presented is no greater than that which meets us in the case of the same doctrine in its connection with the human will. When Mr Knight is able to explain how it is, that the old and familiar force of the human will, working under the crust of familiar appearances, and influencing existing phenomena, does not make the latter cease to act, although they are modified by it; he may then validly adduce his crushing argument:—"Suppose a new and unfamiliar force to appear breaking through the crust of familiar appearances, and influencing existing phenomena, the latter would not cease to act, although they would be modified by it[1]."

We now proceed to another point: "The Duke of Argyll refers us to 'the reasonableness or the unreasonableness of a petition' touching external nature. But who can judge of the reasonableness or the unreasonableness of such petitions?" (p. 25).

This, however, is no answer to the Duke's criticism. Some things we know it would be unreasonable to ask for: the Duke challenges the right of asserting that this knowledge extends to all phenomena, which have nothing

---

[1] It must be observed that Mr Knight is here dealing with another question, but the above quotation affords a fitting opportunity for briefly disposing of those objections in his first article, which are drawn from the doctrine of the Persistence of Force.

It should be mentioned also, that Mr Knight has previously noticed a very obvious objection to his doctrine of the two spheres. "The Duke of Argyll affirms that we cannot reasonably assert that the spheres of the physical and the spiritual are distinct, because we cannot tell where in our own organism the one begins and the other ends" (p. 23). This difficulty is met by a single sentence of studied obscurity; but Mr Knight can scarcely imagine that he has thus disposed of it. If he is in the smallest degree acquainted with the principal results of physiological enquiry, he cannot fail to be aware that, whatever we may think as to the *causality* of the connection, there can be no reasonable doubt that every thought and feeling of ours is *accompanied* by corresponding molecular changes in our cerebral substance. And it is to be observed that this fact is as fatal to the doctrine of the two spheres, as would be the fact of a causal connection, if such were proved to exist. If I pray for an event X in the moral sphere, which can only be accomplished by effecting a corresponding change Y in the physical, it is manifestly immaterial, for the purposes of the Duke's criticism, whether or not Y is causal of X. Either Prayer is ineffectual in either sphere, or it is effectual in both—at least to the extent of bringing about molecular changes in cerebral substance.

in common but their physical character. To reply that in the doubtful class we can never know whether or not any particular request would appear to ourselves unreasonable, were our knowledge sufficiently advanced; is no answer to the question virtually put by the Duke,— Has Mr Knight any warrant to assume such knowledge as he does, when he asserts that *all* such Prayers are unreasonable?

Upon the next page the following sentence occurs:— " The rational prayer of the devout mind in reference to the order of physical events . . . . . . is in all cases, 'Thy will be done.'" Now this statement, taken in conjunction with that quoted from the Duke, serves very accurately to define the position of those who disagree with Mr Knight. They say in effect:—"Some physical changes we do not ask for, because we see that to do so would be manifestly unreasonable : others we do ask for, because we cannot see this. Yet we doubt not that if we could see further, we should perceive that many petitions which we now place in the second class should be assigned to the first: we therefore pray with reference to this section of the doubtful class, 'Thy will be done.' But in the case of any particular request, we cannot tell whether or not a literal fulfilment would be expedient, or even possible,—*i. e.*, to which section of the doubtful class it belongs: therefore in *every* case we pray, 'Thy will be done;' but this 'rational prayer of the devout mind' is a widely different thing from assuming that in *no* case is it expedient that the Divine Will should be influenced by ours." To this Mr Knight will probably answer in the words which occur upon the same page:— "To suggest a change of that physical order, which is divinely and infallibly directed, is to presume that the

hints of our finite intelligence are fit to regulate the divine procedure," etc. This, however, is merely a begging of the question; for who is to know *before the event* whether or not that it is the divinely directed physical order, which leaves human desires and petitions altogether out of account? This fallacy we have had occasion to notice before, and, although it is many times repeated throughout this article, it may here be disposed of once for all. At the close of the paragraph from which the last extract is taken, the following sentence occurs:—
"The sequences of nature and the ordered evolution of events, are a perpetual revelation of the divine will, and it is for the creature modestly and patiently to discipline his wishes in accordance with it." Most assuredly, after the event; but to say that it is the part of a "creature modestly and patiently to discipline his wishes" (in the sense of abstaining from Prayer) to *whatever* may be in store, is merely to make a disguised *petitio principii*. We are constantly hearing of "the spirit of creaturely submission," of "filial dependence," etc., in this sense, without the writer appearing to be aware that his argument is only valid upon the assumption of his own view of the question in dispute. Only if we *knew* that it is not the Divine Will to answer any of this class of petitions, would there be any room for this "creaturely submission." To shew that we possess this knowledge, is the self-imposed task of the writer; but it is clearly absurd to imagine that he can do this by pointing to the rational consequence of such knowledge, if made out, as the proof of its possession.

Mr Knight next deals with an important objection to his case. "I am continually met by the taunt, 'Is man more free than God, because you say he cannot interfere with his own laws?' I accept the alternative. In one sense it is so: in the *non posse peccare* of the schoolmen. The divine will is necessitated to an absolutely perfect administration of the physical universe. The absolute Lawgiver, Artist, Mechanician, cannot undo what He has done, or do otherwise than He does. It is a simple contradiction in terms to suppose, that with a perfect foresight of the whole process of evolution, the divine Evolver should alter that which His omniprescience predetermined, and bring about an equally perfect result." We have already seen that the last sentence here embodies an unwarrantable assumption, viz., that the desires and requests of man have no part or lot in the preestablished harmony of events: the other sentences contain an assumption no less unwarranted. Of course, if the direction of the natural forces by the Deity in response to Prayer is a token of imperfect administration on His part, the whole question is decided—the truth of this assertion being the ultimate question in dispute. When Mr Knight's opponents ask, "Why may not the Deity direct the physical forces in answer to Prayer, when we know that man can do so?" and when Mr Knight answers, "Because, if He did so, it would be a case of *peccare;*" he is merely re-stating his opinion in the guise of an answer. What his opponents want to know is,—*why* should such direction be a case of *peccare*—why should that be the only "perfect administration of the physical universe," which leaves human desires altogether out of consideration? We know that the direction of the physical forces (whether or not in answer to petition) is no sign of error or of imperfection in the case of man, "and we may well decline to accept it as a self-evident truth with regard to God[1]."

[1] Duke of Argyll in *Contemporary Review*. Cf. Chap. v. §§ 10—12.

This dogmatic assumption of Mr Knight's is singularly opposed to other passages in his article, *e.g.*, in the next paragraph :—" The very essence of my whole contention is that the Divine Nature is so singularly revealed in its omnipresence within every element or movement of the physical universe, that whatever comes to pass is the necessary outcome of its agency; every force and every change in nature being an apocalypse of God, and every link in the chain of its sequences attesting the indwelling Presence." Mr Knight has doubtless some good reasons for making this broad distinction between the directive influence of the Deity as universally immediate in all physical sequences, and yet absolutely impotent in responding to Prayer; but if he has such reasons, he surely cannot fail to be aware that their total absence from his writings gives the close apposition of such antithetical doctrines the semblance of a glaring inconsistency.

There is another remark to be made on this last quotation. On the previous page Mr Knight objects to Prayer for physical results, on the score of its requesting "*an alteration of the course of nature.*" But, if " every link in the chain of nature's sequences attests the indwelling presence of God," how can there in any case—*i. e.*, whether or not this kind of Prayer is effectual—be such a thing as "an alteration in the course of nature?"—the "necessary outcome of the Divine agency" being then only apparent when its effects are accomplished. In a transcendental sense, a change may be supposed to take place in the Divine counsels in answer to Prayer (although, if Prayer is effectual, our warrant for this supposition would indeed be hard to establish); but if "*whatever* comes to pass in nature is an apocalypse of God," then, manifestly, it is only to the mind of God, if to any, that the phrase "change in the course of nature" can possess any meaning. The truth is, that Mr Knight, in trying to confine the Physicist's objections to Prayer within the limits of a Christian Theism, has not escaped the calamity which is so liable to attend the putting of new wine into old bottles.

The next point of any importance raised, is the very obvious "demand of the scientific world why we should separate a class of physical phenomena from the rest,... —why we should regard the rain-law as more amenable to fresh direction, than the sun-law or the force of gravitation." It will be remembered that this "demand" has already been fully answered, both by the Duke of Argyll and by the present criticism[1]. Nevertheless, as Mr Knight again presents the same argument in the disguise of an altered phraseology, it may not be superfluous to refute it yet more thoroughly. The argument, then, is palpably illogical, because it clearly has no bearing whatever upon the question in dispute,—it being believed by everyone that Prayer of this kind is only effectual (if at all) in a hidden manner. The supposed argument is therefore nothing more than the statement of an irrelevant fact,— it being no argument against a belief, to make assertions which are admitted as axiomatic by those who hold that belief. The question between Mr Knight and his opponents is not, Are flagrant manifestations of Divine power ever vouchsafed in answer to Prayer? but, Is Mr Knight's classification of the "two spheres" a legitimate one? Are requests for small physical changes as "unreasonable" as requests for large ones? Is it the mere fact of an event having a physical character at all (independently of its magnitude), that renders petition for it unavailing?

[1] See p. 216, and pp. 220—1. Also *Burney Essay*, pp. 95—6.

And, in answer to these questions, the burden of proof lies with Mr Knight to shew that his classification *is* legitimate,—*i. e.*, that things which it is reasonable and unreasonable to ask for, correspond respectively with the moral and physical spheres;—and to do this it can be of no avail to point to *some* things within the physical sphere, which his opponents concede to be unalterable; for this in no wise assists him in establishing his classification—that is, in proving *all* things within the physical sphere to be similarly unalterable. The point which Mr Knight has to make out is, that those things which agree in possessing a physical character, likewise agree in possessing an unalterable character; and it is no more a proof of this point to shew that some physical things are likewise unalterable things, than to shew that some animals have four legs would be any proof that all animals are quadrupeds. In short, the analogy which Mr Knight endeavours to institute does not support his argument, but depends for its existence upon his argument being made out.

On page 30 there is a good opportunity afforded for discussing an argument of which Mr Knight is particularly fond. "The evolution and succession of phenomena are so infallibly adjusted, the balance is so perfect, that when what we desire to be present around us is absent, it is because it (or its equivalent) if present would be misplaced," etc. etc. This argument is frequently repeated, without the writer appearing to know that it is itself incapable of proof. The most celebrated of our Natural Theologians tells us that in Nature he saw Beneficence, but not Optimism; and if the poll of the present generation were taken, I think he would have the majority. Be this how it may, there can be no doubt that the mere assertion of a disputed fact is but of small assistance to either side of a disputed question. In the words of the Duke of Argyll; "That what we mistake for banes may often be really blessings, is very true, and ought always to be remembered. But that all we enjoy, and all we suffer, are given to us in measure absolutely fixed, and absolutely incapable of any other distribution than that which is determined by a purely physical necessity, has not been proved, or even indicated by any fact of science or any analogy of nature" (p. 469).

It is a curious fact that Mr Knight himself, a page or two further on (33), expressly negatives his own argument, by conceding the falsity of the Optimism theory. He says;—"Nor do I deny the legitimacy of petitioning God for the removal of disease, or of all that is interfering with the perfection of terrestrial life. On the contrary, I affirm and enforce the duty of doing so. I maintain, however, the unlawfulness of seeking alterations of nature which are interferences with existing law." If these sentences mean that disease is not amenable to "law," it is evident that this term must here be used by Mr Knight in some unintelligible sense, or, more plainly, that he is writing nonsense: if otherwise, he flatly contradicts his own assumption as to the truth of Optimism; and, I may add, dissolves all his previous distinctions between "the two spheres."

A few pages further on Mr Knight again returns to his Optimism argument (36), but as he throughout supposes that "the felt wants of the suppliant" expressed in Prayer, can in no case, by the mere fact of their presence, render a certain course of events preferable to some other one, which in the absence of such wants might be most so; even if we grant him his argument, it is invalid except upon the assumption of the whole question in dispute.

The next paragraph is occupied with the same assumption in another form, viz., that Prayer in the sense of petition for physical changes is not acceptable to the Deity;—an assertion whose only value in the absence of argument (and no argument is here possible), is to shew that if the writer were in the position of "the omnipotent Administrator," he would altogether disregard such "irregular petitioning[1]."

Another argument is set forth on page 37. "We can never be certain that, if we receive any particular physical blessing, others, who have a better right to it than we have, may not be deprived of it." This is undoubtedly true, and would be a valid objection to Prayer for such blessings, were Mr Knight's definition of "the warrant for presenting petitions for physical benefits," a legitimate one. This definition is, "the felt wants of the suppliant," but such a definition is not complete. To make it so we must add, "together with his belief in the power and wisdom of God." Now this addition destroys the force of the above objection; for it expresses the fact that the petitioner, in detailing his "felt wants," does not do so unconditionally—feels that to do this "would be to invade and not to pray." Consequently, if the interests of two petitioners clash, in so far as they are *petitioners*, there is no difficulty, for each re-

---

[1] "People in general seem to think that they have used a very powerful argument, when they have said, that to suppose some proposition true, would be a reflection on the goodness of the Deity. Put into the simplest possible terms, their argument is, 'If it had depended on me, I would not have made the proposition true, therefore it is not true.'"—Mill, *On the Fallacies of Simple Inspection.*

quests that what upon the whole is best may be that which his petitions shall effect. They both express their desires, yet both agree in leaving the disposition of results to the "wisdom of God"—pray, in the sense previously explained, "Thy will be done[1]."

But this introduces us to another mock-argument. Mr Knight perpetually speaks as if the mere fact of petitioning for a physical change were tantamount to asking for that which the petitioner knows to be against the Divine Will. Throughout both his Essays he assumes that requests for physical benefits are incompatible with "the suppressed premise of all true Prayer," *i.e.*, desire for the accomplishment of the Will of God. But no one is foolish enough to pray for that which he believes to be against the Divine Will. The point that Mr Knight has to establish is, that the results expressed by such petitions *are* against the Divine Will; and the mere assertion of his own belief cannot influence the belief of those who think otherwise. The reservation, "if it be possible," cannot be shewn incompatible with requests for physical changes, unless it has previously been shewn that the granting of any such request is in the nature of things impossible.

Mr Knight then proceeds to another point: "Stress ought also to be laid upon the non-verifiable character of all alleged answers to Prayer for physical good...No record of *coincidences* can prove a causal connection, or

---

[1] It is no doubt true (as may legitimately be urged), that petitions for physical benefits are, from the nature of the case, much more liable in this manner to clash, than are petitions of any other kind. This fact, however, has clearly no bearing upon the only question with which we are concerned, viz., Are *all* petitions for physical changes unavailing?

even suggest it, unless the instances are exceptionally numerous, and unless other causes leading to the result are excluded by the rigid methods of verification." Conversely, no record of failures are of any avail on the other side (see p. 34), so long as any of these apparent answers remain—unless it could be proved that the causal connection between Prayer and its answer, if it exists, must be unconditional. As this position likewise can never be proved, or even suggested as probable, verification upon either side is clearly rendered impossible by the conditions of the case. Still this argument is valid so far as it goes, and will require to be examined at greater length hereafter. As presented by Mr Knight, however, it is not of much value, seeing that those who believe in the physical validity of Prayer, do not regard such validity as the equivalent of miraculous power. The argument, as it here stands, is at best a negative one; since it cannot be proved, or rendered in the smallest degree probable, that if Prayer is of any physical validity, it must therefore of necessity be amenable to the "rigid methods of verification." And here we may repeat, that it is no effectual argument against a belief, to make assertions which are admitted as axiomatic by those who hold that belief. On the other hand, those who hold that belief are fully entitled to challenge the right of asserting that any particular coincidence is *only* a coincidence, unless those who make the assertion are able on independent grounds to demonstrate, or to render probable, the falsehood of that belief.

Mr Knight concludes the list of his arguments by affirming, that the only sense in which we are told to pray for our daily bread, is that of "including within the request all the specific particulars by which the petition could possibly be answered;" and that in praying "Thy will be done," "our request is substantially, though indirectly, met by whatsoever comes to pass." Surely, then, Prayer for physical benefits ceases, not only to be a duty, but to be an exercise worthy of rational creatures. There can be no doubt that Prayer for Bread refers directly to numerous complex physical changes, necessarily involved in the bringing about of the result. If these changes are not believed by the petitioner to be in any way influenced by his petition, where is the sense or the piety in his making it? As regards himself, his Bread would come to him in exactly the same manner whether or not he asked for it: as regards the Deity, is it reverent to suppose that He looks with favour upon a petitionary form of Prayer, uttered by one who regards all such petitions as "the most miserable of mockeries"? Surely we may appropriate another sentence from the next paragraph[1], and add, "that if Prayer be absolutely powerless as a 'physical' agency in human life, there is not only a logical inconsistency in all 'such petitionary forms,' there would also be a latent hypocrisy in their use." Yet Mr Knight adds, "In short, since all unselfish prayer touching outward things contemplates the universal good along with the individual benefit, our special [observe, *special*] requests (say for rain, or an abundant harvest) may be responded to by the descent of the former, or the ingathering of the latter, *anywhere over the whole area of the globe.* We petition for rain, and it falls

---

[1] This paragraph deals with another class of petitions, viz., those for spiritual benefits, uttered by men disbelieving in the efficacy of *all* Prayer—a precisely analogous case, it seems to me, to the one above commented on, although Mr Knight in the latter case advocates petition, and in the former condemns it.

amongst the Andes: we ask for fair weather, and the sun shines out upon the plains of India; but our requests are fulfilled as truly, and much more wisely, than if we experienced what we sought at home." That our requests may be thus fulfilled "more wisely," all will admit; but that they can be thus fulfilled "as truly," all will deny. If the element of *relation* is not satisfied by answers to Prayer, it is only by the most violent of metaphors that such answers can be said to be given at all. To tell an agonized farmer that his often and earnestly-repeated Prayer for rain, has been answered by the merciful Jehovah, in the form of a copious descent amongst the barren steeps of the Andes; will convey the impression to his unsophisticated mind, either that his request has been strangely misunderstood, or that he might as well have addressed himself to Baal and Ashtaroth. Philosophy, however, has a widening influence upon the mind; and those who have pursued its study with the same degree of success as Mr Knight, cannot fail in all things to drink the sweet comforts of religion; for only by the tutored intellect can that profound consolation of a Scriptural faith be realized, which is so pathetically rendered in the lines

> "The Sun by night thee shall not smite,
> Nor yet the Moon by day."

Mr Robertson sets forth his views regarding the physical efficacy of Prayer, in a sermon upon the text, "Not as I will, but as Thou wilt." I may observe that this sermon contrasts favourably with the articles we have just examined, in respect of its temperate tone. It is also marked by that pleasing lucidity and terseness of style, which is so eminently characteristic of this author.

The portion of the sermon with which we are concerned is Section II.—" Erroneous notions of what prayer is."

Mr Robertson begins by asserting that all these "erroneous notions" "are contained in that conception which He negatived, 'As I will'......In the text it is said distinctly that this is not the aim of prayer, nor its meaning. '*Not* as I will.' The wish of man does not determine the Will of God." The entire argument, then, is, that because Christ was refused an answer to His petition on one occasion, therefore Christians are not to expect an answer to their petitions on any occasion. Let not this be thought a false representation of the argument: it is merely a statement of its logical basis. If the fact that Christ was once refused an answer to His petition, proves that "the wish of man does not determine the Will of God (*i.e.*, on no occasion exerts any influence upon that Will), then it necessarily follows that all petitions— whether for temporal or for spiritual benefits—are invalid. The fact that Mr Robertson on the next page expressly repudiates this position, does not in any wise preserve his argument: it merely shews, either that his premises are erroneous, or that they prove more than he desires. Fortunately, it does not require much penetration to see which of these alternatives represents the truth. The premises are manifestly erroneous. If the Prayer of Christ that the cup should pass from Him had had exclusive reference to any one physical sequence, and if no other Prayer of His relating to physical sequences had been recorded; then Mr Robertson might have logically pointed to this position—singular then both in nature and result—as indicating (though not even then as proving), that the Divine Will makes a clear distinction between petitions for physical, and those for spiritual, well-being. The Prayer of Christ, however, on this occasion was *not* for the accomplishment of any particular physical sequence; but rather that some change should take place in the minds of His persecutors—a province in which, according to Mr Robertson, even human Prayer is abundantly effectual. On the other hand, no one can say that when Christ prayed for any particular physical result, it was ever denied Him. On the contrary, it is a remark of Paley's that none of our Lord's miracles were tentative; and they were nearly all preceded by Prayer.

Thus, no argument can be gathered from the fact that Christ was once denied the specific result He prayed for, to prove that any distinction exists in the Divine Mind between prayers for physical benefits and those for spiritual. The only doctrine that can be gathered from this fact is, that in *no* case can we be certain whether or not we shall receive the specific thing for which we pray.

The statement of this doctrine serves to introduce us to another point. Mr Robertson throughout his sermon very unfairly assumes, that belief in the physical efficacy of Prayer necessitates belief in its *unconditional* efficacy; and from this assumption proceeds to shew, that because Prayer for physical results cannot always be *necessarily* answered, therefore such Prayer can never be answered at all. Stated thus baldly, the argument is self-evidently absurd; but any one who will carefully read the sermon in question, will perceive that such is the essence of the discussion. A few quotations will suffice. "What we ask is, whether the good derived has been exactly this, that Prayer brought the *very thing* wished for." "It is enough for the disciple that he be as his master, and the servant as his lord." "What Christ's prayer was not efficacious to do, that ours is not *certain* to effect."

"Consider the danger of vanity and supineness resulting from the fulfilment of our desires as a *necessity*." "Two Christian armies meet for battle—Christian men on both sides pray for success to their own arms. Now if victory be given to Prayer, *independent of other considerations*, we are driven to the pernicious principle, that success is the test of Right." Of course, if we set out with the assumption that Prayer for physical results differs from other forms of petition, in that, if it is efficacious, it must be so *necessarily;* then the task of proving it non-efficacious becomes childishly easy ; for no man in his senses would imagine himself competent to direct even a portion of the physical Universe. What our warrant for this assumption is, however, I am unable to divine. If "it is enough for the disciple that he be as his master," and if that Master's petitions were not responded to of necessity; why should the disciples assume that their petitions must either in every case be responded to of necessity, or never in any case be responded to at all? In short, because those persons who disagree with Mr Robertson, believe that Prayer for physical benefits resembles Prayer for other things, in being a factor conducive to the accomplishment of desired results in *some* cases ; they are not therefore held to the belief, that Prayer for physical benefits differs from Prayer for other things (such, for example, as that set forth in the text of Mr Robertson's sermon), in that the desired results must necessarily ensue in *all* cases.

Mr Robertson's other arguments need not detain us long. The division occupied by that from general laws, must, in accordance with our design, be here passed over. The argument "Try it by fact" has been so much more ably presented by Mr Galton, that we may here neglect it. The argument drawn from "the prejudicial results of such a belief," is not so much an argument as a statement of opinion[1]. The argument that the belief in question "would be most dangerous as a criterion of our spiritual state," is only valid upon the assumption already discussed, viz., that if physical sequences are ever modified by petition at all, they must always be so "*infallibly.*"

Mr Brooks expounds his opinions on the Prayer-question in two sermons[2]. His mode of argumentation is as simple as it is dogmatic. He begins by tacitly assuming that his conception of the Divine method of government undoubtedly represents the truth, not only in a scientific, but likewise in an absolute sense. In other words, he tacitly assumes that natural law as we conceive it, must necessarily represent the whole and the only manner in which the Deity sees fit to govern His physical Universe. By thus dogmatically asserting that the mode in which the Deity governs the Universe is, to our faculties, fully conceivable, and accurately conceived; Mr Brooks opens the way by the further assertion, that any action on the part of the Deity in response to Prayer would amount to a different kind of causation from that ordinarily employed—or, to use his own term, to a miracle. It will thus be seen that Mr Brooks' view is substantially that with which my other Essay has to deal; and so can only be properly refuted by examining his right to assume that our conception of natural law represents the absolute truth, and further, his right to assume that natural law, even as thus conceived, stands in precisely the same relation to the Deity as it stands to us. This

[1] Cf. *Burney Prize Essay*, 1873, p. 125.
[2] *Christ in Modern Life*, 6th ed., pp. 132—159.

question, as before observed, has been exhaustively treated elsewhere; so we must here content ourselves with remarking that Mr Brooks has no shadow of a right to assume that an answer to Prayer, supposing it vouchsafed, would entail any deviation whatever from the ordinary modes of the supreme causative influence, absolutely considered. For all that Mr Brooks, or any other man, can logically assert to the contrary, even a miracle may be to the Deity precisely the same, so far as its causation is concerned, as any other physical phenomena whatever,—the mere fact that to our very partial vision, the causation *appears* different in the two cases, being no logical warrant for concluding that it must therefore of necessity be so in an absolute sense.

The doctrine of the conservation of energy is the stronghold on which Mr Brooks mainly relies. It is desirable, therefore, to enter into this subject more fully than we did in the passing allusion we made to it when treating of Mr Knight's opinions.

It is said, "Force can be infinitely converted, it cannot—unless we suppose the intervention of a miracle—be created." If the word "miracle" here were only intended to signify a mode of causation not usually *perceived*, there would, of course, be no objection to the statement. But if, as is evidently the case, the word "miracle" is intended to signify a mode of causation which does not usually *take place*, then the statement is highly objectionable, because pretending to endow a wholly unwarrantable assumption with the character of scientific accuracy. Mr Brooks is merely violating his rational faculty, when he presumes to assert that the doctrine of the persistence of force has anything other than a relative signification. The mere fact that force is, in its relation to us, persistent, affords no shadow of a guarantee for supposing that it is likewise so in its relation to the Creator; for we are unable to shew that any similarity subsists between the nature of man and that of the Deity, in respect of creative power. Could any such similarity be demonstrated, we might have some feeble analogy on which to rely: as it is, we have not even an analogy to appeal to. Hence, for anything that man can ever know, creation may be a continually-acting prerogative of Deity; and so far from the scientific doctrine of the conservation of energy being any impediment to the scriptural doctrine of the efficacy of Prayer, it has, I think, been made sufficiently evident, by the lengthy argument devoted to this subject in my other Essay, that so far as the one doctrine in any way affects the other, its influence tends wholly in the opposite direction. This much, at any rate, we may safely assert :—until Mr Brooks has shewn us some satisfactory reason why the Deity, if ever He exerts creative power, should exhibit the fact of His doing so to man, we must conclude that the fundamental argument goes for nothing[1].

[1] Compare Mill, *Fallacies of Generalization*, *Logic*, II. pp. 360—1. "There are certain generalizations which *must* be groundless: experience cannot afford the necessary conditions for establishing them by a correct induction,".etc.'; and of such the above is as good an example as could be adduced. Compare also, *Fallacies of Simple Inspection*, ibid. p. 323.—"It is strange that any one, after such a warning, should rely implicitly on the evidence *à priori* of such a proposition as that nothing can be made out of nothing....Such a doctrine is no more a self-evident truth, than the ancient maxim that a thing cannot act where it is not, which probably is not now believed by any educated person in Europe...*Ex nihilo nihil fit;* why? because having never known any physical product without a pre-existing physical material, we *cannot*, or think we cannot, *imagine* a

Having thus assumed that the creative energy is now of necessity in a state of abeyance, Mr Brooks next proceeds to assume that even were this not so, creative energy does not admit of degrees[1]. "There is nothing little or nothing great in the motions of the universe. The demand for the creation of the smallest conceivable wave of new force, is as serious a demand as that for the creation of force equivalent to that which builds up a volcano in a night." Truly Mr Brooks appears to possess an enviable amount of insight regarding the capabilities of the Divinity. According to the doctrine just set forth, the creation of the Solar System was not a whit more difficult, so to speak, than that of any one of its smallest constituent atoms! Perhaps this is so; but if it is so, we should at all events like to hear from what source Mr Brooks has derived his information[2].

After adducing a very hackneyed illustration, our author proceeds to reflect, "When I think of these things, I find it absolutely impossible, without the grossest creation out of nothing. But this may in itself be as conceivable as gravitation without an intervening medium, which Newton thought too great an absurdity for any person of a competent faculty of philosophical thinking to admit: and even supposing it not conceivable, this, for aught we know, may be merely one of the limitations of our very limited minds, and not in nature at all." Compare also *Burney Essay*, p. 156 and p. 161, foot-notes.

[1] Cf. p. 143.
[2] It will be observed that this statement of Mr Brooks differs from a somewhat similar one of Prof. Tyndall's:—"Without the disturbance of a natural law quite as serious as the .... rolling of the river St Lawrence up the Falls of Niagara, no act of humiliation ... can call one shower from heaven." Prof. Tyndall is perfectly justified in making this assertion; for it relates to a merely human conception, and is therefore strictly scientific. Mr Brooks is wholly unjustified in making the assertion above quoted; for it refers directly to the Deity and His relation to the Universe, and is therefore super-scientific.

violation of my reason, to pray for or against rain." Clearly so, if we grant him his premises; but we have just seen that *we* cannot do this "without the grossest violation of reason." The next sentences run, " But you will say that God could do it if He liked. I do not say No to that, but I have no hesitation in saying that I should not dare to ask Him to change the order of the universe at my desire." Mr Brooks, then, does not deny the possibility of creation; but merely the will of the Deity to create—or, which is the same thing, the fact of creation taking place,—and this, as we shall immediately see, because of the consequences involved. " Once a man is acquainted with the processes of nature, and realises what the conservation of force means, and the results which would follow from the smallest possible amount of new force—results, the end of which he could never see, which little here might be stupendous elsewhere (for the fall of a miraculous shower here might necessitate an earthquake (?) elsewhere and destroy 20,000 souls)—he would not dare to pray for five minutes rain which was not naturally coming." Any argument that there is here would clearly apply with equal force to human action of any kind, unless it could be shewn that physical results consequent upon Prayer spread further into the nexus of natural phenomena, than do similar physical results effected by the ordinary action of human will—and to maintain this doctrine would be to destroy that of the conservation of energy. Further, even if this doctrine could be made out, it would not militate against belief in the physical efficacy of Prayer, unless it could be shewn that the directive ability of the Supreme Being is inadequate to provide for the fractional addition, which such physically-availing prayers would make to the already enormous complicity of physical sequences. Next we come to the question, "And if he believed that God would grant his prayer, would he dare, ought he to dare, to meet the tremendous responsibilities involved? I could not ask God to create new force, even if I believed He would do so." It is hard to know whether this is written in earnest or in jest. I have heard it urged as an objection against marriage, that "the tremendous responsibilities involved" in undertaking the endeavour to produce an indefinite number of rational, responsible, and immortal beings, more than compensate for any advantages which may attend the wedded state. Doubtless the balance would fall on the side indicated, if such quaint conceptions regarding human responsibilities were supposed to be rational; and if Mr Brooks' readers will bear this illustration in mind, they are not likely to be much affected by his present argument[1].

The sermon proceeds: "It may be urged that as human will can modify the future results of things occurring now by changing the conditions under which those results will develope themselves—as, for example, I could change the future climate of a country by cutting down its forest—so it may be a spiritual law that the human will, acting on God's will through His appointed channel prayer, may cause God to interpose conditions which will change the mode in which existing results are taking

---

[1] This argument is also employed by Mr Knight (joined with his argument from fore-ordination,) and is alluded to in my other Essay thus:—"It is no more difficult to believe that any fresh increment of force should have its functions for all time assigned to it, than that any equal quantity of previously existing force should originally have had its eternal cycle of transformation foreordained." See p. 157.

place. But the two members of the comparison are not equivalent. The modification of climate by man is the result of natural forces naturally used, through a period of many years. The modification of existing climatal phenomena—the heat which now prevails, for example—would be the result of a sudden interposition; it would not be natural but præternatural—it would be a miracle." Here again Mr Brooks assumes, that the Deity stands to physical sequences in the same practical relation as he himself does—that, practically, natural law is to the Deity what natural law is to man. By branding with the hard term " præternatural," any action on the part of the Deity which is not supposed exactly similar in kind or method to that possible to man, Mr Brooks is merely deceiving us with the semblance of an argument; for the only question in dispute is as to whether or not the implied analogy is a fair one. Had Mr Brooks said, "the two members of the comparison *may* not be equivalent," there could have been no objection to the statement—only in this case, of course, there would have been no answer to the perfectly logical objection, "it *may* be a spiritual law that the human will, acting on God's will through His appointed channel prayer, *may* cause God to interpose," etc. In other words, Mr Brooks is not a whit more justified in his dogmatic assertion, "the two members of the comparison *are* not equivalent," than would the supposed objector be in stating, "it *is* a spiritual law," etc. The mere fact that *if* the members of the comparison were equivalent, the action of the Deity would not be through the same set of laws as the action of man, in no wise justifies us in assuming that the action of the Deity would *therefore*, even in that case, require to be miraculous, *i. e.*, extraordinary. The mere fact that "the modification of climate by man is the result of natural forces naturally used, through a period of many years," in no wise justifies us in assuming that the same result may not be attainable by the Deity in other ways, equally "natural," and just as "naturally used"—the word "natural" being understood in the only sense that is here philosophically legitimate, viz., that of "ordinary," so far as the Deity is concerned. In brief, wherever Mr Brooks has occasion to suppose the Deity producing any series of effects in any other way than is possible to man, he employs the term "miraculous." Yet, for anything that Mr Brooks can ever know, there may not be the slightest analogy in any case between human causation and Divine—the mere fact of our being conditioned under a given code of general laws, affording no indication that the Deity is likewise so conditioned. Even the most startling miracle may not represent any deviation from the ordinary modes of the supreme causality—the mere fact of its appearing unusual to us, not affording the faintest shadow of a logical probability that it represents any unusual mode of action on the part of the Deity.

Mr Brooks virtually concedes this in the next paragraph:—"But it may be again replied: God could do it within the sphere of His own laws. He could introduce a higher law, or rearrange existing laws in a new combination, and so modify the fall of rain or banish the pestilence, and doing so without a violation of law, it would not be a miracle. I am sure, that the only true statement of a miracle that can be received, is that it is the result of a prearrangement by which the ordinary course of nature changes step, as it were, for a moment, by the will of God, for some great spiritual result. A miracle conceived of as a violation of order is an absolute impossibility. The alteration, therefore, of the course of the weather by God's rearrangement (?) into a new combination of existing phenomena *is* a miracle...In whatever way we look at the question, then, we pray for a miracle when we pray for the slightest change in the normal state of the universe." Assuredly, when the word "miracle" is thus defined; but this definition eviscerates every argument in which the word occurs. The definition of a miracle here given is, "the result of a pre-arrangement by which the ordinary course of nature changes step, for a moment, by the will of God." Clearly, in this definition, the changing step must be intended to signify a change *in relation to man;* for to suppose that nature changes step *in its relation to God*, would simply be "to conceive of a miracle as a violation of order" (the mere fact of disorder having been pre-arranged, in no wise tending to alter its character), and this is declared "an absolute impossibility."

According to Mr Brooks' own shewing, then, there is no reason why we should not pray for physical benefits with the reasonable hope of being answered. Let it be fully granted that "we pray for a miracle when we pray for the slightest change in the normal state of the universe," and the proposition is meaningless if, on the one hand, the word "miracle" is expressly guarded from the imputation of referring to any change in the Divine methods of procedure, and if, on the other, as of course must be granted, answers to Prayer for physical results, supposing them vouchsafed, must be inconspicuous.

Understanding, then, that the word "miracle" as used by Mr Brooks simply means an instance of ordinary causal action on the part of the Deity, whether or not appearing extraordinary to man, we proceed to the next paragraph:—"Are such unknown miracles now continually performed at the call of individual men who do not see beyond the present? Those who still believe that the miraculous is common in nature may pray with perfect consistency for rain, or fair weather, but they ought clearly to understand that they are asking God to perform miracles." Doubtless this remark is intended to startle, but it fails of its effect if we refuse to allow the word "miracle" to be played upon at pleasure. According to the definition just examined, a miracle, so far as the Deity is concerned, is precisely the same in its causation, as is any other effect of the Divine activity; so that, in this sense, every Theist is bound to "believe that the miraculous is," not only "common," but universal "in nature." The word "miracle," however, is here evidently intended to depart from the definition of it just given; for in the next sentence we read, "But those who cannot believe this, those who hold that a miracle is derogatory to the true idea of God, unless it is performed for great and ascertainable spiritual ends—ends which appeal to our reason and excuse the miracle—cannot pray for rain, or for fair weather, or for the sudden removal of a pestilence, without idolatry." This mode of varying the signification of a word essential to an argument is highly reprehensible—especially when the latter concludes with so dogmatic a piece of effrontery.

Mr Brooks next commits himself to the fallacy already pointed out as occurring in Mr Robertson's discourse. If the Deity ever answers Prayer with a physical equivalent, "natural laws," it is said, "would be then at the mercy of every religious man. Some extremely good and spiritual persons are very imprudent in the practical work of the world. If their prayer about rain, fine weather, thunderstorms, pestilence, and other things, were answered, and answered in accordance with a spiritual law, so that, in fact, by the hypothesis, *it must be answered*, what a state of utter confusion we should be in! We could not be certain of the sun rising at its proper time," etc. The italics are Mr Brooks', and are apparently adopted for the sake of throwing out the fallacy into the strongest relief. As it has already been sufficiently explained, we need not return to it here.

The first sermon sums up with the assumed conclusion (grounded on the equivocal use of the term "miracle" already pointed out), that if the Deity ever regulates the course of nature at the instance of Prayer, such regulation must, for this reason, be "an interference in an extraordinary manner with its usual course." "I do not think that prayer can check the cholera or divert the lightning. At the same time I believe that God could stay the rain and dismiss the pestilence, if it were His will, at the voice of prayer. He may do so for all I know, but it would make me miserable to think it were so." I have quoted the closing sentence of the argument, for the sake of hailing it as the most philosophical one that is to be found throughout the course of the discussion. It is only a pity that this philosophical admission at the close of the argument, should so ill accord with the other expressions we have had to examine.

The sermon concludes with drawing a distinction, similar to that which Mr Knight draws between the two spheres. We are told that "directly we ought not to pray for interference with the course of nature;" but that we may reasonably expect petition to affect the course of nature "*indirectly;*" since "God is the source of all thought in the brain," and may create thoughts in man which in turn may affect the course of nature. Now we have already seen, when examining Mr Knight's views, that any such distinction as this is wholly untenable—the mere fact that every thought and feeling of ours is accompanied by a physical change of cerebral substance, being sufficient to annihilate the distinction. If, as we have just been told, "there is nothing little, or nothing great, in the motions of the universe," how are we to believe that the molecules of brain-matter are more amenable to the influence of Prayer than are the "forces which build up a volcano in a night"? Mr Brooks meets this criticism in the next sermon (pp. 148—9) with the words, "But this goes upon the supposition, of which no proof can be given, that motion in the brain *is* thought and feeling." In this statement, however, Mr Brooks is entirely wrong[1]. All that the objection need assert is that which physiology fully entitles it to assert, viz., that thought and feeling are invariably *attended* with "motion in the brain." When Mr Brooks says, "Because the thought that two and two make four is accompanied by

---

[1] He is wrong, not only with reference to the nature of this objection (*vide supra*), but also with reference to the whole logical *status* of the subject. "Our *notions*, a configuration of fibres! What kind of a logician must he be who thinks that a phenomenon is *defined* to *be* the condition on which he supposes it to depend? Accordingly he says soon after, not that our ideas are caused by, or consequent on, certain organic phenomena, but 'our ideas *are* animal motions of the organs of sense.' And this confusion runs through the four volumes of the *Zoonomia*; the reader never knows whether the writer is speaking of the effect, or of its supposed cause; of the idea, a state of mental consciousness, or of the state of the nerves and brain which he considers it to presuppose."—MILL, *Logic*, II. p. 341.

an atomic change, it does not follow that that atomic change is the thought;" the answer, supplied by implication, is—Clearly not, but the fact of *accompaniment* is all that the objection requires. Mr Brooks, indeed, proceeds to confuse himself and his readers, by introducing the wholly distinct question as to the nature of human will. The question, however, is not, Is human will "a mode of physical force"? but, Can the Deity originate a train of thought in man, with the accompanying series of physical changes, without causing a "touch of new force"? The analogy, "this is done every day by man to man," if it proves anything, proves a great deal too much. What are the factors of the problem? Thought is accompanied by molecular change, and the will of one man can cause such molecular change in the brain of another. In so doing, is the will of man interfering less with physical nature, than it is when producing an exactly similar amount of molecular change in any other department of physical nature? To answer Yes, would be to deny the conservation of energy. Therefore, if any analogy obtains between the action of human mind and that of the Divine mind in this particular section of physical nature (*i. e.*, molecular changes in the brain of man), we cannot but conclude, unless we deny the conservation of energy, that a similar analogy obtains between the action of human mind and that of the Divine mind in other departments of physical nature—*i. e.*, that there is nothing more antecedently incredible in the supposition that the Divine mind affects physical nature at the instance of petition, than that human mind similarly affects it. In other words, the argument has nothing whatever to do with the question as to the *nature* of the human mind, but merely with the *physical effects* it is able to produce; and if, as cannot be denied, the production of physical effects is a necessary condition to the production of a train of thought, nothing more is gained to the argument by pointing to the ability of the mind to produce this particular kind of physical effect, than would be gained to it by pointing to the ability of the mind to produce any other kind of physical effect whatever. On the contrary, as just observed, if this analogy between the action of the human mind and that of the Divine mind could be made out, it would tend to annihilate the argument altogether; for it would concede more than the foregoing examination has found sufficient for the destruction of the argument, viz., that no analogy can be positively said to subsist between the Divine mind and the human, in respect of their action upon physical nature.

It is refreshing to turn from the loose reasoning and rhetorical dogmatism of these reverend gentlemen, to the strictly logical and strongly convincing argument of Mr Galton, conveyed as it is in a style at once clear, concise, and impartial. The logical cogency of this argument, however, may be best appreciated, if we allow ourselves to be introduced to it by a brief consideration of the other *à posteriori* objections which have been advanced against the doctrine we are considering.

The first of these is the well-known "hospital test," which, although advanced in the form of a proposal, is entitled to rank as an objection; seeing that those who proposed it must well have known that it never could be seriously tried. Now the authors of this proposal no doubt supposed that in making it, they were adhering closely to what is called the Method of Difference. A moment's thought, however, is sufficient to shew that a fallacy is involved by the very supposition that this Method could be of any validity, if applied to this case and in the way suggested. Experimental verification of any theory whatever is only valid upon the supposition that the forces with which we have to deal are constant; and as physical forces always are constant, this is equivalent to saying, that in all cases of purely physical causation the experimental methods are valid. But those who believe in the physical efficacy of Prayer, are not as a consequence committed to the belief that Prayer is a physical force. On the contrary, what of necessity they do believe is, that if Prayer is thus effectual at all, it can only be so by directly appealing to the Author of all Force to modify the action of existing Force—by its influence, that is, upon the Being who transcends Force. Hence we are plainly in a different province here, from that in which Experiment may validly be instituted. Only if we had some previous assurance that the Deity would answer every petition according to the letter, and only if this previous assurance were as high as that concerning the persistence of force; only then would the institution of Experiment be as valid in the one province as in the other.

As there is no escape from this criticism, it is needless to elaborate it; only it is worth observing that the anonymous author against whom it is urged has himself conceded its validity. He says, in effect, that according to his conceptions regarding the Divine nature, such petitions as he proposes ought certainly to be answered; seeing that they are only made with a view of ascertaining truth. Now, without pausing to shew that this purely *à priori* expectation is in direct opposition to what would be the *à priori* expectation of those who are invited to perform the experiment, we are only concerned with the fact that the expectation in question *is* purely *à priori*. If the author of a proposal to institute experimental verification as a final and decisive solution of a controverted question, in the very face of the proposal itself, flaunts the fact that the method cannot be applied at all, without assuming the necessary truth of a purely *à priori* supposition (where experience is impossible); are we not justified in "referring this gentleman to his logical studies for three months," and in pronouncing his argument self-condemned?

A kindred fallacy occurs in a letter addressed to the Editor of the *Pall Mall Gazette* by Prof. Tyndall, whose vast powers of physical research appear to have developed at the expense of those essential to the accurate conducting of metaphysical analysis. The whole argument of this letter may be summed up in the words, Because vaccination has proved itself a more effectual agent than Prayer in the case of small-pox, therefore the latter agency can never have exerted any curative influence at all in that disease. If the Professor, in taking the wonderful leap which is here observable at the "therefore," is thought to have surpassed even his far-famed athletic abilities, the reader may learn how desirable it is to throw an argument into the form of a syllogism before taking the trouble to develope it. That vaccination is more effectual than Prayer in the case alleged, no one would think of denying, any more than they would deny that a screw-propeller is more conducive to progression than is a prayerful crew, or than they would deny any other one of the countless instances in which man has been able to help himself through the agency of general laws.

But the question at issue is not regarding the constancy of general laws in their relation to us, nor the consequent benefit of increasing our knowledge concerning them; but it is regarding the benefit of Prayer considered in itself, and not in comparison with other benefits. There may be a thousand reasons why Prayer should not be as certain in its effects upon disease as is medicine: it clearly does not follow that in no case of disease has it any effect at all[1].

The question then arises, Is it possible logically to apply the scientific methods in any way to the case of the Prayer-controversy? Let us state the problem. It is required to measure the physical influence of Prayer, by ascertaining the difference which its presence occasions in a given set of conditions, precisely resembling some other set of conditions, save only that in the latter Prayer is absent. To do this, it is clearly futile, on the one hand, to adopt Prof. Tyndall's method of comparing the influences of Prayer with that of some other recognized influence—notwithstanding this method avoids the fallacy of appealing to experiment: on the other hand, it is equally futile to adopt the method of direct experiment—notwithstanding this avoids the fallacy of comparing one influence with another. What we want is some middle course between these two fallacious methods: we want to compare the physical results respectively ensuing upon petition, and upon the absence of petition, under precisely similar circumstances; and yet so to compare them without the intervention of experiment. One, and only one, solution of this problem is logically possible; and this has been afforded by Mr Galton.

[1] Some other fallacies which occur in Prof. Tyndall's writings upon this subject have been pointed out in the *Burney Essay*.

To say that Prayer is physically availing, is to say that Prayer is capable of effecting observable results. Consequently, if we choose some easily observable set of facts, such as the comparative duration of men's lives, and take statistics of many cases in which petition has been offered for prolonged life, and likewise statistics of many cases in which petition has not been so offered; then, on averaging the two sets of cases, we ought certainly to detect the influence of Prayer in prolonging life, if Prayer really has any such influence. For, be it observed, according to this method, the presence of Prayer is compared with the absence of Prayer, and compared in such a manner that the agency of direct experiment is dispensed with. In other words, the experiment has already been made on an immensely varied and extensive scale, and made in the unexceptionable spirit of those who had no intention of experimenting. To insinuate that in this case the physical results of Prayer are imperceptible, would merely be to insinuate that Prayer can have had no such results at all; for, if our averages are honestly taken over a sufficient number of instances, such results, if present, must become apparent.

Such is a brief abstract of Mr Galton's argument; and very admirably has it been elaborated. First is pointed out the obvious fallacy of relying on individual instances. Next, the statistics are not confined to any one physical benefit for which the pious are likely to pray for; but extend to all such benefits concerning which it is possible to collect statistics. Clergymen, "whose profession it is to pray," are not conspicuously longer-lived than other men: sovereigns, for whose lives prayers are universal, are actually shorter-lived. Insurance companies make no difference in their rates between the pious and the impious; nor do underwriters between missionary-vessels and traders. Medical men do not recognize Prayer as a remedial agent; and the birth-rate is not affected by it. Several other examples are given, and the whole case has been made out with considerable care; so that we cannot help thanking Mr Galton for the trouble he has evidently taken in collecting his evidence.

Now there is no use blinking the fact that this inductive argument is one of very great weight. Supposing then, what there seems no reason to dispute, that Mr Galton's statistics have been honestly compiled—*i. e.*, that no statistics adverse to his argument have been suppressed; and consequently that if we collected any number of statistics, the result would still be a negative one; I shall endeavour to lay before the reader the only considerations which, so far as I can see, can fairly be opposed to Mr Galton's arguments. Whether or not these considerations are sufficient to neutralize these arguments, I must leave the reader to judge. This much, however, I may state as my own impartial decision upon the value of Mr Galton's enquiries, viz., while these enquiries may properly be taken as confirmatory of the opinions held by those who already disbelieve in the existence and action of a special providence; these enquiries have little or no logical bearing upon the opinions held by those who already believe in the existence and action of such a providence. The following are my reasons for coming to this decision.

Belief in the efficacy of Christian Prayer clearly presupposes belief in the Divine origin of the Christian revelation. In other words, if we reject the latter belief, we also of necessity reject the former; and if we hold the latter doubtful, we must also deem the former proportionably so. Hence, as Mr Galton's investigations have only yielded negative results, it is only those who accept the utterances of revelation as authoritative, that are concerned with his argument. Now I have elsewhere shewn —I think conclusively—that the utterances of revelation concerning the physical validity of Prayer are unequivocal; so I may here assume this point as established. Therefore, if this assumption is granted, the issue resolves itself into a contest of *à posteriori* probabilities: the question is, Is it more probable that the teaching of Divine revelation should be false, or that Mr Galton's statistics should be wrong? Or, thus, If statistical enquiries into the physical efficacy of Prayer are theoretically capable of yielding results as trustworthy as are the results yielded by similar enquiries into other things; and if the results yielded by such enquiries into this subject are negative; and, lastly, if, as assumed, the teaching of Scripture regarding this same subject is unequivocally positive;—then the facts established by Mr Galton's statistics would not only militate against belief in the efficacy of Prayer, but likewise against belief in the Divine authority of revelation. The work before us, then, is to examine into the validity of what we may call the statistical method, as applied to the present case.

The value of statistical enquiries clearly depends upon the *observability* of that to which they are applied. In other words, the trustworthiness of the results afforded by statistical enquiries varies directly with the assurance we possess, that the cause or causes into the degree of whose efficiency they enquire, have not been confounded with other causes similar in their observable effects. Two complementary examples will render this clear. Suppose it were required to ascertain by means of statistics whether cancer or consumption is the more fatal disease. All that we should have to do would be to consult the books of the two large hospitals in Brompton, which are devoted to the cure of these two diseases respectively—taking care to select for comparison patients of the same age and sex; and generally to keep the two sets of examples as closely similar as possible. If such statistics were taken over a sufficient number of cases, no suspicions could be cast upon the result. Next, suppose it were required to ascertain by means of statistics alone whether or not "honesty is the best policy"—whether or not, as a whole, honest people succeed better than dishonest. It is easy to see that this case would present vastly greater difficulties than the other. A patient suffering from cancer or consumption could not conceal the fact from the surgeons and physicians, even were it his interest to do so; while, on the other hand, the motive for concealing dishonesty, and the ease with which it can be done, are matters of every-day experience. Our statistic-maker would therefore be unable to know how far the individuals classed under "honest," really fell within that category. Of course, if he took the trouble of making himself well acquainted with every individual he admitted into his tables, his results would then be somewhat more satisfactory; but in this way he could not obtain a sufficiently wide basis for trustworthy results, statistically considered. What, as a statician, he would require to do, would be to fix upon some other character more easily observable than honesty, and with which honesty is, as a general rule, associated. Wealth would be such a character, because, as wealth increases, the inducement to be dishonest, as a rule, decreases. Wealth, however, would not do, because the object is to ascertain whether honesty or dishonesty is the more conducive to wealth; and it would clearly be no enquiry into this at all, which set out with making wealth the test of honesty. Education would be free from these objections; but it is evident that education and honesty are much too laxly associated, for the former to be taken as a trustworthy test of the latter. Similarly criminal punishment would be clearly out of the question; for this only represents unsuccessful dishonesty. Upon the whole, then, it would be an exceedingly difficult thing to decide by statistics alone, whether a man of ordinary ability has a better chance of success in life when of a scrupulous, or when of an unscrupulous, disposition.

Now of these two complementary examples it is to be observed, that the *results* tabulated by the statistics are equally observable—it being as conspicuous a fact whether a man is in a state of affluence or poverty, as whether he is in a state of health or disease. Far different, however, is it with the *causes*, which it is the supposed object of the statistics to examine. In the former example these are altogether uncompounded with other causes, and their effects are such as not to admit of being confounded with the effects of other causes; so that a mere tabulation of the observable effects is all that is required. In the latter example the causes to be taken cognizance of are so inextricably compounded with other causes, and their effects (whichever way they tend) are so easily to be confounded with those due to other causes, and moreover, the causes investigated (viz., honesty and dishonesty) are of so secret a description, that on this latter account alone any statistical enquiry into their respective merits would be rendered almost nugatory. Hence we see that the value of the statistical method varies greatly in different cases.

In no case, probably, is the value of the statistical method less than it is in the case of Prayer. This arises from the fact that Prayer, more than anything else that can be named, is *secret*. Prayer is more secret than anything else that can be named, because it is a matter between the petitioner and the Deity exclusively. That is to say, although a man may pray audibly in the presence of others, none but the Deity can know whether or not he really prays. Again, thoughtless or formal prayers, we are repeatedly told, are no prayers at all: nay, the Biblical standard of Prayer is so high, that however fervent *petition* may be, it is declared nugatory, unless we have previously ceased to regard iniquity in our hearts. We must forgive our debtors, before our request to be forgiven can be entertained. Even upon the very altar we must leave our gift, if we remember aught our brother has against us. Who then but the Deity can know whether the heart is pure enough to pray? But this is not all. Prayer is so easy to the prayerful, that genuine petition from them is always ascending, embracing with a world-wide charity all kinds of human interests. Even the most profligate cannot altogether escape from the guarding influence of petition. Hence, in no case are we justified in assuming that this influence is altogether absent; while, conversely, in no case are we justified in assuming that it is certainly present.

Thus far no one, probably, will be more willing to go with us than Mr Galton himself. 'All this being granted,' he would say, 'and surely we may still conclude that, upon the whole, *more* genuine prayers occur among the professedly prayerful classes of men, than among the professedly prayerless.' No doubt; but this concedes the outposts of the position—shews that genuine Prayer is so far an unobservable influence (if it is an influence at all), that statistics can only take cognizance of it by including large masses of men; in the hope that, as a general rule, this protecting influence will be confined to those who pray, and will not escape to those who do not pray, even although they may be prayed for. I do not think this too strong a statement of the case; for all who believe in the efficacy of Prayer would assent to the proposition, that they ought to pray for the unrighteous and profligate—even though these be their enemies and persecutors,—if they hope to receive answers to their petitions for themselves. Thus, although it is true that more genuine prayers occur among the professedly prayerful than among the professedly prayerless, yet we are unable to say what comparison subsists between the influence of Prayer upon the physical well-being of the pious, and the physical well-being of the wicked. Doubtless we must suppose that, upon the whole, the balance largely preponderates in favour of the pious: all that is here contended for is, that we are unable to assert *à priori* to what degree the balance so preponderates; and until we can do this, we are unable to *measure* the strength of Mr Galton's *à posteriori* argument, although we may perceive that it possesses some indefinite degree of value.

Thus far, then, we have seen that there are three objections to the statistical method as applied to the case of Prayer. First, If even the petitioner himself cannot know whether his prayer is genuine (*i.e.*, acceptable to the Deity), much less can a statistic-maker. Thus

Prayer may be absent when it appears to be present. Second, General prayers for the unconverted are universal among Christians, and particular prayers of the same kind are exceedingly common. Thus Prayer may be present when it appears to be absent. Third, Consequently, although it is true that Prayer is more common among the pious classes of men than among the wicked, nevertheless we are unable to anticipate the comparative influence which Prayer exerts upon the physical well-being of these two classes respectively.

We must now add that all Prayer, in so far as it is genuine, is conditional. As before observed, " Thy will be done" is the "under-tone"of every petition, in so far as it is a true petition. Now this fact, in its present connection, is of immense importance. If Christians regarded the influence of petition as equivalent to a *physical cause*, then, notwithstanding the three objections above adduced to the employment of the statistical method in this case, that method would certainly be valid; although, for the reasons given, the strength of the arguments founded upon it would be undeterminable. But Christians do not regard the influence of petition in this light. They deem it a duty to ask for all things they desire, physical benefits included; but they also deem it their duty to expect no benefit but such as the Divine Omniscience sees it best to bestow. Who, then, but the Deity can here be competent to take the statistics? One man prays for death, and receives long life instead: another man prays for long life, and instead receives a few working years of health. One man asks that his son may obtain material prosperity, and instead his son brings honour on his name: another man prays that his son may achieve a lasting celebrity, and instead he obtains health and prosperity. All such cases, by balancing each other, elude the cognizance of statistics.

What, then, is the whole state of the case? To illustrate it most fairly, we shall take the strongest of the examples supplied by Mr Galton, viz., that of the Clergy. As Mr Galton truly observes, in no other class are we so likely to obtain men of Prayer. Suppose, then, for the sake of calculation, that one-half of the clergy are sufficiently prayerful to admit of their petitions influencing the course of physical phenomena. Next, let us suppose that one-half of their successful petitions for physical benefits, are offered on behalf of individuals other than themselves: this is equivalent to reducing the number of the prayerful clergy to one-fourth of the whole number. Here we ought to add, that in whatever degree this section of successful prayers influences the prayerless classes of the community, in that degree is the comparison still further vitiated. Neglecting this point, however, let us lastly suppose that one-half of the petitions for physical benefits offered on the petitioner's own behoof, are answered by physical benefits of some other kind, such as to neutralize (so far as statistics are concerned) other physical benefits petitioned for by other clergymen: this is equivalent to reducing the original number to one-eighth. Now, I do not think that any of these suppositions are extravagant. Let us see the result of applying them to Mr Galton's tables. According to these tables, the clergy as a class live, on an average, two years longer than men of any of the other classes quoted, notwithstanding we are repeatedly told that, as a class, they are the most poorly constitutioned of all. Now, neglecting the last-mentioned point, and also the fact that all clergymen do not pray for long lives; still, even on the above data, an average of two additional years over all the clergy, allows, when concentrated into one-eighth of their number, an average of 16 additional years of life to every pious divine.

Of course this illustration is not adduced in order to prove that Prayer has in this case been observably effectual. The greater length of life enjoyed by the clergy may be conceded due to the cause assigned by Mr Galton—viz., the repose of a country life—or to any other cause, without in any way affecting the present argument. All we are here engaged in shewing is, that the statistical method is not a trustworthy instrument with which to gauge the physical efficacy of Prayer; and the above illustration has been adduced to shew, that even if the petitions of the pious clergy for lengthened days were somewhat more effectual than that of Hezekiah, still statistics would be so far unable to take cognizance of the fact, that the observable average increase of two years over the entire body of the clergy, might reasonably be attributed to other causes. Yet length of days is perhaps the most conspicuous, and therefore the most easily tabulated, of all physical benefits for which it is possible to pray.

I have said that the above illustration is not adduced in order to prove that Prayer has in this case been observably effectual. To have so adduced this illustration, would have been to cut away the ground from the strongest of my arguments against the employment of the statistical method to the discussion of the Prayer-question. The brief enunciation of this argument will serve to conclude the present examination.

To those who believe in the efficacy of Prayer, no single proposition can be more self-evident, than that the presiding influence of Providence should not admit of scientific demonstration. Without pausing to shew that the fact of man being in a probationary state, is postulated by the supposition of a supernatural revelation being imparted to him; or that the only conceivable instrument of a moral probation is afforded by the spirit of Faith; it is enough to point to the undeniable fact, that if the system which those who believe in the efficacy of Prayer accept as a supernatural revelation is such in reality, then no two doctrines are to them more certain than those just mentioned; for there are no two doctrines more unequivocally deducible from Scripture. Now where would be the room for the exercise of faith, if the efficacy of Prayer could be scientifically demonstrated? Such a demonstration would amount to a full and perfect proof of the Divine origin of Christianity; so that to withhold our belief as to the latter fact, would no longer be a token of spiritual faithlessness, but of intellectual incapacity. All that is distinctive in the Christian religion would of necessity disappear; for pious rectitude would then require to degenerate into mere intellectual prudence. Thus Mr Galton might have spared himself the trouble of carrying his statistical enquiries into the province we are contemplating; for those who believe in the physical efficacy of Prayer (and who therefore accept revelation as of Divine authority), must have been even more prepared to expect negative results from such enquiries, than those who disbelieve in such efficacy. It thus becomes difficult to perceive the object with which Mr Galton's statistics are taken. Had he never been at the pains of collecting them, his opponents in this matter would have been perfectly ready to concede *à priori*, all that he has established by a somewhat laborious induction. Mr Galton will perhaps retort, 'To have done this would have been tantamount to abandoning the whole position; for to assert that Prayer is not to be supposed capable of producing observable results—no matter from what cause such incapacity is supposed to proceed,—is merely to assert that Prayer is not physically efficacious.' Not so. The question at issue is not, Can the existence and the action of a special Providence be experimentally proved? but, Supposing the existence of such Providence, can its action be rationally supposed capable of eluding the scrutiny of science? This is a question as old as philosophy; and having thus shewn that the issue raised by Mr Galton (and also by Prof. Tyndall), which has been deemed by many so eminently novel, is merely an old acquaintance in new dress, we may fitly leave it to be discussed by the more elaborate treatises into which it is thus merged. One quotation, however, should be laid to heart, as proceeding from the father of those methods, to which science owes all her victories in the past, and all her hopes for the future:—"I believe that God......doth accomplish and fulfil His Divine Will in all things, great and small, singular and general, as fully and exactly by Providence, as He could by miracle[1]."

[1] Bacon's *Confession of Faith*.

www.ingramcontent.com/pod-product-compliance
Lightning Source LLC
Chambersburg PA
CBHW031943230426
43672CB00010B/2029